ORGANIZATIONAL BEHAVIOR
Bilingual Teaching Case

组织行为学
双语教学案例

主　编　吕惠明　王　威
副主编　季　浩　国维潇　陈士慧

内 容 简 介

本书共分为13个案例,基本涵盖组织行为学的相关内容,案例从个体、群体、组织3个层次进行采编。

本书采用中文和英文两种语言,既可作为中国学生学习"组织行为学"的辅助教材,也可作为以英文为主要语言的国际学生学习的辅助教材。

图书在版编目(CIP)数据

组织行为学:双语教学案例/吕惠明,王威主编.—北京:北京大学出版社,2023.7
ISBN 978-7-301-33732-5

Ⅰ.①组… Ⅱ.①吕…②王… Ⅲ.①组织行为学—双语教学—教案(教育)—高等学校 Ⅳ.①C936

中国国家版本馆CIP数据核字(2023)第025138号

书　　名	组织行为学:双语教学案例 ZUZHI XINGWEI XUE: SHUANGYU JIAOXUE ANLI
著作责任者	吕惠明　王　威　主编
策划编辑	李娉婷
责任编辑	赵天思　陶鹏旭
标准书号	ISBN 978-7-301-33732-5
出版发行	北京大学出版社
地　　址	北京市海淀区成府路205号　100871
网　　址	http://www.pup.cn　　新浪微博:@北京大学出版社
电子信箱	编辑部:pup6@pup.cn　　总编室:zpup@pup.cn
电　　话	邮购部 010-62752015　发行部 010-62750672　编辑部 010-62750667
印刷者	河北文福旺印刷有限公司
经销者	新华书店
	787毫米×1092毫米　16开本　20.25印张　304千字 2023年7月第1版　2023年7月第1次印刷
定　　价	58.00元

未经许可,不得以任何方式复制或抄袭本书之部分或全部内容。
版权所有,侵权必究
举报电话:010-62752024　电子信箱:fd@pup.pku.edu.cn
图书如有印装质量问题,请与出版部联系,电话:010-62756370

前　言

随着经济的振兴、公司的发展和组织的健康成长，如何有效地发挥组织的效能、激发个体的潜能、提高团队凝聚力已经成为管理人员高度关注的焦点。组织行为学是研究如何提高组织有效性的一门重要学科，它采用系统分析的方法，综合运用管理学、心理学、社会学、政治学等学科的理论、方法和手段，了解组织中人的行为的决定因素。学习组织行为学有利于管理人员提高对组织成员行为的预测、控制和引导能力，及时协调个体、群体和组织之间的相互关系，充分发挥组织成员的积极性、主动性和创造性，从而提高组织的管理效率，实现组织的战略目标。

本书从个体、群体、组织3个层次构建框架，选取国内本土公司的案例，应用组织行为学的理论知识，对案例公司进行描述和分析，帮助学生更好地理解和掌握相关理论，提高理论联系实际的解决问题的能力。

案例教学的目的在于培养学生观察、分析和解决实际问题的能力。学生通过阅读案例，理解案例背景，结合组织行为学的理论知识，分析案例中存在的问题，并应用理论给出适合的解决方案。在案例教学活动中，学生是研讨的主角，老师负责提供案例背景介绍，提出案例研究的问题，引导学生进行小组讨论，最后进行概括和总结。

本书由宁波大学吕惠明、河南财经政法大学王威担任主编，由宁波大学季浩、国维潇、陈士慧担任副主编。具体编写分工如下：吕惠明编写案例1、案例3和案例7；王威编写案例2、案例5、案例8、案例10、案例13；陈士慧编写案例4；季浩编写案例6和案例11；季浩、朱聪、周伊莉、余轶男、周楠和郑曙萍共同编写案例9；国维潇编写案例12。全书由吕惠明审校、统稿。本书的顺利出版，得益于宁波大学工商管理国际化专业建设项目的支持，在此表示感谢。北京大学出版社做了耐心细致的编辑工作，在此特别表示感谢。

鉴于编者水平限制，本书存在不足之处，敬请同行、读者批评指正。

编　者

2023 年 5 月

Preface

With the revitalization of economy, development of enterprises, and healthy growth of organizations, how to effectively improve the efficiency of organizations, stimulate the potential of individuals, and enhance team cohesion has become a focal point for managers. Organizational behavior is an important discipline that studies how to improve organizational effectiveness. It uses a systematic analysis approach, integrating theories, methods, and means of management, psychology, sociology, political science, and other disciplines to understand the determinants of human behavior in organizations. Organizational behavior helps to improve managers' ability to predict, control, and guide organizational members' behavior, timely coordinate the relationships between individuals, groups, and organizations, fully play the enthusiasm, initiative, and creativity of organizational members, and thus improve the management efficiency of the organization and achieve the strategic goals of the organization.

This book constructs a framework of the three levels of individual, team, and organization, uses cases from domestic companies, and applies theoretical knowledge of organizational behavior to describe and analyze the case companies to help students better understand and master the relevant theories, and improve their ability to solve practical problems in theory and practice.

The purpose of case teaching is to cultivate students' ability to observe, analyze, and solve practical problems. Students read the cases, understand the case background, combine the theoretical knowledge of organizational behavior, analyze the problems in the cases, and apply theory to give suitable solutions. In case teaching activities, students play the main roles in the discussion, teachers are responsible for providing the case background information, posing the case research questions, guiding students to have group discussions, and summarize their work in the end.

The editors-in-chief of this book are Lü Huiming (Ningbo University) and Wang Wei (Henan University of Economics and Law). The associate editors-in-chief are Ji Hao, Guo Weixiao and Chen Shihui, all from Ningbo University. Writers of the cases include Lü Huiming (cases 1, 3, 7), Wang Wei (cases 2, 5, 8, 10, 13), Chen Shihui (case 4), Ji Hao (cases 6, 11), Guo Weixiao(case 12). Case 9 is jointly written by Ji Hao, Zhu Cong, Zhou Yili, Yu Yinan, Zhou Nan and Zheng Shuping. This book is finally edited by Lü Huiming. For the publication of this book, the Business Administration Internationalization Program of Ningbo University provided great support and Peking University Press carried out careful and patient editing work. We would like to express our appreciation for them.

Inadequacy is inevitable due to limited proficiency. Any criticism and suggestions from the peers and readers are appreciated.

Editors
May 2023

目　录

案例 1　BE 公司面临的问题 1

案例 2　AC 航空公司空乘人员的情绪劳动 9

案例 3　成为教师和学生的朋友 17

案例 4　L 公司人事部管理困境 27

案例 5　HC 公司的知识型员工与非物质激励 35

案例 6　杭州"那天·手工艺主题民宿"团队创业的曲折经历 43

案例 7　B 公司员工管理困境 57

案例 8　该怎样和 90 后员工打交道？ 65

案例 9　新创企业如何在传统行业中实现数字创新——斑马仓的创业故事 75

案例 10　VT 公司文化冲突导致的人才流失 89

案例 11　"以不变应万变"——记 X 会装公司组织结构的变迁 105

案例 12　JNSP 物业中心的组织变革为何困难重重？ 117

案例 13　ZL 公司的组织变革之路 129

Case 1	Challenges Faced by BE Company	143
Case 2	Emotional Labor—Flight Attendants of AC Airlines	153
Case 3	To Make Friends with the Teachers and Students	163
Case 4	Management Dilemma Faced by the HR Department of L Company	175
Case 5	Knowledge Workers and Non-material Incentives in HC Company	183
Case 6	Tortuous Experience of Natian · Handicraft Theme Homestay Entrepreneurial Team	193
Case 7	Employee Management Dilemma of B Company	209
Case 8	How to Deal with the Post-90s Employees	219
Case 9	How a Start-up Realizes Digital Innovation in the Traditional Industry: The Entrepreneurial Story of Zebra Warehouse	229
Case 10	Brain Drain of VT Company Caused by Cultural Conflicts	249
Case 11	"Response to Change"—Changes in the Organizational Structure of X Decoration Company	267
Case 12	Why Is the Organizational Transformation of JNSP Property Center So Tricky?	283
Case 13	Organizational Transformation of ZL Corporation	297

案例 1

BE 公司面临的问题

知识点：

人格理论、能力理论、态度理论、工作满意度理论、激励理论

案例目的：

本案例通过对 BE 公司进行分析，引导学生理解并应用个体中的人格理论、能力理论、态度理论、工作满意度理论和激励理论。

案例正文：

1. 引言

宁波 BE 公司成立于 2007 年 1 月 9 日，主要从事家用纺织产品的加工和出口，下设研发、营销、财务、生产、管理、运营 6 大部门，在职员工 180 人。内贸方面，BE 公司主要为一些在电商平台经营的客户供货；外贸方面，主要出口至美国、德国、加拿大等发达国家。经过近十年的不懈努力，BE 公司在宁波外贸市场站稳了脚跟，获取了稳定的销售渠道。2016—2017 年，BE 公司销售利润保持稳步递增，整体销售状况良好。如今，BE 公司已经从最初的小作坊稳步发展成为一家中型纺织企业。但是，BE 公司还在不断筹备多项工程，打算扩建并加大生产投入，将投入更多的时间与人力在开发新产品方面，充分发挥公司的生产技术优势。

2. 公司概况

下文将从公司的内部资源方面介绍 BE 公司概况，内部资源是公司在生产运营过程中拥有的各个环节的资源总和，它是一家公司获得产出，并得以与其他公司竞争的基础。内部资源分为有形资源与无形资源，有形资源主要包括财务资源、物质资源、技术资源等；而无形资源主要包括组织资源、声誉资源、创新资源、人力资源等。

2.1 有形资源

以财务资源和物质资源为例介绍 BE 公司的有形资源。

（1）财务资源

财务资源，也就是公司资金的流动和运作状况。财务资源能否得到合理开发和利用，直接关系到公司能否正常运营，关系到公司的生存和发展。BE 公司 2014—2018 年的主要财务数据如表 1-1 所示。BE 公司的财务数据呈现出两个特点。第一，负债虽然比较稳定，但总体上呈现增长态势。第二，利润稳定但没有大幅增加，近几年的销售收入增长率有所下降。如果生产营销状况没有成功的新的尝试，那么 BE 公司盈利的局面也可能不再长久。

表 1-1　BE 公司 2014—2018 年的主要财务数据

项目	年份				
	2014	2015	2016	2017	2018
总资产 / 千万元	9.39	9.80	10.10	10.80	11.10
总资产增长率 /%		4.66	3.02	6.78	2.74
所有者权益 / 千万元	4.70	4.90	5.00	5.20	5.30
负债 / 千万元	4.00	3.80	4.40	4.30	4.50
资产负债率 /%	43.29	39.45	43.22	39.89	40.58
销售收入 / 千万元	9.21	9.32	9.42	9.54	9.72
销售收入增长率 /%		1.51	1.82	1.14	0.81
利润 / 千万元	1.20	1.10	1.30	1.20	1.50

（2）物质资源

BE 公司环境优美，干净怡人，建有标准厂房、办公楼和员工宿舍楼，另建有多个标准化车间。公司拥有先进的棉胎制作流水线和化纤流棉、铺网等设备，实现了生产流程的自动化。公司还拥有国内外先进的电脑多针缝纫机、单针缝纫机以及电脑刺绣机等良好的硬件设施，为生产品质优良的纺织用品奠定了坚实的基础。公司设有生产厂房、原材料仓库、成品仓库，还有梳棉、绗缝、缝纫及包装检验四大车间。公司设备有梳棉自动生产流水线 1 条、普通梳棉机 2 台，年生产棉胎 15 万条、云丝被 10 万条；高速缝纫机 50 台，年生产床单、被套各 20 万条；电脑缝纫机 2 台；枕心自动灌装机 1 台。

2.2 无形资源

以组织资源和声誉资源为例介绍BE公司的无形资源。

（1）组织资源

BE公司的管理实行逐级负责制，各部门权责明晰，由总经理负责总体事务。各部门有不同层次的工作和职责，生产部门对企业常规生产运作负责，下设梳棉、绗缝、缝纫及包装检验四大车间，车间主任对各车间生产环节负责；人事部门负责员工的招聘、培训，绩效和考核机制的设立；财务部门负责员工工资的发放及日常生产销售的资金运转管理；营销部门分为国内营销部门与国际营销部门，负责国内和国际市场的开拓；生产研发部门一方面通过生产设备及生产技术的创新研发来实现产品的功能性研发，另一方面通过引进国外的先进设备对公司的旧生产设备和生产技术进行改造升级；后勤部门负责管理员工的日常就餐、住宿问题，成立工会保障员工的权益，设立医务室保障员工的就业安全。

（2）声誉资源

BE公司永远将产品品质放在第一位，并建立了完善的服务体系。BE公司以"品质第一、科学作业、顾客第一位"为公司目标；秉承"对产品用心、对客户贴心、对员工关心、对社会尽心"的理念；追求"做文明职工、创良好产品、建和谐公司"的发展愿景；树立"素质优化、信誉优良、环境优美、秩序优良"的BE形象，全力做精做强公司。

3. 公司存在的问题

（1）设计研发能力和生产技术创新能力较弱

设计研发能力和生产技术创新能力的缺乏严重影响了BE公司的发展，导致公司只能以中低端产品为主进行生产销售，这大大降低了公司的竞争力。由于缺乏设计研发的能力，公司的产品很难与其他公司的产品有所差异，产品趋于同质化，缺少品牌特性，很难有竞争优势。而生产技术创新能力的缺乏导致公司很难提高产品质量与工艺水平。第一，公司没有设立自主设计研发团队，这方面的经费投入严重不足，而一些有名气的大型家用纺织公司都会对设计研发投入大量人力、财力，这直接导致公司的竞争力与其他公司存在差距；第二，纺织作业设备落后，没有引入新型设备，也就没有创新的产品，缺少科技含量；第三，没有配备掌握专业技术的人员。这些都限制了 BE 公司的发展。

（2）人力资源管理水平低

BE 公司是一家家族企业，约有百分之六十的管理成员来自家族内部和成员的亲朋好友，管理层通过招聘进入的比例很小，不利于吸收社会中优秀的人力资源，限制了用人范围。这种用人唯亲的管理方法导致公司出现对家族内部员工违规的不处理现象，执行能力缺失。这种不公平现象的产生不仅直接导致公司利润的减少，也让其他员工有所微言，不利于公司内部团结。公司要提高人力资源管理的水平，可以通过对生产过程中员工的分配和构成进行分析，按照员工的能力特点，结合工作需求，最大限度地整合资源，建立一套清晰的培训、调选、奖惩、反馈的流程，从而实现成本最低化、产品最优化生产，为各个部门输送最匹配的员工。BE 公司只有摒弃这种落后的管理层组建办法，加快调整升级，强化内部管理，通过公开招聘选拔和培养高水平的优秀专业型人才，才能使得整个公司的人力资源管理水平得以提高。

（3）薪酬考核机制不完善

BE 公司的人事部门只是建立了简单的薪酬体系，并没有将员工的各项考核表现与薪酬挂钩，也没有将考核目标与公司目标结合，不利于公司的发展。首先，这会导致一线作业员工的离职率很高，不仅直接降低了生产率和产品质量，还加大了人事部门招聘新员工的工作量和相应的资金投入，导致生产成本上升。家用纺织公司对一线员工的操作熟练度要求极高，若是频繁更换操作人员，会大大影响生产效率与生产质量，新员工作业前需要进行系统培训，这不仅耽误了老员工的工作时间，还会导致生产原料的浪费。其次，由于考核结果对员工的收入不会产生影响，所以员工不重视绩效考核，工作中责任感不强，工作热情不高。

（4）员工满意度调查结果较差

尽管财务报表显示，BE 公司总资产正以大约每年 10% 的速度增长，国内市场和国际市场都在不同程度上得以拓展，生产订单饱满，公司前景十分乐观。但是公司的员工满意度调查结果却不尽如人意。调查表分为3个部分，一是员工对薪资福利待遇的满意度；二是员工对个人职业生涯发展的满意度；三是员工对工作环境及企业文化的满意度。调查结果显示，在总分为100分的情况下，员工对薪资福利待遇的满意度为52分，对个人职业生涯发展的满意度为27分，对工作环境及企业文化的满意度为40分。这两年，BE公司的人才流动率为38%，也说明了公司在人才激励、员工薪资待遇及企业文化等方面存在一些问题。

（5）员工流失率困境

近两年，公司有38%的员工辞职，加入同行业竞争对手的公司，尤其是很多新加入的大学生，一旦完成培训，掌握了主要的管理经验或项目开发经验，就被竞争者用高于本公司的工资吸引过去。

根据人事部的工作满意度调查表，可以发现员工的满意度不高。因此有很多员工跳槽，且公司内部大多数员工缺乏工作热情，没有以前那么积极主动。

这一困境可以从一些部门体现出来。在人事部门，经理具有绝对的权威。在实际运作中，各组组长都对经理直接负责，因此在很大程度上，主管成了一个摆设。人事部门经理王浩在2016年从一个高校跳槽来公司，他一向对下属要求很严，事无巨细都要进行过问，在布置工作任务时，他不但要求新员工必须按其设定的工作程序进行操作，而且老员工的工作方法和程序也必须得到他的认可后才能实施。他认为，这样可以避免不必要的摸索过程，提高工作效率。他一味注重过程的控制，不但使下属感到压抑，常担心在细节问题上出错而遭到责备，而且令下属的工作没有创造性和自主性，做出来的成绩也似乎全是经理的功劳，下属根本没有成就感。另外他在批评下属时，从不允许下属申辩，他认为下属首要的是服从，申辩只是寻找失败的借口，这样的员工是不会认真地改进工作的。员工的工作一旦出现差错，往往轻则受责备，重则受处分。在员工的工作做出成绩时，王浩却很少给予当面的赞扬，因为他觉得，工作做好了是本分。下属除非有非常突出的贡献，否则很难晋职加薪。为此下属都很怕他，但在公司内，他却因其严谨干练的工作作风而赢得了高层管理者的称赞。

面对各种各样的问题，公司应该如何制订管理规划呢？公司准备召开高层管理人员会议，讨论如何解决公司的困境。

思考问题：

1. BE 公司员工离职率高和工作满意度低的原因是什么？如何解决这一问题？

2. BE 公司在员工管理中存在什么问题？如果你是管理人员，将会如何解决这些问题？

分析要点：

1. 应用工作满意度理论、激励理论对第 1 个思考问题进行分析。

2. 应用态度理论、激励理论、人格理论、能力理论对第 2 个思考问题进行分析。

案例 2

AC 航空公司空乘人员的情绪劳动

知识点：

情绪劳动、情绪管理的相关理论

案例目的：

本案例通过对 AC 航空公司进行分析，引导学生理解并应用情绪劳动、情绪管理的相关理论。

案例正文：

1. 引言

　　AC 航空公司是一家以客运为主要经营业务的航空公司，如何为乘客带来良好的乘坐体验，一直是 AC 航空公司关注的重点。空乘人员无疑肩负着完成这个任务的责任。一般来说，空乘人员指的是包括乘务长、客舱服务人员在内的空乘服务员工。为了提升航空服务质量，AC 航空公司针对空乘人员制订了许多相关的绩效和评比等考核方法。

　　然而，这些考核方法效果并不好。一方面，考核的标准和实际工作之间联系并不紧密，且一部分工作内容无法量化；另一方面，采用这些考核方法只会增加工作压力，非但无法让空乘人员更好地开展服务，反而会进一步消耗他们的服务热情。

　　金色航班的乘务长阿丽非常细心，在每次航班结束后，都会及时地将一天的飞行任务记录下来。五年多的飞行生涯，她已经写完了十几本厚厚的飞行日志。阿丽的飞行日志中有一项内容，就是记录员工们在开展服务工作时，到底需要付出什么样的劳动。

2. 特殊工作要求下的情绪劳动

　　阿丽回想起自己过去五年的工作生涯。在正式工作之前，她认为自己的工作既体面又风光，然而真正开始工作之后，她却发现在光鲜亮丽的背后，有许多不足为外人道的艰辛和困苦。空乘人员的平均年龄在二十岁左右。然而，即使是这样的年轻人，高强度的飞行任务也给他们的身心带来了极大的负担。

除了要长时间的站立，国内热门航线、热门航班一天多次的起落，也使得他们作息极不规律。同时为了保持形象，他们的体重也被严格限制。一方面是劳累的工作，另一方面是小心翼翼的饮食，都在加速透支着空乘人员的身体。

虽然公司为了保护空乘人员的基本身体健康，出台了一系列保障性措施和政策，例如规定空乘人员每年的总飞行时间不能超出1200小时；一天同一航班的乘务组成员最多执飞4个起落，并且在起落间至少保证连续2小时以上的休息；平均每周的工作时长不超过40小时。但是，这些措施只保障了空乘人员身体的基本健康，却没有办法解决他们由内而外的疲惫。

阿丽认真思考这背后的原因，甚至去请教了一些管理学、心理学领域的学者朋友。她发现，空乘人员之所以会感到如此疲惫，是因为工作性质决定了他们需要付出比常人更多的情绪劳动。众所周知，空乘人员不论在任何情况下都需要保持足够的礼仪，提供良好的服务。在这一过程中，他们自身的真实情绪是不能表露出来的。可阿丽的心理学朋友告诉她，人不可能一直保持在良好的情绪状态之中。情绪会受到各种各样的内外部因素的影响，而如果所处的工作场所对所表达出的情绪有期望或者有要求，就必须要付出相应的情绪劳动。

经过这样的咨询和思考，阿丽认为自己发现了问题的关键所在。她在之后的工作时间里，认真体会、观察和记录了自己工作过程中的相关事件，希望从中找到更多的信息和线索。

3. 反面的例子

阿丽在飞行日志中记录了一些反面的例子。

其中比较典型的情况是，对于新员工来说，实际工作和设想之间存在较大的偏差，这会导致他们不适应工作。三年前阿丽刚刚晋升为两舱乘务员时，遇到了自己乘务组的一位新员工。这位新员工沟通、表达等各方面能力都很突出，刚执飞时工作劲头也很足，可是没多久她就开始懈怠起来。阿丽趁着休息的时间和她聊过，从她口中得知，她认为这份工作完全不像她最初想象的那样光鲜亮丽，实际上就是端茶倒水、看人脸色的服务员。她时不时抱怨，更是把这种不好的情绪迅速传到整个乘务组。最后，这位新员工辞职了，阿丽也由于升职成为乘务长而调到了其他乘务组。

不过阿丽在一定程度上是能够理解这种抱怨的。空乘人员的工作性质，决定了她们需要服务各种各样的乘客。而乘客们既有非常尊重她们的劳动付出的，也有高高在上、颐指气使的。遇到态度恶劣的乘客，空乘人员还是需要用积极阳光的态度来应对，这确实是一种很高的要求。这也是为什么阿丽会特别关照刚刚入职的员工，来尽可能帮助他们适应这种工作要求。阿丽不止一次劝说过那些被乘客骂哭的员工。她记得有一位刚刚执飞不到两个月的空姐，被一名乘客无端辱骂了好几分钟。但她还是全程保持微笑，对这名乘客进行劝说和安抚。虽然最终事情得到解决，但是阿丽能够看出她透露出的疲惫。阿丽认为她已经做到了最好，可是在执飞第二次起落时，她却因为疲惫被乘客投诉假笑。这次投诉成为压垮她的"最后一根稻草"，让她忍不住抹了几把眼泪。然而哭过之后，她还是需要调整好自己的精神面貌，去服务下一批乘客。

而阿丽印象最为深刻的例子，是她的同事有一次和乘客之间发生了剧烈争执。阿丽记得这次争执发生在春节期间，他们在执飞从北京飞往哈尔滨的航班。由于天气原因，航班发生了延误。空乘人员此时最重要的工作就是不断安抚坐在座位上无法动弹的乘客们。虽然空乘人员竭尽全力，但是随着延误时间的拉长，乘客们的不满情绪也越来越多。然而空乘人员即使再疲惫，也仍旧需要耐着性子、保持微笑，不厌其烦地向乘客们解释。

因为国内航班都实行机长负责制，所以飞机延误等信息，往往是机组能够最先了解和跟进。同时，机组由于种种原因，不便将最新信息透露给空乘人员。但是直面乘客压力的却不是机组，而是乘务组。这就导致空乘人员需要不断安抚乘客，但是却给不出任何有价值的消息，这使得乘务组往往面临着来自航空管制和乘客的双重压力。在这种情况下，一旦有一点风吹草动，加上个别空乘人员缺乏经验、工作失误等原因，就很容易产生严重的纠纷。由于一次工作疏漏，阿丽的同事未能及时照顾到一位乘客的需求。这时另一位同事及时去补救，却被该乘客无故刁难和辱骂。这位同事无法忍受，和乘客扭打在一起，最终造成了非常恶劣的影响。

阿丽事后对这件事进行了复盘。她觉得这次事件是众多因素汇集在一起之后的必然结果。第一，由于长时间的延误和安抚工作，空乘人员都身心俱疲。第二，当时阿丽所在的乘务组出现了离职员工，普遍工作氛围和工作满意度都受到了负面的影响。第三，当天正值春运期间，乘客数量较多，素质也参差不齐，大家回家心切，对于延误的不满情绪也就更加高涨。第四，乘务长本应该及时制止纠纷的发生，同时处理好机组和乘务组之间的关系，与机组保持有效的沟通。第五，也是阿丽认为最为关键的，她认为乘务长对于空乘人员过于严厉，总是拿公司的绩效考核和评价来压制大家，导致大家无法形成良好的团队氛围，工作没有积极性，甚至存在敌对紧张情绪。

4. 良好的参照

阿丽也记录了很多较为积极的例子。

阿丽进行过总结，最需要付出情绪劳动的情况往往是应对飞机航班延误或飞机上发生突发事件的时候。其中，最为常见的就是飞机延误了。由于各种原因，飞机发生延误是一种较为普遍的现象。阿丽不仅对自己所经历过的各类事件进行了回顾，还特地查阅了公司内部分享的一些参考案例，希望从中找到涉及情绪劳动的内容。

她首先想到的是，在她刚刚升任为金色航班乘务组的乘务长时遇到的一次飞机航班问题。金色航班主要执飞北京和上海之间的往返航班，该航线是国内最为繁忙的航线，因此，金色航班也几乎不会有太多空座。然而有一次突发情况，AC航空公司的另一架飞机出现突发故障，导致机上一部分乘客不得不转移到金色航班上来。这就为阿丽的工作开展带来很多问题。一方面，由于航班问题，乘客已经对航空公司非常不满；另一方面，很多商务舱或头等舱乘客，转移后却只能被安排在普通舱。于是也就出现了一部分乘客故意刁难空乘人员的情况。在这时，阿丽及时站了出来，她认为应当充分考虑到这些乘客的情绪不稳定性，因此不能针锋相对，而是想办法解决他们的问题，从根本上赢得他们的尊重。阿丽尽可能地照顾到了所有乘客的需求，也以身作则给其他空乘人员做了表率，激发了他们的服务热情，最终避免了矛盾的激化。

除了自己的亲身经历，阿丽也在公司内部的分享中找到了一些优秀案例。其中一个也是关于飞机延误。该航班的乘务组负责人叫周丽佳，执飞北京至广州的航班已经有五年多的经验。该航线也是 AC 航空公司的热门航线，并且有很多商务人士乘坐。在一次航空管制造成的延误中，周丽佳成功地化解了一次潜在的空乘人员与乘客之间的冲突。在延误等待中，一名乘客不断询问起飞时间，周丽佳不厌其烦地进行解答，并一直和机组保持良好沟通，及时将她所能够获取到的信息反馈给该名乘客。然而由于该乘客要去广州参加会议，担心迟到，且无法获取准确的回答，一直非常不满，并以下飞机作为要挟。乘客的不满情绪也很快蔓延到整个机舱中。周丽佳非常冷静地处理应对，在尊重该乘客的同时，主动为其提供服务，并持续关注乘客的后续行程，最终成功安抚该乘客，化解了可能出现的不良情况。

飞机在飞行中遭遇突发事件，往往是所有人都不愿意看到的情形。然而空乘人员必须具备处理突发事件的能力。在一次北京飞往南昌的航班中，飞机起飞不久，空乘人员就突然接到机组通知，飞机遭遇了严重的机械故障，需要立即返航。乘务长强迫自己冷静下来，迅速召集乘务组开了一次小会，把情况向大家说明，并安排好了各种应对措施，展现出了一名优秀乘务长所必须具备的各项心理素质和工作能力。在向乘客通报情况时，这名乘务长也充分利用自己的专业能力和诚恳态度，成功安抚了乘客。在飞机返航的过程中，乘务长不断与机组沟通，并及时将机组方面的信息总结和反馈给乘客，获取了乘客的充分信任，使得乘客能够在返航过程中保持必要的冷静，最终在机组及全体乘客的共同努力下，飞机顺利返航并重新降落在了北京首都国际机场，成功化解了这次危机。

另外一个让阿丽记忆深刻的例子是她的同事刘嫚，刘嫚在 AC 航空公司是毋庸置疑的金牌乘务长。她身上有很多值得空乘人员们学习的地方。刘嫚在一次重庆飞往上海的航班上，遇到了赶往上海做手术的一家人。一家人中的小姑娘罹患骨癌，刚刚做过化疗手术，但是病情并未好转，还需要赶往上海做截肢手术。刘嫚得知该情况后，协调其他乘客，为这家人调换了更好的位置。考虑到这家人的不易，刘嫚还在行程中开展了一次募捐活动。当飞机抵达上海时，刘嫚带领的乘务组获得了全体乘客的尊重。

5. 尾声

经过一段时间的认真记录和深入思考，阿丽发现她对于情绪劳动有了更加深入的了解。对于空乘人员的绩效考核与评价，并不能真正解决空乘人员的情绪劳动所引发的各类问题。阿丽又陷入了新的思考，是否还有什么更好的办法，能够在根本上解决这些问题。阿丽相信，解决问题的方法一定可以找到。

思考问题：

1. 从案例中来看，你认为哪些因素会影响情绪劳动？

2. 从案例中来看，当乘客有不满情绪时，空乘人员应当如何更好地提供情绪劳动？

3. 从本案例来看，空乘人员想要提高服务质量，提升情绪劳动的效果，应当具备哪些素质？

4. 情绪劳动给员工和顾客分别带来了哪些影响？

5. 从公司的角度来看，应当采用什么样的措施来保护员工的情绪资源？

分析要点：

1. 应用情绪劳动的理论对第1个思考问题进行分析。

2. 应用情绪劳动的理论对第2个思考问题进行分析。

3. 应用情绪管理的理论对第3个思考问题进行分析。

4. 应用情绪管理的理论对第4个思考问题进行分析。

5. 应用情绪管理的理论对第5个思考问题进行分析。

案例 3

成为教师和学生的朋友

知识点：

人格理论、能力理论、态度理论、激励理论、情绪管理理论、领导理论

案例目的：

本案例通过对宁波 RA 实验中学进行分析，引导学生理解个体中的人格理论、能力理论、态度理论、激励理论、情绪管理理论、领导理论。

案例正文：

1. 引言

周梅 2004 年到宁波 RA 实验中学工作，2014 年起担任校长之职。周梅可谓是 RA 实验中学的元老，见证了学校的发展壮大。周梅见证了一茬茬学生如园中青葵，在阳光雨露中成长，以这里为起点，走向远方。而她一直以来坚持的管理方式是，成为教师和学生的朋友。宁波 RA 实验中学新建不久时，规模小、底子薄，教师来自全国各地，绝大多数是缺乏教学经验的年轻教师，而且有的教师身在学校，眼观远方，待机高飞，教师队伍的不稳定性尤为突出。面对这种情况，身为校长的周梅，敢于改革创新，以身作则，为学校创建了一支素质良好、相对稳定的师资队伍，也为学校这几年优异的高考成绩奠定了基础。

2. 学校概况

宁波 RA 实验中学是由 RA 集团创建、直属宁波市教育局的一所全日制民办普通中学，是全国教育科研重点研究课题"尝试教育"理论研究的实践基地和先进单位，是全国民办先进学校、浙江省质量诚信品牌优秀示范单位、宁波市"5A"级平安校园。学校有在校生 1500 余人，教职员工 172 人，其中专职教师有 130 人。

学校实行中小班化教学，每班 40 余人，班级都配备多媒体设施，运用最先进

的现代教学手段开展教学。学校专注于中学生的教育和管理,这对提高教育质量,起着至关重要的作用。学校实行"自爱""自律"的自尊教育,每一个学生都能得到人格上的尊重与个性的发展。学校崇尚"做人第一"的教育思想,引导学生克服自身的各种陋习,与文明社会接轨;实行封闭式管理与开放性办学相结合的制度。

3. 成为学生的朋友

3.1 平等、尊重地和学生相处

"我们开展的一切工作,都是以学生的进步和成长为中心。因为家长选择RA实验中学就是对我们的信任,绝不能辜负家长的信任。"温柔的周梅在说这句话的时候,显得特别铿锵有力。

和学生相处时,周梅强调平等和尊重。她说,平等,可以让我们看到真实的学生;尊重,可以激发学生身上不一样的潜能、个性,帮助他们成长。

有一件事至今让她记忆犹新,她做班主任时,班上有个学生叫吴浩,他性格外向,活泼好动,喜欢探索外部世界,对新鲜事物充满好奇,喜欢追问为什么。他在课堂上坐不住,容易受到外界事物的干扰,老师上课时,他经常在下面讲话,影响老师上课和同学听课。周梅在了解这个同学的特点后,并没有直接公开地批评他,而是给予他足够的尊重。平时,她注意关心这个学生,有时和他聊天,谈谈他的兴趣爱好。上课过程中,如果向学生提问,周梅有时会叫吴浩回答,回答后会给予适当的肯定和表扬。通过一段时间的接触,她和吴浩关系融洽,能像朋友似的聊天。在课堂上,吴浩认真听讲,积极回答问题,基本能控制自己不讲话,如果周围有同学在闲聊,他还会提醒同学不要影响老师上课。

3.2 多看学生的困难,少看学生的问题

RA实验中学除了常规的班主任以外,还推行导师制,每位导师负责3～5位学生。导师要负责对结队的学生进行思想上的引导、学业上的辅导、心理上的疏导、生活上的指导。周梅也是其中一位导师。

周梅在处理学生问题时的方式是:多看学生的困难,少看学生的问题。曾经一

位学生在手机上用花呗进行巨额消费，被家长发现、批评后，这个学生想要离家出走。家长担心孩子走极端，他们处理不好，于是和周梅说了这件事。周梅二话不说联系到这位学生，仔细询问缘由。原来这位学生和同学周末结伴出去玩时，看到大家都穿了名牌运动鞋，心理不平衡，就想自己去网上购买几双。但是他没控制住自己，还买了很多其他东西，导致收到"天价账单"。父母强硬的批评又让他心里非常难受。周梅了解事件的原委后，温柔地开导了这位学生，学生马上意识到了自己的错误。

"如果你想管住学生，就须尊重他们，让他们感受到温暖，他们就会主动让你管，特别省劲儿。"周梅说。

王刚，周梅曾经担任他的导师，他个性要强，非常喜欢顶嘴，跟谁都要较真。有一次，周梅去观看全校的诗朗诵表演彩排，这位学生正好站在中心位。

彩排结束后，周梅悄悄地走到他身边，说："你可以把装着诗歌的文件夹稍微往下移一点，让观众看到你的表情，这样朗诵的效果就更好了。你在上面没有感觉，我在下面看就不一样。"学生有点惊讶，原来校长不是来走个过场，竟然还能看到旁人注意不到的细节。

于是，这位学生按照周梅说的话上去试了一遍，果然效果不一样。他偷偷地看着台下的周梅吐了吐舌头，露出了开心的笑容。

"孩子在长大的过程中，对外界的体验很重要，特别是在中学时期，心理非常敏感。我们做老师的一定要特别留意青春期孩子的心理特征。"周梅说。

这么多年，周梅最喜欢去的地方就是课堂。"心安之处，是课堂。"这是周梅十多年来从未改变过的教育初心。只要有空，她便会走进一间教室，坐在后面或挤在孩子们中间随堂听课，认认真真地与孩子们一起学习。

周梅听课绝对不是走过场。听完课后，她会细心总结，密密麻麻地做着笔记，下课后仔细询问学生学习的难点。

好多学生毕业多年后，仍旧惦记着那个亦师亦友、会帮自己解决难题的校长。

3.3 激发学生的潜能

每个学生都有自己的喜好与特长,但不是每个人都有足够多的机会去展示。这是资源分配的不合理,也是当代教育的尴尬之处。如果缺少尝试的机会,就降低了学生成功的可能,久而久之他们的潜能就会受到压抑。如何激发每一个孩子的潜能?教育界有各种尝试。

"我们坚持什么事情都让孩子先尝试,而不是老师先灌输。课堂要以学习为中心,以引导为抓手。"周梅说。

在这样的教育理论的指导下,RA实验中学根据学校的实际情况,不断进行调整和改革,最终形成了"三导四学"的课堂教学法则。三导即引导、督导和指导,四学即自主学习、合作学习、探究学习和体验学习。以一堂课为例,"三导四学"倡导先练后讲、精讲多练。让学生在预习的基础上发现问题、提出问题,老师收到学生的问题反馈后再确定教学目标,随时进行课堂教学的调整。"我们的课堂,是在充分了解学情基础上的教学,宁可一堂课的内容容量稍微少一点,也要以让学生掌握为核心。然后,辅以当堂检测、单独辅导等,从起点看终点,从入口看出口,成效慢慢就显现出来了。"周梅说。

4. 成为教师的朋友

4.1 共情管理

对于学校员工的管理,周梅认为,教师愿意找她倾诉就是最大的信任。RA实验中学现有员工172名,其中专职教师130名,中高级教师106名,中高级教师占专职教师的比例约为82%。教师平均年龄40岁,已逐步形成了一支素质良好、相对稳定的师资队伍。但在此之前,RA实验中学的师资稳定性面临很大的考验。RA实验学校虽然是宁波第一所享有事业单位法人身份的民办学校,但在教师的职业稳定性上,还是无法跟公办学校相比。前几年,有很多培养多年的骨干教师跳槽,这让周梅感到头疼。

在强化教师队伍这件事上,周梅十分注重与每一个教师"搭建关系"。首先,是学会倾听。"教师喜欢找我倾诉,就是对我最大的信任,不管是孩子的学习问题,还是日常管理的建议，我都非常乐意倾听。"在周梅看来，教师愿意跟自己讲真话，表示他们真正建立了一种好的关系。

其次，除了倾听，还要解决问题。周梅在员工管理中会站在人文关怀的角度看待问题。比如学校有一个中年教师，她孩子正好面临高考，学校就会适当考虑调整她的工作分配，允许她不用坐班。"教师只有心情愉悦，才能更好地投入工作。"周梅说。

罗红是英语组老师，来RA实验中学四年，之前，由于习惯性流产，她一直未能拥有自己的孩子。最近，罗红欣喜地发现自己怀孕了，周梅知道这个消息后，主动找到罗红，首先恭喜她怀上小孩；然后告诉她，让她暂时在家静心休养，保护好孩子，目前她的课，学校想办法让其他老师代课。校长的暖心安排瞬间感动了罗红，产假后，她全身心投入工作，如今，罗红已成为学校的明星老师。

同时周梅在管理教师时因人而异，针对不同的群体采取不同的方法。慢慢地，RA实验中学的教师队伍形成了一个巨大的磁场，吸引着全校教师投入全部的精力开展教学工作，学校的教学质量也越来越好。

4.2　薪酬体系管理

"努力为教师谋福利，解决他们的后顾之忧，是提升教师幸福指数、增强教师归属感的重要方式。"周梅说。

近年来，学校改革了薪酬分配体系，采用底薪加绩效工资的形式。底薪可以保障教职员工的基本生活，根据员工的职位、职级，学校每个月发放固定的金额；绩效工资和工作量相关联，可以激励教师们发挥自己的潜能，多上课，多做指导学生的工作。改革薪酬分配体系后，教师的平均年收入不断提高，社保基数翻了一番，学校中级、高级教师的社保基数已达到市直属公办学校同级教师的平均水平。

另外，在节假日前，学校都会采购不同的物品作为节日福利，比如，新年前发新年大礼包；五一节发水果；国庆节发月饼、糕点；等等，让员工能感受到学校实在的关怀。

4.3 员工培训管理

RA实验中学一直崇尚培训是送给员工最好的礼物这一理念。因此，有关教师的培训事项，会被明确地写到学校管理细则中。

学校通常组织四种类型的培训。第一，新入职员工培训。每年七月份，学校会招聘一些刚毕业的学生有针对性地组织新员工培训，培训内容包括：学校的概况、使命、愿景、价值观；学校的工作模式及规章制度；学校的薪酬福利待遇；等等。除此之外，还为每一位新教师指定导师，有利于新员工快速熟悉学校的环境，适应学校生活，也有利于他们的成长。第二，教学技能培训。学校会定期针对全校教师展开教学技能培训。另外，学校会针对不同教研室，组织具体科目的教学技能培训，邀请资深的校内外教师，在教研室进行研究讨论，共同探讨有价值的教学方法及教学模式。第三，教学比赛强化培训。学校鼓励教师们参加各种教学比赛，以此促进教学质量的提高。在比赛前，学校会举办培训讲座，邀请有经验的名师到校进行辅导。第四，校外培训。学校鼓励教师利用寒假或暑假参加相关的高品质培训项目。

近5年来，教师人均培训时长达到360学时，学校专职教师职称也得到大幅度提升。民办学校花巨资去外面请教师的事件经常发生，但周梅认为学校更应该花时间和精力去培养自己的人才队伍，这样的队伍才有归属感。RA实验中学这几年涌现出许多敬业爱岗、潜心教育的优秀教师，荣获"市教坛新秀""市优秀教师""市优秀班主任""市政治优质课一等奖""市数学说题比赛一等奖""第十九届语文报杯全国中学生作文大赛指导教师特级奖、省一级奖"等多项荣誉。

4.4 以身作则

周梅大多数周末就在学校。"既然是分管教学，那赶上学生上课，我肯定要在，有什么情况老师也能找到人处理。"周梅说。

暑假是建设学校的黄金时间。随着教育经费投入的增加，RA实验中学这几年每年暑假都有不少建设项目。所以假期时，周梅也依然像往常一样，过着家庭、学校两点一线的生活。轮到值周的时候，周梅通常早晨六点半就到学校，组织、指导住校学生晨操；晚上从一楼到五楼巡视36个班级的晚自习，在巡视完男、女生宿舍后才回家。

因此，赶上值周，她回家后只能看看孩子熟睡的脸孔，没有同孩子说话的机会。"儿子没抱怨过是不可能的。有段时间他一直不太理我，说我不和他交流。我就跟他说，你有你要做的事情，妈妈有妈妈要做的事情，我们把各自的事情做好。"周梅说。

后来，周梅的孩子被重点中学录取，过上了寄宿生活。母子俩见面更少了，但彼此关系却比之前更加融洽了。每周日下午，周梅都会尽量抽时间送儿子去学校，也借这一点车程的时间和他聊聊。

"妈妈，原来老师需要关注这么多事情，以前我还真是错怪你了，你有这么多学生要管。"孩子的理解，让周梅倍感欣慰。

5. 再创辉煌

近两年RA实验中学的高考升学率为100%，本科升学率达到45%，其中一些班级的本科升学率达到90%以上，每班次都有至少5名学生被一本院校首批录取。这些成绩的取得得益于学校近几年不断提升的教学质量。尽管与重点高中比，RA实验中学还存在一定的差距，但在民办高中里独树一帜，给同学们树立了强大的信心。

思考问题：

1. 根据组织行为学的概念，分析周梅在人格、态度、情绪管理、能力等方面的特点。
2. 联系案例分析周梅的领导风格。
3. 联系案例谈谈周梅是如何提高员工的工作满意度与参与度的？
4. 为什么学生和老师都喜欢找周梅交流？

分析要点：

1. 应用人格理论、态度理论、能力理论、情绪管理理论等对第1个思考问题进行分析。

2. 应用领导理论对第 2 个思考问题进行分析。

3. 应用激励理论、领导理论对第 3 个思考问题进行分析。

4. 应用激励理论、领导理论对第 4 个思考问题进行分析。

案例 4

L 公司人事部管理困境

知识点：

知觉理论、情绪智力理论、激励理论、工作满意度理论、能力理论

案例目的：

本案例通过对 L 公司进行分析，引导学生理解并应用个体中的知觉理论、情绪智力理论、激励理论、工作满意度理论、能力理论。

案例正文：

1. 引言

现今，经济飞速发展，各行各业也繁荣发展起来，竞争也变得剧烈起来。L 公司在发展的同时，不断创新管理模式，加快人才培养，实现工程项目的规范化管理，积极扩大业务范围，获取更多的市场份额。公司在各地设有多家分公司，各分公司独立经营。但是由于行业的规定，资质和工作人员须统一由总公司管理。

公司总经理郑海涛坐在办公室，思考公司近期出现的问题，并发消息给人力资源部经理郑玲，让她过来一起探讨。

2. 公司概况

L 公司位于宁波市，成立于 2003 年，拥有住建部核准的监理资质，包括建筑工程、市政工程、水利水电工程、机电安装工程、人防工程、工程招投标代理等，可以承接各类建筑工程监理业务、项目全过程咨询管理、招投标代理等业务。公司年产值名列行业前茅，是行业诚信纳税大户之一。已完成总建筑面积超过 2000 万平方米的工程，总造价达到 450 亿元。

L 公司实行在董事会领导下的总经理负责制。公司员工有两百多人，大部分为技术人员。这些技术人员中有多名行业专家和精英，其中中级以上专业技术人员占比超过 65%。同时，有多名专家入选行业专家库，为行业发展建言献策。

L公司目前的发展需要大量的高素质技术人员。这些技术人员必须符合公司的需求岗位和所需的知识结构。精准的人才需求定位，有利于招聘活动的开展、招聘渠道的选择，从而满足公司的招聘目标。

3. 公司人事部经理的烦恼

L公司的人力资源部门分为资质管理部和人事部。资质管理部主要负责企业和人员的资质管理，包括职业资格证书、职称证书、经营资质证书、行业协会资料等。人事部主要负责招聘工作。各分公司的招聘由分公司人事部员工使用总公司的招聘渠道，和总公司一起进行。

3.1 核心人才流失问题

最近人事部经理郑玲遇到一件烦心事，技术部的项目主管黄波提出了辞职。黄波从小一直保持很好的成绩，高考考入了985高校，在大学里，他成绩突出，是一个有自信和抱负的学生，毕业后，他顺利进入L公司。两年后，他由于出色的工作业绩被任命为技术部的项目主管，负责一个新项目的开发。他手下有10个技术员，他相信只要努力，就一定能顺利完成新项目。

半年后项目组新来了一位技术开发人员，叫秋明。秋明很快就投入到工作中，工作能力也很强，逐渐崭露头角。

工作几天后，秋明向项目组成员谈了他的想法，又给大家讲了一些相关的数学模型和人工智能方面的知识。项目组成员对秋明刮目相看，认为秋明很有能力。整整一天，黄波感到心情郁闷，他自己也说不清为什么。

一个月后，项目组召开项目论证研讨会，黄波首先提出了自己的方案，大多数成员对他的方案表示认同，同时也提出一些完善修改的建议，黄波感到很开心。但是轮到秋明发言时，他提出了一个与黄波完全不同的方案，大家听完后认为不可行。秋明并没有被大家的反应吓倒，反而兴奋地向大家解释方案的具体细节，他出色的表达能力与严密的逻辑推理能力使大家觉得他是一个不可多得的人才。最后，大多数成员都表示理解和支持他的方案。

公司最后采用了秋明的方案，同时准备在一个星期后请专家来公司对这个新项目方案进行论证。按常规，黄波作为项目组主管应该在论证会上做主要发言人，于是他就试探性地问总经理："秋明是新方案的主要贡献者，有研究经验，是不是让他做主要发言人？"总经理看着他，高兴地说："你的建议很好，就照你说的办吧，让秋明做主要发言人。"黄波感到很失望。

论证会上，秋明的汇报获得了巨大成功，他清晰的思维、精辟的论证和杰出的表达能力给全体与会者留下了深刻的印象。黄波心里佩服秋明的能力，但同时也有一种说不出的难受感觉。

论证会后，有些项目组成员对秋明冷淡起来，他们认为他太爱表现自己。秋明也因此开始变得沉默起来。与此同时，黄波也有点闷闷不乐，一个月后，他向人事部提出辞职申请。当郑玲收到辞职申请时，她陷入沉思，黄波为什么要离职呢？公司该如何留住人才呢？另外，公司在进行新员工招聘时是否存在问题呢？

3.2 团队协调管理问题

近几年，随着公司的发展，项目组成员越来越多，团队之间的协调管理出现不少问题。

郑明是客户维护部技术人员，他比较内向，技术能力较强，做事积极。最近，公司接到几次客户方领导对郑明的投诉，这对他的工作情绪和积极性打击很大。客户维护部经理去客户方了解到，客户方提出需求后，郑明不和他们商量就直接开始工作。两方沟通不畅，导致后面来来回回做，浪费时间，影响工作效率。

郑明的工作和为人，团队里是认可的，但也有人认为他不会说话办事，工作方式方法有问题，情绪智力一般，有时会造成一些负面影响。

团队里另外一个员工胡军，他做事认真，执行力高，从不拖延，而且坚持原则，公司总经理也有意培养他。但是胡军有一个比较突出的问题——他说话很直，不懂得变通，经常和别的团队争吵，闹得大家都不开心。因此，他经常遭到投诉，认为他推诿、不知变通等，导致胡军虽然平时工作认真，但业绩却表现平平。

安装部黄磊是一个项目的负责人，这个项目的其他员工都经常加班，他却每天早早就走了，即使马上到交付时间了，也依旧是这个样子。发给他的消息经常出现一直未读的情况，有时到第二天已读后也没有回复。而且他上班经常迟到，据人事部统计，迟到次数在技术部排名第一。目前团队人手不足，黄磊技术能力在部门还算不错，他工作最久，经验也是最丰富的。

3.3 培训项目没有效果

受新冠疫情影响，公司的业绩大幅下降，为提高公司的经营效率，公司领导层决定对公司全体员工进行培训，从整体上提高员工素质。人事部主管阮萍接手了这个培训项目，她从外部请来几个有名的培训师，为公司组织了几场培训。受训人员包括高层管理者、部门经理、主管、技术人员、行政管理人员等。培训内容包括基本技术、沟通能力和管理能力等方面。培训一般安排在周末，所以一些员工总是找理由不来参加，或者来培训现场报到后，中途离开。培训后，对参加培训的人员没有设立考核制度，对培训师的教学质量也没有设立评估制度。员工们参与培训时也极其懒散。连续培训几个月后，公司的整体业绩非但没有任何改观，反而又出现了下滑，而公司却花费了大量的培训费用。对此情景，公司领导层得出结论：培训没有效果！

4. 尾声

总经理郑海涛与人事部经理郑玲谈话后，眉头紧锁，脸上没有丝毫笑容，他意识到公司目前面临着一些困境，对外，新冠疫情不知道何时能过去；对内，却出现越来越多的问题。

思考问题：

1. 你认为黄波为什么要辞职？L公司应该如何留住核心人才？
2. 你认为胡军是否能胜任工作？为什么？
3. 简述L公司在招聘过程中出现的问题，给出你的建议。
4. 结合案例谈谈情绪智力对工作业绩的影响。

分析要点:

1. 应用工作满意度理论、激励理论对第 1 个思考问题进行分析。

2. 应用能力理论、知觉理论对第 2 个思考问题进行分析。

3. 应用知觉理论对第 3 个思考问题进行分析。

4. 应用情绪智力理论对第 4 个思考问题进行分析。

案例 5

HC 公司的知识型员工与非物质激励

知识点：

知识型员工理论、企业文化理论、激励理论

案例目的：

本案例通过对 HC 公司进行分析，引导学生理解知识型员工理论、企业文化理论、激励理论。

案例正文：

1. 引言

林丽是 HC 公司的人力资源部门总监。她原本是温州一家制鞋厂的人事部门经理，早些年她的老领导出来创业，最近请她过来辅助。出于对老领导的信任和感谢，林丽二话没说就从制鞋厂辞职，来到了新成立的 HC 公司。

2. 公司概况

HC 公司是一家科技制造型企业。它主要生产工业机器人的核心部件，包括伺服电动机、控制器和减速机。这三个零部件是工业机器人最为重要的基础零件，早些时候完全被国外垄断。HC 公司决定在这个领域进行深耕与突破，成长速度非常快。HC 公司的产品逐渐替代了部分进口的核心部件，同时也在不断提高产品质量和技术。

HC 公司在成立之初，凭借衢州市政府的大力支持和创始人自身的影响力快速建立了一支包括研发、生产和销售的高效团队。随着公司的成长和快速扩张，团队从最初的 100 多人增加到近 800 人，其中研发人员占比接近 40%。对研发的重视是 HC 公司能够快速崛起的重要原因之一。目前，HC 公司在伺服电动机领域已经是国内当之无愧的第一，控制器和减速机方面也在快速发展，有望在未来五年成长为行业领域的领头羊。

然而过快的成长,以及对于研发的依赖,也给公司带来了一些问题。首先,虽然衢州市政府非常重视 HC 公司,也给予了大量的扶助和优惠政策,但是 HC 公司对于相对高层次的人才来说,还是严重缺乏吸引力。而 HC 公司又需要大量的高层次研发人才。这使得 HC 公司创始人之一的徐东非常头疼。其次,HC 公司人员规模迅速扩大,原有的人事管理方法已经不再适用,亟须改革。林丽也因此来到 HC 公司,想办法解决徐东现在最关心的问题——如何吸引和留住高层次的人才。

3. 林丽的挑战

虽然林丽毫不犹豫地来到 HC 公司,但是在真正开始工作之后,她心里还是有些担心。因为她没有信心解决好 HC 公司目前所面临的问题。而她目前所面临的工作情况也确实给她带来了极大的挑战。

这个月林丽已经接到了三个离职申请,而且这些离职申请都来自研发部门。刚刚递交离职申请的是研发部门的小肖。小肖从毕业起就开始在 HC 公司工作,已经有三年了。林丽对小肖的情况有一定了解,于是拉着他询问了很久。

经过沟通,林丽发现小肖对公司的薪资待遇和工作节奏都比较满意,他离职更多是因为衢州的地理位置,他希望去更大的平台试一试。

小肖的说法让林丽陷入了沉思。这让她联想到前两个本月辞职的同事——研发部门的小赵和小李。他们辞职有一个共同的原因,就是认为衢州这个地方平台较小。

这三个人的离职让林丽意识到,HC 公司人才流失最大的原因就是区位问题。HC 公司的员工们来自全国各地,普遍比较年轻。而且最为重要的是,他们都拥有较高的学历,研发人员中有半数拥有研究生学历。林丽也明白,这些人思考的问题和看重的内容,和生产部门的操作工人们完全不同。林丽看着桌上的辞呈,陷入了沉思。

4. 知识型员工

小肖走后,虽然一切都仿佛回归了平静,但是林丽的焦虑丝毫没有减轻。然而林丽并没有这方面的经验,一时间无从下手。她想到自己有一个高中同学,现在正在大学里做管理学专业的老师。于是,林丽便联系了这位多年未见的老同学,准备向他取取经。

林丽很快就找到了在宁波大学工作的张翔。林丽一见张翔便向他说明了来意。听完林丽的描述，张翔沉思了片刻，便开口说道："其实你们的问题，用一句话描述，就是怎么留住知识型员工。"

原来，HC 公司的研发人员属于一种特殊的员工类型——知识型员工。知识型员工，是指那些掌握知识并将知识运用到实际工作中的员工。知识型员工在企业中从事生产、创造和应用知识的各项活动，他们拥有知识资本这种生产资料。

与张翔的沟通使林丽获益良多。她决定回去后，按照老同学的指导，总结知识型员工的特点并做出相应的解决方案。

5. 林丽的分析

林丽做的第一件事情，就是对 HC 公司知识型员工的特点进行分析。经过一段时间的观察和了解，她对知识型员工有了更深的认识。知识型员工主要有如下特点。

5.1 较高的个人素质

研发部门员工都拥有本科及以上学历，所以他们在学历水平上明显比其他部门的员工要高很多。除此之外，HC 公司的研发部门员工在技术层面也具有很明显的优势。这些员工主要来自计算机及电子信息等专业，很多都拥有自己的专利，一些员工还有发表学术论文的能力和经历。这些特点显著区别于其他部门的员工。

5.2 很强的自主性

林丽还发现，知识型员工是一群相当有活力的人。他们和生产部门的流水线操作工的工作特点具有显著的不同。比较来说，生产部门的流水线操作工需要被动地适应设备运转。流水线操作工对于工作的态度很难有自主性。然而研发部门有所不同，研发部门的员工普遍具有主动性，愿意主动去发现工作中存在的问题，也不太需要领导的约束和管教。

5.3 高价值的创造性劳动

最为重要的是，研发部门的员工所从事的工作对于公司来说具有很高的效用。HC 公司能够迅速从一家小型科技公司成长为细分领域内的明星企业，显然得益于实力强劲的研发部门。这些研发人员不仅打破了国外企业长期以来在伺服电动机领域的垄断地位，也在此基础上开发出一系列具有竞争力的新技术，能够在专利领域和国外传统优势企业进行竞争。这些也是 HC 公司把"五年内将控制器和减速机发展成为行业领头羊"作为目标的底气。

5.4 劳动过程难以监控

负责研发部门的绩效专员不止一次向林丽抱怨自己的工作很难做。林丽发现，问题的症结在于，研发部门员工们的工作成果很难用一套固定的绩效考核方案进行衡量。研发部门的负责人也不止一次向林丽反映，HC 公司开展绩效考核之后，研发部门的员工存在很多不满。因为他们的工作难以监控，有些技术开发工作，并不是简单的重复性工作，劳动过程往往是无形的，劳动成果也难以衡量。采用一般的绩效考核方案来对研发部门员工进行评价，显然是不公平的。

5.5 渴望实现自我价值

最让林丽头疼的是这些知识型员工带有强烈的实现自我价值的愿望。这种愿望当然是好的，但是对于管理者来说也意味着很多麻烦。比如之前离职的三个研发部门同事，他们离职的原因有一个共同点，就是他们对于现状的不满足，以及对于更高层次发展的追求。这些员工喜欢有挑战性的工作，对于日常的一般性的工作很容易厌倦。离开公司，并不一定是因为公司给他们的物质待遇不好，也可能是因为他们觉得 HC 公司不能给他们带来更多的挑战和乐趣。

6. 应对策略

从知识型员工的特点来看，劳动过程难以监控和渴望自我价值实现这两个特点增加了管理难度。林丽觉得在对这些知识型员工有了更充分的认识之后，制订相应的策略就更容易了。于是，她又专门花了一个星期，和所有的研发部门员工进行了面谈，希望了解他们的真实需求。她相信，在了解这些人的真实需求之后，如何激励和留住他们就不是问题了。

林丽的应对策略从以下几个方面入手。

首先，改革研发部门的绩效考核体系。她发现最为研发部门员工诟病的就是现有的绩效考核体系。根据当前的绩效考核体系，研发部门员工需要按照人力资源部门制订的目标开展工作。然而，一方面，人力资源部门对于研发工作并不了解；另一方面，研发的实际工作过程是难以监控和衡量的，现行的考核方式显然不合适。林丽认为，研发部门需要实行个性化的绩效考核方案。经研究，公司决定在研发部门试行互联网企业常用的目标与关键结果模式（简称为OKR模式），给研发部门更高的独立性和更大的自由空间，鼓励他们进行探索。

其次，提供更多精神层面的非物质激励。林丽了解到研发部门员工对现有的薪资报酬较为满意。然而物质激励并不是他们看重的全部，他们更需要精神层面的非物质激励。在这方面，林丽制订了很多相应的方案：加强公司文化建设，提高研发人员对于公司的认同感；提高研发人员在公司内部的地位和受尊重程度；积极开展关于研发人员职业生涯规划的培训和指导，为研发人员在公司内部的成长道路提供更加明确的方向和路径；等等。这些方案是对当前物质激励的有效补充。

最后，采用更加有针对性的按需激励方案。林丽认为，知识型员工和一般员工最大的区别在于他们的需求是多样化的。因此，激励方案要有针对性。虽然这给人力资源部门带来了很大的工作压力，毕竟想要实时动态地掌握研发部门员工的多样化需求，需要投入大量的时间和精力。然而林丽认为这一切都是值得的。因为研发部门的这些员工是HC公司最大的财富。只有研发团队稳定，才能确保HC公司取得长足的发展。

7. 尾声

林丽制订的应对策略已经试行了一段时间，效果还是比较令人满意的。然而，这对于林丽来说仅仅是工作的开始，后面她需要面临的挑战还有很多。例如，衢州的区位劣势仍然无法得到解决，虽然现阶段能够比较好地留住以及激励研发部门的员工，但是未来公司还要发展，也必然需要更多更高水准的知识型员工加入。然而衢州对这些高层次人才确实缺乏吸引力。那么，真正的解决方案应该是什么呢？林丽陷入了新的思考。

思考问题:

1. 什么是知识型员工？他们有哪些特点？

2. HC 公司遇到了哪些问题？为什么会产生这些问题？

3. HC 公司采取了哪些方式来解决知识型员工的激励问题？

4. 你认为还有哪些方式可以用来促进对知识型员工的激励？

5. 你认为未来 HC 公司想要吸引更多的知识型员工，还有哪些措施可以采用？

分析要点:

1. 应用知识型员工理论对第 1 个思考问题进行分析。

2. 应用企业文化理论对第 2 个思考问题进行分析。

3. 应用企业文化理论对第 3 个思考问题进行分析。

4. 应用激励理论对第 4 个思考问题进行分析。

5. 应用激励理论和企业文化理论对第 5 个思考问题进行分析。

案例 6

杭州"那天·手工艺主题民宿"团队创业的曲折经历

知识点：

领导力风格、团队属性、团队决策、团队冲突、权力与政治行为、团队发展五阶段模型、输入—过程—结果模型、间断平衡模型、权力与政治行为

案例目的：

本案例通过对杭州"那天·手工艺主题民宿"团队进行分析，引导学生理解并应用领导力风格、团队属性、团队决策、团队冲突、权力与政治行为、团队发展五阶段模型、输入—过程—结果模型、间断平衡模型、权力与政治行为。

案例正文：

1. 引言

创业是个艰难的过程，不仅要面临各种资源不足的限制，还要面对极高的不确定性（McMullen and Shepherd, 2006）。正因为如此，大多数创业活动都是由团队发起和开展，用集体的智慧和资源来应对创业活动中的困难（Mol, Khapova and Elfring, 2015; Moran et al., 2020）。这种方式虽然有利于克服创业活动中的限制和困难，但是也可能从团队内部产生新的冲突和危机。本案例将通过一个创业团队的真实故事来体现团队创业经历的艰难和曲折。

2. 发端

王女士是杭州小有名气的手工艺人，她拥有一家文创公司，主要销售自己制作的书画、皮包、摆件和笔记本等工艺品。由于公司的办公场所限制，缺乏作品展示的空间，加之杭州民宿市场的火爆，2014年，王女士萌生了开办一家手工艺主题的民宿的想法。民宿的一楼可以展示和销售文创公司的手工艺品，二楼和三楼则可以用于开展住宿业务。通过手工艺与民宿的结合，不仅可以为手工艺品提供展销场所，还可以展示有别于其他民宿的亮点，有利于吸引客户。有了这个想法后，王女士开

始搜寻开民宿的合适地点，经过多方打听和熟人介绍，王女士选择在白乐桥村开设民宿。白乐桥村位于西湖边的灵隐寺脚下，地理位置得天独厚，背靠北高峰，翻过一座山就是西溪湿地，村中植被茂盛，还有一条清澈的小溪从北高峰流下贯穿整个村子，风景十分宜人。白乐桥村中原本只有一些茶农居住，村中有上百栋二至三层的农家小楼，在被民宿从业者发现其地理优越性后，村中的房屋早已陆陆续续出租用于开办民宿。白乐桥村现已成为西湖周边民宿的重要聚集地之一。

3. 团队初建

选定民宿地点后，2015 年初，王女士开始着手准备，但过程中却遇到了困难。

一方面，开设民宿所需要的资金超出了预算。第一，虽然白乐桥村只是一个小村子，但是得天独厚的地理优势使得民宿业的发展非常迅速，由于需求量较大，而村中房屋的供给有限，一栋 300～500 平方米的房屋每年的租金已经从过去的 5 万～6 万上涨到 30 万～40 万，并且租金需要半年一付甚至一年一付。第二，由于村中过去曾被改造过作为民宿的房屋大多早已被其他民宿长期租用，剩下的可租用的房屋需要进行较大规模的装修才能适应民宿的需要。第三，因为王女士想以手工艺为主题，所以进一步加大了装修改造的工作量。初步估计，装修改造的成本将在 60 万以上，总体成本已经接近 100 万，超过了王女士的预算。

另一方面，开设民宿比想象中更加复杂，王女士对开办民宿的相关流程手续，以及后续的管理等都缺乏经验。而在项目推进的过程中，王女士发现开办一个民宿不仅需要租房和装修，还需要办理消防安全许可证、营业执照、卫生许可证、从业人员健康证明等一系列手续和证件。同时需要确定民宿的定价、运营和推广方式，还需要学习员工招聘、管理以及维护上下游关系等一系列工作。这些对王女士而言都是非常陌生的。所以开设民宿的工作量和所需的经验也超出了王女士的预期。

面临上述困难，王女士自知凭借自己的能力和资源难以顺利推进这个民宿项目，为此，她决定招募合伙人，想借助集体的力量来弥补自身资金和经验的不足，进而推进创业项目顺利开展。王女士首先从自己过去的合作伙伴和朋友中寻找到一位愿意加入创业项目的合伙人，然后经人介绍，有另外三位合伙人决定出资加入。这些人的加入不仅补充了民宿项目的资金来源，同时因为有一位新加入的成员有开办经济型连锁酒店的经验，还给团队带来了酒店行业的重要经验。至此，王女士组建了一个包含自己、黄先生、刘女士、白先生和李女士在内的五人创业团队。团队组建成功后，大部分资金需求得到了满足，但是现金和后备经费依然存在短缺。为此，王女士凭借自己在手工艺圈和众多客户中的影响力，对民宿项目发起了众筹，承诺所有参与众筹的人都可以根据自己的出资比例享有民宿的利润分红。该众筹项目得到了许多王女士的亲友和客户的支持，过程非常顺利。至此，创业团队基本解决了民宿项目的资金问题。

4. 困难接踵而至

随着人员和资金的到位，团队开始迅速推进民宿项目。2015年末，团队成功租到一栋位置较好的别墅，该别墅坐落在白乐桥村的中心位置，背后紧邻着从北高峰流下的横穿村子的青溪，并且青溪在别墅侧面形成了一个小型的瀑布，景色非常优美。为了确保长期经营，团队与房主签订了"三年+两年续租"的长期协议，并一次性支付了第一年的租金。接着，团队开始着手别墅的装修改造工作，原本团队预期这项工作能在三个月内完成，但实际上远没有预想的顺利。

因为事先约定将民宿的一楼作为王女士的工作室或文创公司的展销场所，所以民宿的一楼和二楼、三楼的装修被分开来进行。一楼主要由王女士负责，二楼和三楼的装修设计则请了装修公司和家装设计师来负责。当团队期待着装修工作如期进行的时候，问题却接二连三地出现。首先，装修和施工的难度比预想大很多。因为租用的别墅虽然之前也曾被用于开办民宿，但改造并不彻底。原本房屋的结构设计并未考虑到供旅客居住的需要，因此需要从整体上进行改造，但是很多设计和施工由于房屋结构的限制根本无法展开，设计师在考虑原有房屋结构的基础上进行的方案始终无法让团队完全满意。其次，装修公司的施工人员因为迟迟无法确定动工方案，大多数时候都处于无所事事的状态。这给团队成员留下了不良的印象，团队成员开始指责装修公司不负责任、拖延工期。因为对民宿经营者而言，装修的进度直接影响了其回收成本和实现盈利的进度，所以团队与装修公司之间的矛盾日益升级。

在装修了近五个月后,团队成员与装修公司产生了激烈的口头冲突。团队成员对于装修公司工期进度的一再拖延表示了强烈的不满,而装修公司则对于团队事先未与他们有效沟通房屋结构问题,以及过高的设计和施工标准表示不能接受。在双方矛盾激化的情况下,装修公司决定只保留团队已经预付的工程款,并与团队协商决定退出施工。装修公司退出后,为了将装修推进下去,团队成员召开了集体会议商议对策。考虑到后续工程再寻找装修设计师的成本较高,大家一致决定由具备一定工艺经验和艺术品味的王女士来负责民宿进一步的硬装和软装工作,其他成员将全力配合。

5. 内部矛盾激化

让团队成员没有预料到的是,这一安排却让团队内部逐渐出现矛盾。在分工后王女士快速地开展了相关工作,为装修的收尾制订了方案,并且在团队成员的帮助下联系到愿意接手的施工队,开始着手进行收尾工作。为了更快地推进,王女士还加班加点地确定了整个民宿需要的家具、电器和装饰等一整套的软装方案。为此王女士特别召开了一次成员会议来商讨和确定最后的方案,但是会议的过程和结果都并不如意。在会上,除黄先生外,其他三位成员对于王女士的软装方案并不认同。王女士表示原先团队已经授权自己确定软装方案,而此时反对有悖于过去的决策;而另外三位成员则表示王女士的方案花费过高,与原先确定的计划存在极大的出入。双方争执不下,最后只能无奈暂时搁浅软装方案。

此次会议后,团队成员间的裂痕慢慢出现。刘女士、李女士和白先生原本就相互熟悉,过往有一起经商的经历,他们三个人慢慢地形成了一个小团体。三人小团体想拉拢民宿的主要出资人和发起者王女士,并试图将黄先生排挤出创业团队。由于团队的财务工作是由黄先生负责,他们开始质疑黄先生财务工作的能力,将装修花费过高的责任推向黄先生,甚至向王女士散播谣言,称黄先生可能挪用了部分团队的资金用于偿还自己的贷款。王女士并不相信这些指责,她与黄先生在创业前就曾有合作共事的经验,信任其职业操守和品行。并且如果将黄先生排挤出团队,王女士就有被其他三人架空的危险。因此她在三人小团体指责黄先生时经常出面维护黄先生。至此，团队之间逐渐出现了互不信任和相互敌对的苗头。而这一苗头在一个意外的政府行政命令的影响下被彻底引燃。

2016年9月初，二十国集团（G20）领导人第十一次峰会在杭州举办，这一会议是推进杭州城市建设，以及向全世界展示城市风采的重要契机。但也给杭州的城市安保和环境整治提出了高要求，杭州市政府对此高度重视。距白乐桥村不到五百米处有一家五星级的酒店被一个国家的代表团包场入住，虽然G20峰会9月初才开幕，但是从8月下旬开始，就有代表团的先遣人员陆续入住。从安全和环境的角度考虑，市政府要求酒店周边的道路施工和装修施工全部暂停。为此，民宿的装修施工将被延期至少一个月，这对本身时间并不富裕，同时急需现金流的创业团队而言是一个巨大的打击。

面对这一问题，团队成员为了自身的利益彻底分裂开来。三人小团体开始萌生了退出团队另谋出路的打算。而此时恰好白乐桥村中有一家营业中的民宿正在寻求转让，于是他们就想从团队中退股，然后接手这家民宿，这样可以更迅速地实现成本回收甚至盈利。而对于王女士而言，这个手工艺主题的民宿项目是不可割舍的，一方面这关乎她自己的理想和追求；另一方面该项目已经通过众筹得到了亲友的赞助，放弃这个项目或者抛弃手工艺这个主题将让她失信于人，使得长期积累的声誉和人脉受损，因此王女士想联合黄先生继续保留这个项目。团队成员为此争执不下，对于王女士一方而言，三个成员的出资额达到了民宿项目总出资额的40%以上，而民宿装修本身已经花费了大量的经费，这时候三人要求全额退股造成的资金缺口难以弥补；而对于其他三人而言，他们对这一项目的进展已缺乏信心，并且对于王女士和黄先生缺乏信任，要求获得财务管理权才能继续合作。双方难以协调，陷入了僵持。

6.团队重组与重新上路

鉴于民宿迟迟无法开始营业，但是一楼的艺术工作室已经基本装修完毕，王女士开始尝试先承接一些艺术相关的业务，来提升民宿的知名度。为此，王女士一楼的工作室承接了一个儿童绘画大赛的展览活动。但是在展览前一天，当大量的画作和展架运到民宿时，三人小团体的不合作态度彻底导致了团队的分裂。在展览材料运抵后，王女士邀请团队成员一起布置展厅，但是三人小团体采取了不闻不问和冷眼旁观的态度，导致展厅的布置根本无法开展。无奈之下，王女士决定再次召集全部成员开会，会上三人小团体明确表达了不再合作和退股的要求，并且没有转圜的余地。王女士和黄先生见强留三人已经没有意义，只好答应了三人的要求，并在双方协商后退还了三人当初认购股份的大部分资金。至此，创业团队彻底分家。

三人小团体在退股后很快接手了那家转让中的民宿，事实上在团队彻底分家前，他们甚至已经和对方谈妥了接手的细节并达成了初步的协议，因此他们接手民宿的过程非常顺利，反而赶在王女士和黄先生的手工艺主题民宿之前开始了经营。王女士和黄先生则决定继续推动手工艺主题民宿这个项目，这个项目已经和王女士的职业生涯紧密地联系在了一起，王女士不想放弃，黄先生对此也表示支持。经过商议后，他们对于以后民宿项目的管理和决策进行了分工：大部分经营性的决策都由王女士拍板，黄先生只提供建议；而对于经营战略、新项目投资等重大决策，则由两人共同商议决定；其他通过众筹获得股份的小股东将继续不享有经营的权利，只接受盈利分红。从此，团队分裂后，王女士和黄先生两人组成新的团队继续他们的创业之路。

7. 不顺利的开端

重新上路的团队首先面临的问题就是资金不足，三位成员退股后，团队原本就不充足的经费就变得更加捉襟见肘，已经完全无法支持民宿后续的装修和经营。而解决这一问题的可行方案并不多。一方面，上次的失败经历使得团队对于继续招募合伙人已经失去了信心。有兴趣以较高股份比例投资民宿的投资者一般都要求经营权力，而根据上次的经验，想招募能够彼此信任且具有合作精神的投资者非常困难；招募纯粹的财务投资者同样行不通，民宿的利润率并不高，很难吸引财务投资者。另一方面，再次众筹这个方案同样存在障碍，为了民宿这个项目王女士已经开展过众筹，现在民宿尚未开业又要再次众筹，将大大影响她的声誉，并且可能会引发对非法集资的质疑。在缺乏可行方案的情况下，王女士不得不抵押了自己的房产，获得了宝贵的资金来填补创业项目的资金缺口。在人员方面，三个成员的退出也使得民宿人手短缺。王女士为民宿招聘了一位前台和一位保洁，基本上解决了这一问题。接下来的重点工作就是要对民宿的装修进行收尾。

王女士和黄先生商议后很快达成共识：团队全权委托王女士敲定后续的装修方案等相关事宜，并在G20峰会期间确定具体方案。在接近一个月的停工期间，王女士和装修队沟通确定了具体的施工细节，并确定好了后续软装的材料和家具。G20峰会结束后，民宿的装修在王女士与装修队的合作下推进得非常顺利，不到一个月的时间就完成了所有后续的工作。在2016年10月下旬，前期准备工作终于全部完成，"那天·手工艺主题民宿"正式开始对外营业（图6-1）。回想起来，从开始创办民宿到民宿正式营业已经用了接近一年的时间，其中民宿的装修就用了将近八个月，而原本团队预期的装修时长是三个月。

图6-1　装修后的民宿外观

民宿开业后，预想中的火爆场景并没有出现，入住的顾客只有寥寥几人，在非周末时通常一天都没有一个顾客入住，这样的状况让团队成员非常着急。王女士和黄先生分析了顾客少的原因，想从中找到突破口。他们发现，一方面，由于装修进度的拖延，民宿开业时正好错过了暑期和十月份杭州的旅游旺季，导致民宿损失了大量的外地顾客，客源本身不充足。另一方面，这个别墅两年前也曾做过民宿，为了注册等方面的便利，新的民宿依然部分沿用了原民宿的名称——"那天"，只是将"手工艺主题民宿"作为后缀加入到名称中。在各大旅游网站中，民宿继承了原民宿的账号和"那天"的名称，然而原民宿的评价并不高，并且遗留了大量负面评价，诸如"床铺不干净""房间有虫子""服务态度一般"。再加之入住过新店的客户本身就很少，难以在短时间内扭转以往积累的负面评价，这些都导致了民宿一开张就迎来了生意惨淡的困境。

综上所述，民宿刚一开张，如何吸引客户、提高美誉度的难题就摆在了重组后的创业团队面前。如果无法快速地解决这一问题并实现盈利，王女士房屋抵押带来的还款压力、众筹带来的分红压力将进一步威胁民宿项目的生存。

8. 走向正轨、实现盈利

为了摆脱经营困境，王女士和黄先生开始尝试多种举措来吸引顾客。团队最核心的战略是，充分利用民宿的手工艺主题，即不仅仅将手工艺作为民宿的一种外在风格，而是将其作为顾客入住民宿后的一个体验环节。团队分析发现，在此之前，民宿虽然以手工艺为主题，但是并未有效利用这一特点。民宿整体装修都采用了江南手工艺的风格，所有床品都是江南地区具有代表性的扎染工艺制作的蓝印花布四件套，民宿中的家具、摆设和装饰都无一不体现了水墨江南的诗情画意（图6-2）。可惜的是，除了直接造访民宿外，顾客都很难体会到民宿的特别之处，网络酒店平台的宣传广告又十分昂贵，对于艰难起步中的团队而言难以承受。正当团队一筹莫展时，正好迎来了一个较为知名的网络酒店平台的推广活动，如果参与活动为该平台的顾客提供费用优惠或者礼品等，就可以获得免费引流和宣传。团队认为该活动是吸引顾客的重要机会，为此，团队向平台承诺对周日到周四入住的顾客都提供八折优惠，并在此基础上承诺为所有入住的顾客提供一份小手工艺品作为礼物。

图 6-2　民宿客房布置

这一举措起到了立竿见影的效果，民宿的网络预订量获得了很大程度的提升。并且随着已光顾顾客的增加，民宿的江南手工艺风格受到了很多顾客的喜爱和推荐。有些顾客直接包揽了酒店所用的床上四件套，另外一些顾客则对收到的手工艺小礼品表示非常喜欢，要求购买更多作为旅游纪念品回馈给亲友。从中，团队逐渐发现了江南特色手工艺品的商机，为此团队将一楼王女士的手工艺工作坊重新进行了定位和改造，在保留其手工艺展销功能的同时，加大顾客的可参与性。入住民宿的顾客可以以相对优惠的价格亲手在一楼的手工艺工作坊中制作头花、摆件、笔记本、鼠标垫等小工艺品，还能亲手染制具有江南特色的蓝印花布。

这一举措取得了很好的效果，大多数入住民宿的顾客都在一楼的工作坊参与了手工制作工艺品的活动，进而大大增加了民宿整体的营业额；并且这一特色还为民宿吸引了大量的顾客，许多家长都希望带着孩子来民宿体验手工制作，甚至一些小型的旅行团也开始入住民宿。民宿的经营状况得到了很大的改观，周末经常处于一房难求的状态，在非周末时的入住率也有很大程度的提升，通常能保持在八成以上。与此同时，顾客对于民宿的评价也获得了提升，在主流酒店或旅游平台上，即使受到了老店大量低评分累积的拖累，民宿的评分也有显著的提升。

从此，民宿的经营彻底步入了正轨。

图 6-3 民宿摆件图

9. 尾声

正式运营三年多后,"那天·手工艺主题民宿"已经是白乐桥村最具代表性和最受欢迎的民宿之一。现在的"那天·手工艺主题民宿"成为了许多希望感受"江南"情调的游客来杭州旅行的首选落脚点之一。顾客们对于民宿的服务和品位都给予了很高的评价。现在的"那天·手工艺主题民宿"不仅仅是一家民宿,还成为了友谊的桥梁和见证者。很多旅客入住过"那天·手工艺主题民宿"后都对其恋恋不舍,他们会将一些朋友聚会、同学会等也安排到这里。一些顾客还与"那天·手工艺主题民宿"的经营者和员工建立起了友谊,他们托王女士在西湖边购买最正宗的西湖龙井,还有一些外地的游客在回乡后给王女士寄来特产和小纪念品。民宿也不再仅限于住宿和手工艺制作体验的业务,还创办了一家微信店铺,用于售卖王女士手工坊制作的具有江南特色并结合现代审美的服装和配饰,由于手工制作且款式别致,同样受到了民宿住客乃至非住客的欢迎,一款产品上架后基本属于脱销的状态。

本案例讲述了一个创业团队的小故事,从中可以看到,即使是开办一家民宿这样的"小生意",依然要面临多方面的困难,而团队内部的冲突,团队外部环境的变化等都会对创业过程和结果产生重要的影响。如何应对创业过程中的不确定性和各方面的限制，如何组建和发展一个高效的创业团队，都值得研究者和创业者深入思考。

思考问题：

1. 从这个案例中看，团队或群体的发展可以分为几个阶段？
2. 案例中创业团队的分歧和分裂是什么因素造成的？
3. 从本案例出发，你认为应该如何构建一个有效的创业团队？

分析要点：

1. 根据间断平衡模型和团队发展五阶段模型来描述和分析团队的发展阶段，及每阶段的特点。
2. 根据团队冲突、团队属性及团队决策的相关知识，分析哪些因素可能会引发团队内的冲突。
3. 根据领导力风格、输入—过程—结果模型、权力与政治行为的相关知识，分析哪些因素会影响团队过程及团队效能。

资料来源：

MOL E, KHAPOVA S N, ELFRING T, 2015. Entrepreneurial team cognition: a review [J]. International journal of management reviews, 17（2），232–255.

MORAN L, ELLA S M, RAJSHREE A, et al. 2020. Entrepreneurial team formation [J]. Academy of management annals, 14（1），29–59.

MCMULLEN J S, SHEPHERD D A, 2006. Entrepreneurial action and the role of uncertainty in the theory of the entrepreneur [J]. The academy of management review, 31（1），132–152.

案例 7

B 公司员工管理困境

知识点：

能力素质模型、自我效能感理论、工作满意度理论、激励理论、领导理论

案例目的：

本案例通过对 B 公司进行分析，引导学生理解组织中的能力素质模型、自我效能感理论、工作满意度理论、激励理论、领导理论。

案例正文：

1. 引言

B 公司成立于 2010 年 12 月，注册资金 500 万元，投资规模 5000 万元。公司拥有 4000 多平方米的独立实验楼，以及各类先进检测仪器设备 300 多台，可提供电子电器类产品全生产过程的测试，包括计量校准、数据分析、软件测评、质量检测、可靠性分析等技术服务。B 公司具备多项国家资质，凭着专业的技术和优质的服务，赢得了客户的信赖和支持，每年服务企业超过千家，业务范围覆盖华东地区。在服务企业的同时，公司还为所在行业和地方政府提供技术支撑，为检测行业的健康发展和业务覆盖区域的产品质量提升做出贡献。

多年来，B 公司一直保持着良好的发展势头，公司经营业绩持续稳定增长，人员规模逐步扩大，品牌影响力逐年提升。B 公司共有人员 297 人，设有 13 个部门，其中 5 个职能部门，8 个业务部门。

2. 忙碌的总经理

2020 年 12 月的一个晚上，在办公室，公司高层正在举行年末部门绩效讨论会议，受新冠疫情的影响，公司经营业绩比 2019 年同期下降了 30%。公司各部门虽然有 KPI 考核，但实际操作起来很复杂，人力资源部门需要耗费很多的精力来跟进，而且员工也有消极抵制的情绪，不太配合考核。散会后，总经理张军一个人待在办

公室，想起创业的初心和这些年走过的心路历程，陷入了深深的沉思。

张军从浙江大学毕业后，进入政府机关做了两年公务员。2010年带领相关技术团队成立了B公司，经过不断的努力，公司团队也由最初的20多名员工发展到今天的297名员工。张军平时非常注重自身的学习和管理能力的提升，是某商学院的MBA。但最近他感觉陷入了一种困境。

有时，张军会抱怨创业太辛苦了。张军喜欢事必躬亲，当公司采购材料设备时，他会亲自过问，联系供应商，商谈产品型号、要求和材料价格等。当公司售卖产品时，他也会亲自指导员工如何去推销，如何与客户沟通，并给出很多建议。甚至在公司过节采购员工福利礼品时，他也会亲自指挥，给出很多采购建议。这些都使得他感觉特别累，没有自己的个人休息和家庭休闲时间，有时感觉力不从心。

近期，公司高层针对公司管理混乱的现象，聘请了专业咨询公司的负责人李红梅，她经验丰富，为许多大公司做过咨询。李红梅进驻公司，对公司进行了深入调研。

3. 技术部惊雷频现

就在张军焦头烂额之际，技术总监陈海向他提出了辞职。紧接着，张军又接二连三地收到了广告部、市场部等四个部门经理的辞呈。原因竟然也惊人地相似——除了个别人想要继续深造、对薪酬待遇不满意以外，大家都表示近几年公司招的员工很难带。惊讶之余，张军决定找老朋友陈海聊一聊。

陈海表示他也很舍不得这个工作，但这两年新入职的员工让他深感无奈。他建议张军去了解一下这些新员工。

过了两天，张军听从陈海的建议，来技术部"微服私访"，正巧看到四五个人正在一个会议室里争吵不休。他们争吵得太过投入，以至于没有人意识到张军正靠在会议室开着的门边上，默默地看着他们互相推卸责任。

张军悄无声息地离开了会议室，他意识到问题比他想象的还要糟糕。正走着，又传来一阵批评声，仔细一听，声音还有点熟悉。张军抬头一看，陈海正在工位上给一个新员工讲解基础的专业知识，因为员工所犯的错过于基础和明显，陈海有些生气。

张军回到自己办公室，摸着下巴陷入了沉思。在张军的印象里，技术总监陈海总是一副笑眯眯的样子，从来没有跟人红过脸。刚开始创业的时候，他总喜欢拉着自己畅想未来，期待着能够带领自己的核心团队，在产品的技术研发层面做出更高的成就。而现在，他仍然保持着学习的习惯，但是部门员工却连最基础的专业能力都没有。

思绪渐渐拉回现实，张军下定决心打开办公邮箱，给人事部发了邮件，让他们通过技术总监的辞职，又打开了自己的私人邮箱，给陈海发送了一封邮件："此一别，愿你万事顺遂，待你深造归来。"

4. 人事部困境重重

4.1 形式化的招聘流程

张军忽然回想起了他在技术部会议室外听到的争执，再结合各部门经理的辞呈，一个念头渐渐在他心中浮现。他叫来了人事部经理蔡磊，仔细盘问了近两年公司的招聘流程，并面谈了部分新进公司的员工。

王红丽是春季刚入职的技术部员工，据她回忆，第一轮小组非结构化面试时，大家一起讨论，并由小陈进行总结汇报。但小陈把大部分讨论成果直接包揽在自己身上，导致其他成员不服气地进行争辩，并迅速演化成口角斗争，场面一度失控。最后大家对讨论结果进行点评，当有人说到小陈汇报的某一点结论并不是特别准确时，小陈直接对提出这一点的面试者说："还不是因为你提出了这个错误的论点，还要害得我被批评！"

让王红丽意外的是，小陈和她一样进入了第二轮面试。第二轮是个人面试，面对应聘技术部的王红丽，面试官却对她的专业技能避而不谈，只是问一些无关痛痒的问题，最后草草结束面谈。最终，王红丽和小陈都收到了录取通知。张军把小陈也叫到办公室，他一到办公室，张军马上认出他就是那天在会议室里推卸责任的年轻人。

4.2 僵化的绩效管理

今年1月，新季度开始，销售部开始了新一轮的绩效管理。绩效管理总共有4

个步骤，分别是设定目标、绩效考核、绩效面谈和改进提升。

第一，设定目标。和往常一样，销售部负责人张明接到高管下达的指标：本季度销售额提高10%。他没有经过仔细调研就一拍脑门，为下属定了一个大目标：本季度销售额提高20%。他心想，目标定得越高，说不定越能激发员工的工作热情，从而提高销售额。他把这个目标发送到每个员工的邮箱，之后他在员工办公区大声说明了这个目标，还把目标写在了销售部办公室的黑板上。当然，不是没人反对过，以前会有员工尝试和张明沟通目标的设定，但他都一口回绝并表示，他是负责人，他说了算。久而久之，没人再和他沟通目标设定的问题。

第二，绩效考核。很快，第一季度结束了，绩效考核开始了，公司没有明确的考核细则，只有简单的规则。员工的考核分数只有两方面，一个是销售额，一个是日常表现。满分100分，两项各占50%。销售额是客观的，按照排名来进行打分。但是日常表现却非常主观，张明想打多少就打多少，一般来说，和张明关系好的员工，张明给的日常表现分数都很高，不管他们是否有迟到早退等行为。

第三，绩效面谈。张明通常是采取电话沟通的方式。当然，他也面对面谈过几次，但是他觉得面对面比较麻烦。在面谈中，老员工会提出质疑和问题。他认为，重要的不是员工的反馈，而是把自己的想法表达清楚，电话沟通不仅方便，还能节省时间。员工要是提出问题，不想回答也能随便说两句就敷衍挂电话，要是面对面的话，这种情况就很难应付。所以大多时候，张明都采取电话沟通的方式。

在绩效面谈时，张明遇到评分高的员工，就说："表现不错，下个季度继续加油。"然后就挂断电话，不会提及任何的实质奖励，只有简单的口头表扬。当他与评分低的员工谈话时，就采取非常简单的责骂方法，他总说："你怎么回事，评分这么差，赶紧回去自己反思一下，下个季度好好做，现在销售部业绩提不上去，都是因为你们。"如果有员工想说出自己的想法，张明会说："哪来这么多借口，你自己回去好好想想。"李军，他的绩效考核评分较高，他每天都想多努力提高销售额，从而获得高绩效，并希望得到奖励。但张明却只有简单的口头表扬，让他觉得很不满，所以他在工作中越来越懒散，甚至已经提交了调职申请。陈新，他本来是非常努力的，但由于缺乏指导业绩平平，加之平时和张明关系一般，所以他的绩效评分非常低，绩效面谈时，张明通常只会一味地责怪他，却从来没有追问原因或采取一些措施帮助他，陈新也变得越来越没工作热情。

第四，改进提升。对业绩平平，甚至业绩差的员工，张明在绩效面谈过程中，除批评、指责外，既没有理性地为员工分析业绩差的原因，距离目标的差距，以后应该采取何种形式、何种流程提高工作的绩效，也没有关心员工在以后的工作中是否需要支持，是否需要一定的资源以便帮助他们达到绩效目标。

4.3 缺乏激情的团队管理

经过调研还发现，团队的凝聚力不高，没有规范的员工激励制度。比如，一个项目为公司赚了一百万元，但团队获得的奖励只有一万元，相比贡献，绩效奖励太少，导致员工缺乏工作积极性，只求把本职工作做好。

同时项目奖励的分配周期也很长，通常完成项目一年后才能拿到奖励。越来越多的员工对此表示不满，因为项目结算周期长，如果成员离开项目部，通常拿不到分成，或者拿到得很少。

4.4 模糊的工作职责和业绩目标

在面谈过程中，李红梅发现有将近80%的员工对自己的工作岗位职责不明确。技术部老陈，因为人缘好，又是十年的老员工，对公司各部门都熟悉。有时公司人员忙不过来，周边门店送货等事情也要他兼顾。用他的话来讲，同事电话过来要求帮忙，也不好意思推托。在谈话过程中，当被问到在公司日常管理运营中，最痛苦的是什么时，很多员工提到了开会。主要原因是开会的时间长、指令多、领导说了算数导致员工没有参与感等。如果管理者希望开会时让员工思考解决方案，那么管理者可能需要做出改变。

品管部经理邓明也反映，好几次看到一名员工在上班时间对着电脑看微博、网购。刚开始邓明觉得工作压力大，员工想稍微放松一下，也无可厚非。后来在提醒过几次之后，这名员工还是存在这个现象，而且已经影响了工作，产品的抽查数量和抽查率都没有达到公司的要求标准。

5. 尾声

李红梅进驻公司一个月后，收集了所有的面谈和调研数据，整理出公司的现状及问题，正式提交给张军，张军看着报告，思绪万千，他拨通人事部经理的电话，让他立即安排公司高层管理者召开会议，商讨公司未来的发展对策……

思考问题：

1. 为什么总经理反而成了公司最大的业务员和公司最忙碌的人？
2. 根据案例谈谈公司在招聘中出现的问题，如何解决这些问题？
3. 根据案例谈谈公司在绩效管理中出现的问题，如何解决这些问题？
4. 根据案例谈谈员工工作缺乏积极性的原因是什么？
5. 高效的团队管理是什么？结合案例谈谈如何在团队管理中提升领导力？

分析要点：

1. 应用激励理论、领导理论对第 1 个思考问题进行分析。
2. 应用能力素质模型对第 2 个思考问题进行分析。
3. 应用激励理论对第 3 个思考问题进行分析。
4. 应用工作满意度理论、激励理论对第 4 个思考问题进行分析。
5. 应用自我效能感理论、领导理论对第 5 个思考问题进行分析。

案例 8

该怎样和 90 后员工打交道?

知识点：

人格理论、价值观理论、态度理论、激励理论、沟通理论、领导理论

案例目的：

本案例通过对 ZS 银行进行分析，引导学生理解并能综合应用人格理论、价值观理论、态度理论、激励理论、沟通理论、领导理论。

案例正文：

1. 引言

刘丹是 ZS 银行信用卡中心客户服务部的一名经理。她刚刚结束了一天的繁忙工作，处理了几起客户投诉，又接连和几个手底下的员工进行了绩效面谈，连续不断的工作让她倍感疲惫。坐在回家的地铁上，她打开了手机，翻看微信朋友圈，这是她为数不多可以放松的时刻。她最爱看的就是自己部门那些年轻员工们的朋友圈。70 后的刘丹，目前管理着一个 40 多人的部门，其中大多数员工都是 90 后。

刘丹工作已经有快二十个年头了，随着越来越多的 90 后加入公司，代际之间的差异让像刘丹这样的管理者明显有些不适应。近年来，ZS 银行的信用卡业务越做越大，对于产品和服务质量的要求也越来越高。刘丹所在部门也面临着越来越大的工作压力。这也时常让刘丹有些担心，她手下的这些年轻员工们，能够承担起这样的责任吗？

2. ZS 银行信用卡中心员工的新主体

信用卡中心是 ZS 银行的重要一级部门。其中，客户服务部主要负责处理客户投诉及为客户提供后续服务等工作。在信用卡中心的众多部门（见图 8-1）当中，客户服务部是和客户关系最为紧密的部门之一。

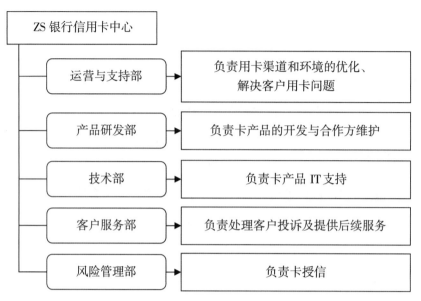

图 8-1　ZS 银行信用卡中心组织架构

自从 2013 年以来，越来越多的 90 后开始进入职场。这一时期也恰好是 ZS 银行信用卡中心快速发展的阶段，因此信用卡中心吸纳了大量的 90 后员工。以刘丹所在的客户服务部为例，共有员工 45 人，其中 90 后有 38 人，而这 38 人之中，又有近一半是 95 后。信用卡中心的其他部门也存在一样的情况，随着年轻员工入职，90 后员工所占的比例越来越高。因此，有一个非常实际的问题摆在刘丹这样的管理者面前，那就是该如何和这些 90 后员工们进行有效的交流和沟通，从而确保工作能够顺利推进。

3. 令人操心的 90 后

在刘丹看来，90 后虽然已经步入社会，甚至有些也已经有了不少年的工作经验。但是很多时候，他们的表现仍旧像是一群还没长大的孩子。他们普遍是独生子女，在家中称得上是"集万千宠爱于一身"。他们的表现让刘丹觉得这些 90 后员工们没有办法较好地进入工作角色。比起能够独当一面的员工，他们更像是嗷嗷待哺的雏鸟。似乎有人照顾、有人帮助，在他们看来是理所应当的事情。

最让刘丹，以及其他部门的一些负责人难以理解的是，新时代的年轻人们，一个个"本事没多大，脾气却不小""能力没多大，心气高得很"。刘丹记得，之前有一个名牌大学毕业、各方面条件都很优异的小姑娘，加入了产品研发部。小姑娘姓赵，各项工作能力都比较出色，很受部门领导的重视。然而在一次与产品合作方进行沟通时，小赵不能接受对方提出的要求，就和合作方产生了冲突。部门领导知道之后就批评了小赵几句。谁知平时看上去温和的小赵竟然大发脾气，觉得自己遭受到了很大的委屈，甚至闹到了人力资源部，导致很难收场。小赵最终也递交了辞呈，离开了ZS银行。

除此之外，刘丹还碰到了一件让她颇为头疼的事情。她倾尽心力培养了一批新入职的年轻员工。然而没过多久，就有两个人向她提出辞职。刘丹花了很久的时间和他们沟通，了解他们辞职的原因。刘丹非常担心是自己工作不到位等原因造成了这些年轻人的不满，或者是给了他们太多的工作压力让他们无法适应。然而结果却有些出乎意料。这些年轻人在工作了一段时间之后，觉得自己并不喜欢这份工作，并不是对薪资不满意，也不是对职业生涯规划有疑惑。其实，从刘丹的部门开始大量接纳90后员工之后，类似让她头疼的事情并不少，只不过最近几年尤为明显。90后员工似乎过于有勇气了一些，说辞职就辞职，完全不给自己留什么后路，也不担心自己的未来。这和刘丹她们这些70后特别不一样。

在刘丹看来，90后成长的环境和自己这代人完全不同。不仅仅自己无法理解他们，相信他们也很难理解自己。刘丹经常怀疑，这些人能够承担得起工作中的责任吗？而ZS银行想要发展，依靠这些年轻人真的没有问题吗？

4. 是偏见吗？

刘丹找了人力资源部的同事，了解了90后员工离职的情况。信用卡中心共400多名员工，其中90后占比已经超过了50%。然而，相比较而言，他们的离职率却是高得吓人，90后员工比非90后员工的离职率高出约20%，近几年还有不断提高的趋势。

不过人力资源部的同事也给了刘丹另外一份数据。人力资源部的工作职责之一，就是例行对具有离职意向或者提交辞呈的员工们进行挽留，并通过一对一谈话的形式，了解他们离职的真实原因。刘丹面前的这份数据显示，相比较而言，90后员工们对于薪资并没有那么在意。他们更加看重的是工作是否能够给他们带来成就感，对于所处的团队是否有归属感等方面。刘丹把这归结为，90后员工们相较于他们这一代人，没有那么"务实"。

这让刘丹觉得，自己越发看不透这些年轻人了。刘丹担心自己对90后有偏见，影响自己的判断和工作开展。于是她决定找其他几个部门的管理者们好好地聊一聊。

5. 个性强烈的90后员工

刘丹趁着快下班的时间，来到了产品研发部。产品研发部的负责人冯天和自己差不多是同一时间进入ZS银行的，也是一名70后。产品研发部有近100人，是个名副其实的大部门。刘丹相信冯天在如何与90后员工打交道方面，会有非常丰富的经验。

得知刘丹的来意后，冯天的脸上流露出一丝无奈，然后便打开了话匣子。原来，冯天是要向刘丹诉苦。

"90后员工，最大的毛病就是批评不得！"冯天觉得最让自己无法接受的就是这一点。冯天觉得批评是有利于进步的，应该虚心接受。但现在，他生怕惹员工不开心，导致他们辞职。

听着冯天的抱怨，刘丹也不知道自己该说些什么。虽然非常理解冯天，但是刘丹又觉得，这种问题也许可以避免。在冯天这里，刘丹显然是无法获取什么有价值的信息了。于是她便告辞，决定第二天再去找运营与支持部的负责人聊一聊。

第二天午餐时间，刘丹端着餐盘坐在了运营与支持部负责人李然身旁。虽然李然前几年才调到信用卡中心当运营与支持部负责人，是个80后，比刘丹资历要轻一些。但是李然工作能力很强，而且两人因为工作原因经常打交道，倒也称得上熟稔。刘丹说明了自己的来意，李然笑了起来："我比你们都年轻些，所以和90后打交道没你们那么多困难。"刘丹听了赶紧让他分享一些经验。

李然认为，90后员工最大的特点就是非常有个性。在工作中如果和领导有争执，根本不会忍着，工作不想做会大胆拒绝，觉得领导有地方不对就会明确指出来。很多时候，这些行为会让自己这个领导有些没有颜面，但是90后员工似乎根本不在意。

但是时间久了之后李然也发现，这些年轻人是没有任何恶意的，这就是他们养成的习惯。在了解了这一点之后，和他们沟通也就容易很多。同时，他们还特别在意自己是不是得到了尊重。李然举了个他在调往信用卡中心之前的例子。当时因为工作原因接待客户，客户要求他们部门的一个小姑娘喝酒。可是小姑娘就是坚决不喝，搞得客户很没面子。最后还是李然作为领导出来调和了一下，才没有让事情太过难堪。李然对刘丹说道，现在的年轻人个性强烈，同时又非常在意是否得到了尊重。幸亏自己比较维护这个小姑娘，事后也没怪她不给客户面子，不然她肯定也会辞职的。

李然还发现年轻人对于边界的意识非常强烈。在工作的时候，他们一般不愿意讲太多私人的事情。同事过度的关心都会让他们特别反感。边界意识还表现在他们对于工作时间和非工作时间的界定非常清晰。李然提到了一个技术部门的年轻人，他技术能力很强，但是极其厌恶加班，也厌恶领导在非工作时间因为工作事项去打扰他。有了这些发现之后，李然在和年轻人聊天时，就特别留意，从不问一些跨越界线的问题。另外在安排培训、组织部门集体活动的时候，也尽量不去占用大家的休息时间。通过这些简单的方法，李然在信用卡中心的几个部门负责人之中最受年轻人的欢迎。

刘丹听了李然的分享，觉得受用很多。她之前对于90后还是有些偏见。与其说90后不值得信赖，不如说是管理者们不得其法。

6. 值得信赖的90后

刘丹必须承认，虽然自己手下的90后员工没少给自己惹祸，很多工作完成得也不尽如人意，但是他们身上也确实有不少闪光点。有一次，部门碰到了一个重点客户投诉的突发事件。这名客户是白金信用卡客户，在用该信用卡购买跨国航班机票时，多次交易失败，显示失败的原因是额度不够。客户十分气愤，表示自己的额度绝对没有问题，要求信用卡中心给他一个说法。在接到投诉后，刘丹带着部门的人去后台查看，但是始终无法找到真正的原因。

这时，部门的几个90后员工站了出来，一方面和航空公司进行联络，一方面和技术部、运营与支持部积极沟通。刘丹就这样看着他们沉着冷静、条理清晰地把问题解决了。原来，交易失败的原因在于，客户在购买机票时，输入姓名的方式有误，导致交易始终无法进行。当然，更重要的问题在于，信用卡中心对于交易失败的归因不够严谨。

最后经过几个部门之间的通力合作，问题得到了良好的解决。这件事让刘丹对于90后员工有了新的认识，他们也是值得信赖的。

7. 尾声

有一个前些天提出辞职的员工，最近又重新回到了工作岗位。经过认真思考之后，他觉得自己还是有些冲动了。他觉得刘丹对于自己的想法非常尊重，在这里工作也能够体会到工作带来的乐趣。在之后的日子里，他成为了客户服务部的后备人才，工作也更加努力。

刘丹在和90后年轻员工们沟通时，也越来越懂得方式和方法，很快在部门中和年轻人打成一片。刘丹也开始思考新的问题，那就是如何更好地领导这支年轻的队伍，更好地帮助这些90后员工成长。

思考问题：

1. 从案例中描述的这些90后员工来看，他们都有哪些特点？这些特点是什么原因造成的？
2. 由于这些特点，90后员工的工作绩效会受到哪些影响？
3. 70后员工和90后员工本质的区别是什么？
4. 与90后员工的沟通有哪些特点？他们在沟通中有什么样的偏好？
5. 冯天和李然的领导风格，分别有哪些优缺点？90后员工偏好什么样的领导风格？
6. 结合案例，谈一谈你对与90后员工沟通的建议。

分析要点：

1. 应用人格理论对第1个思考问题进行分析。

2. 应用价值观理论、态度理论对第 2 个思考问题进行分析。

3. 应用沟通理论对第 3 个思考问题进行分析。

4. 应用沟通理论对第 4 个思考问题进行分析。

5. 应用激励理论、领导理论对第 5 个思考问题进行分析。

6. 应用沟通理论对第 6 个思考问题进行分析。

案例 9

新创企业如何在传统行业中实现数字创新——斑马仓的创业故事

知识点：

创造力理论、创新理论、领导力风格理论、团队属性理论、组织结构理论、企业文化理论

案例目的：

本案例通过对杭州斑材科技有限公司进行分析，引导学生理解创造力理论、创新理论、领导力风格理论、团队属性理论、组织结构理论、企业文化理论。

案例正文：

1. 引言

数字创新是利用数字技术创造新的产品或服务。数字创新对我国的经济发展和人民生活产生了巨大的影响，数字创新不仅仅是企业形成竞争优势的重要手段，同时也对促进产业变革，提升行业质量、效率和管理水平具有重要作用。令人惊讶的是，在许多行业中，承担数字创新主体责任的并不是在行业中占据主导地位的大型成熟企业，而是规模较小的新创企业。例如重塑了零售业格局的阿里巴巴，对餐饮业运营模式产生重要影响的美团和饿了么，以及给出租车行业带来深刻变局的滴滴出行等都是这一类新创企业的代表。新创企业时常需要面对资源短缺和能力不足的困扰，并且由于在行业中缺乏影响力，很容易遇到阻力。那新创企业是如何在这样不利的情况下实现数字创新从而获得企业成长的呢？

目前对于数字创新的研究还处在起步阶段，现有的研究主要关注数字技术带来的影响，但无法清晰地描述和解释新创企业如何实现数字创新。本案例将聚焦于杭州斑材科技有限公司（以下简称"斑马仓"），研究其在家装行业中数字创新的过程机制。

2. 行业背景及公司概况

2.1 传统家装行业

在传统家装行业，无论是客户还是家装公司，都面临着一些行业内固有的难以抵抗的困难和压力。按照管理实践领域的话语体系，这些困难和压力被称为"痛点"。传统家装行业的"痛点"主要有以下方面。

（1）客户方面的"痛点"

① 各个公司报价不统一且没有对照标准。

② 为了低价吸引客户，很多公司在报价时会恶意漏项，而在施工时处处加钱。

③ 没有统一的工程管理体系，装修品质没有保障。

④ 施工周期没有保障，通常只能由客户承担因工期延误带来的损失。

⑤ 装修费用尤其是水电改造费用不量化、不透明，容易超出客户预算。

⑥ 项目经理和家装公司之间合作关系松散，往往不能及时解决问题，导致客户的合法权益无法得到保障。

（2）家装公司方面的"痛点"

① 获取客户的成本过高，抑制了行业的健康发展。因为信息的不对称，客户没有一套有效的方法来挑选、甄别各个家装公司，只能通过市场知名度来选择家装公司。由于没有经济实力的家装公司没有能力进行广告宣传，最终大部分客户都被大公司通过广告效应吸引走了，小公司只能一味地打价格战。价格战使得装修的品质也同时下降，最终导致小公司的经营陷入恶性循环。

② 人才的流动性很大，难以管理。家装公司的用工报酬大多以订单量为基础，而每个公司的订单量存在明显的季节性和间断性，从而造成员工的报酬波动很大。为此，装修人员频繁地跳槽和转行，提高了家装公司的管理难度，也间接影响了装修质量和装修进度。

③ 获取订单方式单一，营销成本居高不下。家装公司缺乏有效的渠道获取消费者的装修需求，只能投入大量人力、物力用于广告宣传，营销成本居高不下。

2.2 互联网家装行业

目前互联网家装占整个家装行业的市场份额较小，但互联网家装更符合人们日益互联网化的消费习惯。互联网家装具有信息透明化的优点，人们可以通过互联网完成洽商、设计、购买材料等过程。不仅如此，互联网家装还可以满足个性化定制，产品和服务的品质都可以得到整体提升。随着互联网家装巨头的崛起，透明化的企业管理、全新的商业模式也会有利于互联网家装行业持续扩大市场空间，对传统家装行业形成冲击。

由图9-1可知，2014年中国互联网家装行业市场规模已突破1000亿元；2017年中国互联网家装行业市场规模达到了2461亿元，同比增长25.7%，保持了2015年以来超过25%的高增长态势；2018年中国互联网家装行业市场规模为2956亿元。但与整个家装行业的市场规模相比较，互联网家装的渗透率仍处于较低水平，发展前景广阔。

图9-1　2014—2018年中国互联网家装市场规模

在这个互联网技术越来越发达、互联网家装前景越来越明朗的背景下，斑马仓这个新创企业凭借高效创新的运营模式，通过资源整合在互联网家装企业中逐渐崭露头角。

2.3 公司概况

斑马仓成立于2017年，注册资本500万元。2019年9月，斑马仓被评为杭州市高新技术企业，入选杭州市雏鹰计划，是未来科技城估值1亿美金的准独角兽企业。斑马仓位于全国互联网技术领先的浙江省杭州市。斑马仓将互联网与传统建材相融合，在泛家居领域独创产业路由器模式，通过先进的大数据、云计算、区块链、AR、VR 技术和 SaaS 系统，整合泛家居领域核心资源，解决了家装行业供应链的痛点问题。斑马仓致力于打造集产品、销售、物流、服务四大平台为一体的一站式家装供应链 S2B2C 平台。

斑马仓在专注浙江区域市场开拓的同时，将公司的服务区域扩展到全国 20 多个省份的 400 多个区、市和地级县。

3. 斑马仓的成功经验

3.1 数字创新过程

通过对斑马仓案例分析发现，企业数字创新过程基本可以分为 5 个阶段。①通过对外部环境的观察识别机会；②通过数字化商业模式的迁移解决客户和企业的需求；③通过数字技术的迁移优化服务并为平台赋能；④根据机会利用的效果对商业模式进行整合与适应；⑤不断对数字技术进行迭代与深度应用。此外，新创企业的背景将影响机会识别过程，而在机会利用中遇到的阻力与新发现将激发企业对商业模式进行整合和适应。本研究将数字创新过程总结为图 9-2。

图 9-2　数字创新过程

3.2 机会识别

在家装行业，传统的商业模式存在弊端并且难以解决。从毛坯房到精装房的装修需要经历选材、设计、施工、验收等众多环节，每个环节都有其内在模式，对于毫无经验的消费者群体来说，要想顺利地完成整个装修过程，着实是一件令人头疼的事情。

随着时代的发展，装修模式也在不断增多，例如半包模式和全包模式。不过棘手的是，无论哪一种，都存在着不少的问题，不少消费者和业内人士都对此头痛不已。

半包模式中，消费者需先自行购买材料，再寻找家装公司或施工团队进行施工。虽然在一定程度上节约了经济成本，但是在选材与寻找装修队伍的过程中，消费者需要投入大量的时间与精力，容易造成工期时间长的后果。另外，一旦装修完成后发现问题，材料商与装修团队之间难免会出现相互推脱责任的情形，消费者权益也就无法得到妥善保障。

全包模式中，所有装修材料的采购与施工都由家装公司负责，节省了消费者的时间与精力。并且一旦后期出现质量问题，消费者可以针对性地向家装公司问责。然而近几年的运营中，全包模式下的问题与矛盾开始逐渐显露。家装公司在装修过程中以次充好、谋取差价，装修进度一拖再拖的事件层出不穷。并且由于消费者对装修具体事项了解甚少，许多公司虚报采购材料价格，更有甚者联合材料供应商在中间环节非法牟利，造成整个装修环节的成本虚高。这极大地损害了消费者的利益和对家装公司的信任度。

而这些状况的存在也一定程度上导致了现如今供应端的困局。消费者对家装公司缺乏信任，对自己的消费者权益能否得到有效保障存在疑虑，导致家装公司获客面临着巨大困难，也因此往往需要投入更多的营销成本。除此之外，由于传统家装设计无法看到未来预期的具体效果，而消费者需求又极具不确定性，所以施工过程中需要时常变更设计，从而导致施工进程曲折、拖延，增加了施工难度与各项成本费用。获客困难、成本加大，这些都为市场乱象埋下了祸根，而市场环境的混乱又消耗了消费者的信任，两者似乎已经进入了恶性循环。供应端与需求端存在着不一致性，两者矛盾不断升级，传统家装模式面临难以规避的发展困局。

斑马仓的创始人林先生出身建材世家，从小耳濡目染，十分了解家装行业的状况。上大学后他积极参与创业实践活动，以大学生的身份参加各类创业比赛并获得了许多奖项。本科毕业后顺利升入硕士研究生的林先生也并未放弃创业的梦想，和一位从事装修行业多年的合伙人共同成立了 e 修鸽公司。该公司是主营老房翻新和维修的互联网平台。通过两年的努力，公司成为了行业内排名前列的公司。林先生凭借自己敏锐的洞察力和互联网思维，发现了新房互联网家装这个绝佳的商业机会。如果能够架构一个平台来充当需求端与供应端的桥梁，很多问题就可以迎刃而解。首先，由平台甄选入驻建材商品质，并为家装公司的装修向消费者提供质量保证，同时家装公司和建材商可以在平台上获取订单，这样供需双方就可以对接起来；其次，平台为消费者保管装修款，待到装修效果达到消费者预期之后，平台再将款项交付给装修厂商。这样大大减少了消费者的顾虑，也降低了家装公司和材料供应商获取订单的成本，从而有效降低了家装行业的交易成本，并且有利于规范装修行业的市场秩序，促进行业的良性发展。

从中国整体的家装行业市场规模来看，这将是一个巨大的商业机会。近几年来，买房逐渐成为刚需，相应的房屋装修话题也持续高涨。随着购房者年龄中枢的下移，年轻一代已成为装修行业的主要消费者群体。习惯于快节奏生活的年轻消费群体，面对装修中的诸多繁琐环节，很容易产生"装修焦虑"，因此整装成为绝大多数人的首选项，尤其是在一线城市。早在 2017 年，一线城市的消费者对整装的接受度已达 60% 以上，且随着发展，这个数字还在不断攀升。在未来，整装规模将继续扩大，成为装修行业的主流，我国的整装市场还存有巨大的发展空间。在这样的契机之下，已经获得上亿人民币投资的独角兽新创企业 e 修鸽决定新成立斑马仓来深耕新房装修市场，由 e 修鸽总经理林先生担任 CEO。初创时期，公司的组织架构主要包括人事、行政、财务、市场、运营、技术等事业部，随着业务线的不断变化，后续成立了社交电商事业部、派单事业部等，以便更好地赋能获客。团队人数也从最初的几十人发展到上百人。随着业务的不断扩大和分工的不断细化，公司的组织结构又进行了进一步的调整与更新，旨在更好地为解决供应端和需求端双方的痛点问题服务，顺应互联网时代发展，助力家装行业升级。

3.3 数字化商业模式的迁移

与传统家装企业自营式的商业模式不同，斑马仓将"美团 + 京东"的数字化商业模式引入到家装行业中，并且制订全品类战略合作，运用 e 修鸽的资源整合了众多一线品牌，致力于实现提供高性价比服务的目标。同时凭借多渠道的运营以及深度的合作与两万家家装公司免费对接，从而实现线上储备客源，线下分流客源。表9-1所示为"美团模式"和"京东模式"应用过程中的实际优点。

表9-1 "美团模式"和"京东模式"应用过程中的实际优点

"美团模式"	"京东模式"
（1）提供订单资源与消费者需求	（1）提供一站式的高性价比材料
（2）降低推广、宣传费用	（2）节省消费者时间与精力
（3）实现家装行业的"共享共建"	（3）解决消费者信任问题

一方面，"美团模式"为家装公司提供了一个线上获取订单的平台。家装公司可以通过这一平台获取宝贵的订单资源和了解消费者需求，大大降低了推广、宣传等获取消费者的成本。"美团模式"的大致流程如下。①消费者在斑马仓平台上下单，订单中包含消费者的基本信息以及对装修的想法、要求和预算等；②平台接到消费者的订单后，根据消费者的需求与消费者进行沟通，而后请室内设计师制订合适的方案，方案呈现后由工作人员与消费者进行交流再修改方案；③等最终装修方案敲定，平台再根据消费者要求分配装修物资以及家装公司。这一新型模式不仅为斑马仓提供了广大客源，还可以根据消费者喜好为消费者分配家装公司，实现精准定位。同时家装公司可以以较低成本获取客源，并且可以从平台上获取消费数据，了解消费者的最新装修偏好和需求，有利于家装公司开发新的设计方案和采用新的装修技术与材料。

另一方面，"京东模式"给消费者提供了一站式、高性价比的装修材料包。通过平台的严格审核和大额统一采购的优惠，消费者可以低成本地获得质量较好的装修材料，节省了消费者的时间和精力成本，同时也解决了消费者对家装公司提供的材料不信任的问题。"京东模式"提供的一站式平台具有品质保证，消费者可以绝对信任在这个平台上所购买的东西，如有不满意的地方，售后保障将服务到底。同时装修材料供应商则可以通过斑马仓平台以较低成本的方式进行材料销售，从而摆脱或减弱对于线下展示或经销店以及家装卖场的依赖，大大降低营销和渠道成本。另外，通过平台的数据支持，装修材料供应商可以在第一时间获取消费者的反馈和评价，也促进了其产品的更新和升级。

这两种模式的组合大大降低了供需双方的交易成本，提升了交易的效率。而斑马仓则可以从每笔装修订单交易中抽成，并从材料供应中赚取差价，从而获取可观的经济利益。斑马仓贯彻"共建共享"的理念，引入"美团＋京东"的商业模式，将消费者的需求与供应商对接从而提高资源的整合利用率，最终形成供需对应的数字化商业平台。这一模式很好地解决了消费者、家装公司和材料供应商的困难。

3.4 数字技术的迁移

在确立了新的商业模式之后，斑马仓又通过应用数字技术来进一步提升自身对于消费者和商家（家装公司及材料供应商）的服务。斑马仓以数字技术帮助消费者获得更好的体验，在贯彻"科技让服务更智慧"理念的同时也很大程度上帮助家装公司提升效率、降低成本。

在消费者层面，斑马仓通过智慧云眼、3D 云设计等技术的应用，极大地升级了消费者的体验感，提升了消费者对于服务的满意度。智慧云眼可以借助人脸识别和智能大数据分析为客户推荐合适的标签，客户可以在这基础上对标签进行自主筛选和添加。后台根据客户的标签推荐适合的装修风格并展现全景 VR 图，让客户可以无死角查看预期的效果。当客户做好选择后，系统会给出预算、工期及建议等，做到每个环节公开透明，所有流程一键完成，不断提高客户黏性与依赖度。3D 云设计则是可以让消费者成为自己房屋的装修设计师，针对自己的喜好设计优质的独家方案，并快速出图，效果一目了然，"所见即所得"，解决了"买家秀"与"卖家秀"的差异问题。这一新颖的设计方式开创了客户与设计师互动和联合设计的方式，最大限度地满足了客户的个性需求，同时也降低了设计师设计和与客户沟通的难度。该技术一经推出，就成为厂商口中的促单神器，设计师口中的高效工具。3D 云设计的出现让客户在虚拟场景中直观地体验装修效果，切实地参与其中，增强了客户的主体地位并营造了归属感。客户满意度的不断提升极大地增加了成单量，也降低了频繁更改设计方案给消费者和家装公司带来的成本和压力。

在商家层面，斑马仓向商家提供客户关系管理（Customer Relationship

Management，CRM)、企业资源计划（Enterprise Resource Planning，ERP）等管理平台与工具，使家装公司能够更好地了解和分析客户需求，更加合理地管理公司内部的人力和物力，以及外部的供应商。CRM 利用信息技术及互联网技术协调企业与客户在营销、销售和服务上的交互，自动为客户匹配最合适的商品和服务，进而帮助公司改善管理方式，提升管理效率。CRM 客户端上提供了一系列的客户服务——自动建档、自动调取标签、立即了解需求、自动获得电话、随时微信聊天、随时跟进签单等，让斑马仓与客户建立长期互相信任的密切关系，从而为企业稳固了老客户，吸引了新客户，也不断地整合客户资源，完善了管理体系，提升了整体的竞争优势。ERP 则是建立在信息技术基础上，以系统化的管理思想，为企业决策层及员工提供决策运行手段的管理平台。斑马仓利用 ERP 全面跟踪施工全流程，实时监控预警，确保工程进度与质量。斑马仓利用这两个管理平台对客户信息进行合理化的管理、对资源进行合理匹配，再将这些信息和数据分享给进驻平台的家装公司。有利于家装公司更好地了解客户需求从而不断提升工作效率和企业竞争力。

3.5 商业模式的整合与适应

斑马仓通过数字化商业模式进军家装行业，并通过数字技术的应用不断改善其为消费者和商家提供的服务，在家装行业受到了好评，获得了订单量的迅速增长。然而经过一段时间的运营，斑马仓发现在家装行业中完全依赖数字技术和数字商业模式还是存在一些阻力和不足。

一方面，装修客户的线下消费习惯根深蒂固，很多消费者还是倾向于亲身触摸和观看装修材料，现场体验装修的样板间效果。在传统家装的商业模式中，消费者可以看到实体的建材展示和装修效果，从而获得更为直观的感受与体验。另一方面，平台上入驻的家装公司和材料供应商的业务也离不开线下的活动和参与。消费者在平台上购买装修材料后，装修材料的交付等还是需要线下的材料供应商来落地，通过材料供应商来交付给消费者，完成整个过程的最后步骤；平台上达成协议的装修订单也需要线下的家装公司来对接和具体实施，平台无法直接参与装修的具体施工。且根据市场调查问卷数据，仍有相当部分受访者不愿意尝试互联网家装，还是觉得线下传统家装更让人安心；大部分受访者选择线上线下相结合的装修方式；没有一位受访者愿意完全使用纯线上的装修服务。

考虑到装修客户对线上装修的顾虑和对线下体验的实际需要，斑马仓又开辟了"线上+线下"的模式：在原来线上平台的基础上，斑马仓在全国主要城市都设立了线下展厅，如图9-3所示。展厅内可以体验3D云设计等数字家装服务，同时也包含了诸如样板设计、装修材料实物等传统线下展览环节。从而为家装公司和材料供应商提供了展销场所，也为消费者了解斑马仓的相关服务，以及观察和体验装修材料、样板设计提供了更加直观的体验场所。这个全新的举措不仅缓解了客户对互联网家装的顾虑，也给材料供应商提供了一个线下的平台来展销自己的材料。

图9-3　线下展厅实景图

3.6　数字技术的迭代与深度应用

"线上+线下"模式确立后，斑马仓还不断革新各项技术服务，应用新的数字技术来为消费者和商家提供更好的服务。斑马仓通过SaaS系统、智慧魔镜、CRM、VR、AR、ERP等数字技术的全面应用及客户和家装公司的大数据反馈，对相关应用的数字技术进行了迭代和更新，为开拓更加广阔的潜在市场奠定了基础。

首先，斑马仓升级了核心的SaaS系统平台和CRM系统。升级的SaaS系统平台可以更为精准地分析客户需求，有效地整合消费者、材料供应商、家装公司的资源。这一平台的结构化升级更好地使SaaS系统与产品、销售、服务、存储物流等各平台全方位深度结合，对平台数据进行精准高效的分析利用，从根本上帮助家装公司提升管理与应用的能力，有利于斑马仓为消费者提供更好的服务。同时，为了更好地协助管理者对接消费者关系，识别和保持有价值的消费者，斑马仓还升级完善了 CRM 系统。斑马仓将升级后的 SaaS 系统和 CRM 系统联合深度应用，更好地引流消费者，深度了解、满足消费者需求并实时更新数据，使得消费者在应用 SaaS 系统平台的过程中，得到高性价比的个性化装修设计方案，提高斑马仓的整体效益与竞争优势。斑马仓 SaaS 系统平台和 CRM 系统的加速迭代与深度应用为企业全方位提升管理和运营效率、发展目标消费者带来了巨大的优势。

其次，斑马仓在线下展厅应用了 VR 和 AR 技术，增加了消费者在现场体验的真实性。通过多可能性的数字技术的操作，VR 与 AR 技术的加入给线下消费者带来了沉浸式、交互式的装修体验。与此同时，VR 和 AR 技术的结合不仅可以实现场景的应用，触摸选材的质感，还可以为消费者定制多种精装样板房，为消费者带来了全新的便捷体验。这一系列的数字技术应用让消费者的方案更为具体化，也更具有可调节性，增强了消费者的装修意愿，更好地全面满足消费者的基本需求，还可以现场根据消费者的个性化要求来调节装修设计方案。模拟体验的 VR 和 AR 技术的更新与应用为斑马仓线下体验注入了活力，可以不断吸引新的消费者来尝试。

最后，斑马仓开发了针对消费者的斑集 App，使消费者能更加方便地获取斑马仓的服务。由于市场正处于获客难、获客贵的流量时代，针对消费者设计的斑集 App 在斑马仓平台化后随即被推出，旨在为消费者提供高品质、高性价比的家居建材服务，为家居建材商家在线推广品牌知名度、获得消费者流量和建材交易量等。

全方位更新数字技术的斑马仓受到了消费者的青睐，而斑马仓巨大的潜在市场也吸引了众多的一、二线高品质家居建材的品牌商和新兴的建材装修小企业，实现了公司业务的良性循环，带动了整个行业的数字技术转型升级与深度应用。

在这之前，斑马仓主要通过共享、共建展厅的智慧云眼扫描、获取消费者需求信息，而斑集 App 可以辅助实现这一环节的信息采集，基于电商理念，更多地获取消费者信息，有利于更好地赋能企业发展。在这一过程中，斑马仓通过信息平台与数据平台协调企业发展资源，引流锁客并引入优质品牌商，提高了整个产业链的效率与资源的利用率；通过 VR 和 AR 技术的线下应用与斑集 App 的开发，从根本上解决了家装行业最初的痛点；以数字化转型升级的思维导向聚焦商业发展模式，加速了企业自身数字技术的迭代与深度应用，形成了共享、共建的良好趋势，为未来行业最终走向提供正确引导与良性竞争循环。在这一过程中，开发、完善与更新从未终止，斑马仓数字技术的更新和迭代一直在持续进行中。

思考问题：

1. 该案例对于新创企业突破行业壁垒有何启示？

2. 从该案例出发，你认为创造力和创新有何区别？

3. 根据斑马仓案例的启发，组织应该如何促进创新？

分析要点：

1. 应用创造力理论和创新理论对第 1 个思考问题进行分析。

2. 应用创造力理论和创新理论对第 2 个思考问题进行分析。

3. 应用领导力风格理论、组织结构理论、团队属性理论、企业文化理论对第 3 个思考问题进行分析。

案例 10

VT 公司文化冲突导致的人才流失

知识点：

管理风格理论、文化冲突理论、文化价值模型、离职心理动因模型

案例目的：

本案例通过对 VT 公司进行分析，引导学生理解管理风格理论、文化冲突理论、文化价值模型、离职心理动因模型。

案例正文：

1. 引言

2013 年 11 月 29 日晚 10 点，VT 公司的人事行政总监 Jenny 终于结束了一天的工作，拖着疲惫的脚步走出了办公大楼。回头望去，整个办公楼只有消防通道灯还在昏暗地亮着，Jenny 不禁长长地叹了一口气。今天是令人盼望已久的周五，本应该早早地完成一天的工作，待下班的时间一到，马上关好电脑，冲出办公室，开始享受周末的快乐时光。可是，这一切对于 Jenny 来说，只能是一个美好的愿望。今年对于 VT 公司人力资源部来说，又是艰难的一年，公司的员工离职率继续攀升，从三年前的 12.19% 达到了现在的 32%。刚刚的电话会议中，当说到今年高达 32% 的离职率的时候，Jenny 明显感觉到了老板对于这个数字的不满。虽然 Jenny 罗列了各种导致员工离职的客观原因，但是，在老板看来，这些只能算是借口，因为相较过程而言，大多数老板都会更加注重结果。于是，Jenny 在报告中，把力图将明年的离职率控制在 25% 作为了目标。但是，老板对这个数字还是不满意，进一步提出了要求。最后经过协商，双方终于达成了一致，那就是将明年的离职率控制在 22% 以内。面对这一目标，Jenny 锁紧了眉头……

2. VT 公司的基本信息

2.1　VT 公司简介

VT 公司成立于 2005 年,母公司 VT 集团是一家知名的美国上市公司、世界 500 强企业。VT 集团的业务范围涵盖了信息技术、影音成像、管理咨询等多方面,在世界各国设有分公司。VT 集团自成立以来,一直秉承"客户至上、结果导向、精工细作、拼搏进取、协同发展"的核心价值观;"用创新的技术与服务,使世界更平坦"的使命和愿景;"以人为本"的管理理念。到 2013 年底,员工人数达到 625 人。其中直接从事 BPO 实际业务的员工人数为 603 人,约占公司总人数的 96%。其他员工分布在行政部、财务部、人力资源部等职能部门,主要为公司的核心业务部门提供服务。

随着 BPO 行业的兴起,VT 集团从 20 世纪 90 年代开始就先后在印度、俄罗斯等国家设立了外包服务中心。随着日本在亚太地区位置的重要程度提升,集团相关部门经多方考察及研究后决定成立对日的外包服务中心 VT 公司,选址大连。2005 年 VT 公司成立,成立之初主要负责日本业务中可流程化、可标准化的业务。虽然大连已有通用电气(现在的简柏特)、埃森哲、IBM 等知名企业入驻,但是由于 VT 公司尚处于起步阶段,发展前景可观,工资水平和福利待遇极具竞争力,所以一度被在校大学生认为是大连最好的外资公司。自 2005 年至 2013 年,VT 公司走过了 8 年不平凡的发展历程。无论是质量控制,还是客户满意度,均领先于集团内部的其他外包业务中心。并且在 2009 年和 2010 年,连续两年获得"大连市十佳雇主"的称号。VT 公司成立以来,公司规模迅速扩大,业务范围不断拓宽。2012 年,VT 集团日本分公司中可流程化、可标准化的所有业务全部被转移到了大连。在国内从事 BPO 业务的公司中,VT 公司脱颖而出,成为一个年交易额突破一亿的专业流程外包服务公司。

2.2　VT 公司的组织架构

尽管 VT 公司组织规模不断扩大,员工人数已经达到 625 人,但仍然是以直线职能的组织结构为主(见图 10-1)。

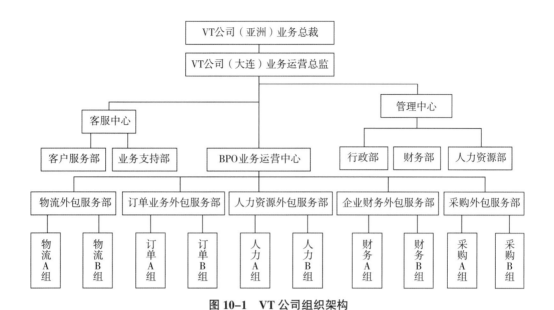

图 10-1 VT 公司组织架构

在 VT 公司的组织架构中，最高层管理者是业务总裁，业务总裁下面是业务运营总监，业务运营总监具体主管三个部门：客服中心、BPO 业务运营中心和管理中心。其中，客服中心分为客户服务部和业务支持部；管理中心分为行政部、财务部和人力资源部；主管一线运作的 BPO 业务运营中心分为物流外包服务部、订单业务外包服务部、人力资源外包服务部、企业财务外包服务部和采购外包服务部。

在组织层级中，组员是具体业务的实际操作者，主要是按照既定的操作手册进行工作；助理经理和组长，由更具经验的员工承担，是各个业务组中对业务知识最熟知的人，不但需要熟悉基本的操作，还需要精通业务背景，可以说是整个业务持续进行的重要保证；经理级别的员工主要负责团队的管理，不需要精通具体的业务。因此，对于整个业务运营部来说，涉及具体业务的主要是各个业务组的组员、组长和助理经理。

2.3 VT 公司发展的行业背景

VT 公司刚刚成立的时候，BPO 行业才刚刚兴起，由于公司属于新兴行业，极具成长潜力，工资水平和福利待遇也很有竞争力，所以吸引了很多人才。然而随着 BPO 行业的快速发展，大连有了更多新公司的加入。公司间为了争夺人才，不惜大力提高工资待遇。于是，VT 公司原本富有竞争力的薪酬福利变得不那么吸引人了，公司最初成立时规定的起薪，虽然随着物价的上涨也略有调整，但是终究竞争不过其他公司。与此同时，各公司都出现了一个奇怪的现象，那就是从同行业其他公司挖来的员工，因其有相关的工作经验，即使职位和现有员工相同，工资也要比现有员工高出许多。在这种情况下，员工忠诚度逐渐下降。由于工资差距，很多人为了工资而跳槽，甚至有人跳槽到其他公司一段时间后，还会重新跳回原来的公司。从某种程度上来说，整个行业已经进入了一种不健康的发展状态。

3. VT公司突如其来的人事变动

3.1 "以人为本"的Rajesh式领导

Rajesh自VT公司成立时就担任业务运营总监，是集团总部为了大连BPO业务的发展特地从印度的外包中心调配过来的。虽然Rajesh是印度人，但海外经历使他的领导风格深受美国文化的影响。Rajesh不仅在流程管理方面经验丰富，还是质量控制专家，是六西格玛的黑带大师。虽然服务对象由印度转为日本，但是Rajesh凭借其丰富的经验将部门的业务做得有声有色。在对待员工方面，Rajesh始终本着人性化的管理理念。他在和员工交谈的时候总是强调员工才是企业的主人，没有团队的合作，没有员工们夜以继日的努力就不会有今天的VT公司。为了能够和每一个员工进行充分的沟通，Rajesh将办公室的窗户全部改用透明的玻璃窗。Rajesh认为管理者应该以身作则，在监督员工的同时，更应该接受员工的监督，和员工奋斗在一起。Rajesh的管理充分展现了"以人为本"的公司文化和管理理念，得到了全公司的认可。在2012年末，Rajesh退休的时候，VT公司已经成功地将物流、订单、财务三个项目从日本移管到大连。

3.2 令人"依依难舍"的Rajesh退休

虽然VT公司并没有正式将Rajesh退休的消息发出公告，但是这件事却早已在公司传得沸沸扬扬，几乎无人不知。很多人都觉得Rajesh不应该在这个时候退休，Rajesh在职7年，在他的领导下，VT公司已经成功地将项目从日本移管了过来。Rajesh带领大家熬过了最困难的时期，现在公司各项业务都稳步发展，他却要退休，大家都觉得可惜。如果没有Rajesh，VT公司的业务根本就无法进行。员工集体致信集团总部要求 Rajesh 继续任职，Rajesh 虽然心里很感动，但不想因为个人的感情影响了公司整体的规划。公司也希望 Rajesh 能够公开地给全体员工一个合理的解释，从而避免给公司带来一些不良影响。

作为集团的元老之一，Rajesh 带领新公司步入正轨正是集团给他的任务，目前这个任务已经顺利完成。VT 公司在 Rajesh 的带领下已经从弱不禁风的小苗长成了参天大树，所以是时候离开了。Rajesh 考虑许久，从自己、员工和公司发展的角度，向大家做出了声明。最终大家只好投入了下一阶段的工作。

3.3 "风格迥异"的 Nakamura 式管理

对于继任者的人选问题，VT 集团进行了多方面的考量。最后，考虑到已经将日本地区的可流程化、可标准化的业务全部移管到大连，集团认为还是由日本管理者直接带领整个团队比较好，于是指派了日本分公司的 Nakamura 来到大连接替 Rajesh 的工作。Nakamura 在日本业务部担任业务经理，在他的领导下，日本分公司的业绩在集团中也算是数一数二的。而且 Nakamura 对工作的态度严肃认真，集团觉得他既能整顿 Rajesh 退休后 VT 公司运营部一盘散沙的状态，也可以让公司的员工能够紧张起来去共同应对当前激烈的竞争环境。Nakamura 自从担任 VT 公司业务运营总监以来，一直奉行典型的"日式"管理风格，不仅对细节锱铢必较，等级观念和时间感也非常强。Nakamura 认为赏罚严明才可以让员工积极主动地工作。自从 Nakamura 来到了大连，VT 公司的工作氛围变得和以前不一样了。Nakamura 严厉的领导风格、强烈的等级观念招致了很多人的不满，越来越多的人开始怀念 Rajesh 在任时的工作氛围。

4. 新人的离开

4.1 VT 公司的新人培训

Liz 是 2012 年加入公司的应届大学毕业生，彼时 VT 公司正在 Rajesh 的带领下逐渐羽翼丰满。加入 VT 公司后，Liz 被分到了订单流程组。刚进入订单流程组的时候，主要由业务熟练的前辈们负责给 Liz 等新人培训。由于 Liz 业务流程学习得很快，负责培训的同事们都认为这个新人招得很成功，将来一定会成为业务能手。Liz 也对工作信心十足。

培训了大概一个月之后，Liz 第一次参加了由 Rajesh 主持的会议。"我觉得大家在入职培训这段时间已经对 VT 公司的基本情况有了一定的了解，所以今天召集大家开会的主要目的有两个，一是感谢大家的加入，二是想了解一下大家对公司的认可程度。"听到这里，一直绷着一根弦的 Liz 终于松了口气，心里暗暗觉得这个总监很是平易近人。接下来 Rajesh 还和大家讲了自己在集团的工作经历，"今天我为大家讲述我的经历，只是想让大家明白机会永远是掌握在自己手里的，公司是不会放弃任何一个员工的，除非你自己放弃了自己！来到 VT 公司，大家就是一家人。在 VT 这个大家庭里，每个人都有平等的发展机会，我会关注你们每一位新人的发展，所以我希望大家可以互相帮助，共同进步。"公司能够为员工提供平台，当然自己更要加把劲，Liz 想。

"大家累了一天了，今天就到这里，大家回去休息吧！我的办公室就在培训室隔壁，如果工作上遇到什么问题随时可以来找我，当然生活上的问题也可以向我咨询。"虽然整个会议时间不长，但是 Liz 感受到了公司的关注，也感受到了 Rajesh 的亲切。

4.2 操作手册的修改风波

2012 年 12 月，Liz 来 VT 公司已经半年多了，工作表现很出色，可是自从 Nakamura 来后，Liz 却一点也轻松不起来。

前不久，Liz 所在的订单流程组发生了一个操作错误。日本前端的负责人知道这次的错误之后，不但要求大连方面写报告说明原因、经过、结果和对策，还要求重新做一个详细的操作手册来避免今后出现同样的问题，而这个任务恰好落在 Liz 身上。Liz 很快就做完了操作手册，但是日本前端的负责人并不满意。由于双方工作方式和文化的不同，导致原本很简单的工作，Liz 修改了好几版才最终完成，这让 Liz 感到身心俱疲。

4.3 Liz 下定决心离开

后来发生的一件事情成为促使 Liz 下定决心离开的最后一根稻草。事情要从一个周一的上午说起，当时整个办公室的人都在忙着处理业务。Nakamura 从自己的办公室走出来，径直走向了 Liz 隔壁组经理 Todd 的座位旁，突然不顾自己的身份地冲 Todd 大发脾气。偌大的办公室，除了 Nakamura 持续的吼叫和辱骂，完全听不到其他的声音。大家都很惊讶，没有人敢朝着 Nakamura 的方向看，只能低着头假装继续工作。

Liz 也被吓傻了，心脏怦怦直跳，半天也没缓过神儿来。她完全没有经历过这样的事情，她认为即使是领导，也不能这样冲下属发脾气。之后，Nakamura 仿佛意识到了这样做的影响，带着 Todd 进了自己的办公室，但是依旧持续着之前的声音和语气。后来终于传来消息，原来 Nakamura 是因为 Todd 没有及时向他汇报问题而大发雷霆，而 Todd 当时正忙于处理那个紧急的问题，原本打算处理完后，再将详细情况向 Nakamura 汇报。就这样，Todd 由于没有及时进行汇报而遭到了一场严厉的批评。

Liz 无法想象，如果这样的事情发生在自己身上，她会怎么面对。Liz 越发茫然了，难道这就是自己想要的工作吗？想到这里，Liz 决定辞掉现在的工作，去外面闯一闯。

5. 公司中坚力量的流失

5.1 Norah 在 VT 公司的发展之路

2014 年的 2 月份，VT 公司发生了"一件大事"，物流 A 组的 Norah 离职了！Norah 是物流 A 组的助理经理，不但业务能力强，而且团队管理能力也很强，在 VT 公司及日本客户方面都有很好的口碑。因此，Norah 离职的消息一传出来，立刻引起了轩然大波。Norah 是在 2006 年大学毕业后加入 VT 公司的，经过她的努力奋斗，2012 年 6 月成为公司里最年轻的助理经理。

但是新的职位并不像 Norah 想的那么简单，挑战接踵而至。日本分公司计划更换物流业务系统，这对 Norah 的组来说，意味着整个工作流程都要顺应新系统做出改变。新系统已经开发完毕，接下来 Norah 需要研究怎样利用新系统进行操作，制作新的操作手册，并在组内进行培训。距离新系统的启用只有两个月的时间，Norah 只好加班加点，带着两个业务组长，没日没夜地研究。两个月后，新的系统顺利启用，Norah 的组受到日本分公司的大力肯定，称赞大连的员工对业务知识理解深刻，值得信赖。

努力并不是白费的，付出会得到回报。12 月份的某一天，Norah 突然得知自己的月薪破例涨到了 4200 元。在接下来 2013 年 2 月份的工资调整中，因为 Norah 被评为优秀员工，又按照优秀员工的加薪标准将她的月薪涨到了 5000 元。在 VT 公司，她已经成为一颗耀眼的新星了。

笼罩在光环下的 Norah 感到很幸福，她认为，虽然自己在工作中付出了很多，甚至流过眼泪，但是所有的努力和付出，Nakamura 和其他公司领导都是看在眼里的。Norah 又一次感到了 VT 公司的伟大，决心要在这个公司工作一辈子。

5.2 Norah 对 VT 公司态度的转变

物流组根据具体业务的不同分为 A、B 两个小组，Norah 所在的组是 A 组。2013 年 8 月份开始，B 组业务量激增，员工不得不每天加班到晚上 10 点以后，公司虽然按照规定给予了加班费以及相应的补助，但还是有员工受不了这样的工作量，陆续提出离职申请。B 组员工的离职造成了人手紧张的现象，Nakamura 决定从 Norah 的物流 A 组借调两名员工到 B 组支援。Nakamura 的领导风格属于任务导向型的，业务的顺利开展是第一位。虽然 Norah 并不是很乐意，但是她知道在 Nakamura 看来，不论是哪个组遇到困难了，其他组都要全力支持以确保工作的顺利进行。于是，Norah 选了组内两名优秀的业务能手到 B 组支援，组里少了两名能干的员工，Norah 只能想尽各种办法来提高 A 组的工作效率，希望 B 组能够尽快渡过难关，自己借调出去的两名爱将能够早日回归。

但是两个月过去了，B 组似乎毫无起色。据派往 B 组的员工反映，B 组虽然业务量有所增加，但是本身的工作效率也存在很大的问题，员工根本没有齐心协力做出最大的努力。对于这一点，Norah 最近也有所察觉，她偶尔会看到 B 组员工在 Nakamura 不在的时候，浏览与工作不相关的网页。Norah 虽然心里觉得很不公平，但这毕竟是其他组的事情，也不好直接向 Nakamura 反映情况。于是，Norah 找了一个机会试探性地和 Nakamura 提了一下这个问题，谁知 Nakamura 信誓旦旦地向 Norah 保证，B 组的员工每天都全力以赴。Norah 也不好再说什么，但心里有些委屈。

不久，在公司的季度表彰大会上，B 组被评为"优秀团队"，理由是在业务量增多，人员较少的情况下，B 组依旧能够团结一致，顺利渡过难关，而 A 组却没有受到任何嘉奖。Norah 对此很失望，A 组在 Nakamura 的高压管理政策下派出两人支援，自己不得不在人手短缺的情况之下艰难度日，但是在成绩上公司却丝毫没有考虑到 A 组，自己的下属兢兢业业，结果到头来得到的还不如那些滥竽充数的人！更令 Norah 心寒的是，Nakamura 对下属的失落好像丝毫没有感知。

5.3　Norah 的辞职

转眼又到了年底评定的时候了，Nakamura 给的评级意味着工资的涨幅，这次 Norah 依旧被评为优秀。这几年，公司不断强调要降低成本，缩减开支，因此工资的涨幅也没有前几年那么大了。Norah 心想，既然今年又被评为优秀，最少也能涨 5% 的工资吧，然而，公司只给涨了 1% 的工资。

Norah 觉得自己对未来不是那么有信心了，她突然觉得 Nakamura 最初给自己的加薪只是他新官上任的举措，而不是出于对自己的重视。Nakamura 的等级观念让 Norah 觉得同他争论工资会是徒劳，这一切都不会因为自己的不满而有所改变。在经过反复地思考之后，Norah 决定离开这个自己热爱并付出了 8 年的公司。

6. VT 公司离职员工的调查

6.1　Jenny 的离职员工调查和统计

面对人才流失的现状，Jenny 召集人力资源部的全体员工讨论对策，最终决定先对离职员工进行离职去向、工资满意度、管理风格满意度、工作压力、工作成就感这五个方面的调查和统计，以便更好地解决问题。

第一，对离职员工的离职去向进行调查和统计（图 10-2）。

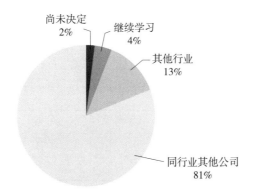

图 10-2　离职去向调查和统计图

第二，对离职员工的工资满意度进行调查和统计（表10-1）。

表10-1 工资满意度调查和统计表

工资是否满意	不满意的原因	调查结果	
		人数/人	比例/%
满意	—	7	8.86
不满意	低于同行业其他公司	43	54.43
	低于其他行业	11	13.92
	低于自己的付出	18	22.79
	低于其他同事	0	0.00

第三，对离职员工的管理风格满意度进行调查和统计（表10-2）。

表10-2 管理风格满意度调查和统计表

管理风格是否满意	不满意的原因	调查结果	
		人数/人	比例/%
满意	—	14	17.72
不满意	管理者与员工之间缺乏沟通	9	11.39
	管理方式与公司文化不匹配	9	11.39
	管理者要求高、吹毛求疵	16	20.26
	管理者对员工缺乏尊重	26	32.91
不确定	—	5	6.33

第四，对离职员工的工作压力进行调查和统计（表10-3）。

表10-3 工作压力调查和统计表

工作压力程度	压力非常大的原因	调查结果	
		人数/人	比例/%
一般	—	12	15.19
非常大	服务质量要求高	20	25.32
	工作生活不平衡	35	44.30
	管理者要求高	9	11.39
	工作气氛紧张	3	3.80
没有压力	—	0	0.00

第五，对离职员工的工作成就感进行调查和统计（表10-4）。

表10-4 工作成就感调查和统计表

工作成就感	没有成就感的原因	调查结果	
		人数/人	比例/%
强烈	—	3	3.80
没有	工作内容重复性大	26	32.91
	工作参与度低	17	21.52
	工作缺乏挑战性	13	16.46
	工作缺乏创新性	15	18.99
一般	—	5	6.32

虽然通过连续两周的努力，人力资源部终于对公司离职人员进行了初步的调查和统计，但是仅仅进行统计，无法解决目前离职率居高不下的问题。为了更准确地了解员工离职的真正原因，Jenny觉得有必要与部分已经申请离职的员工进行访谈。

6.2 离职员工的访谈

人力资源部随即组织了集体访谈，召集了30名已经申请离职的员工进行下一轮的离职原因调查。访谈结束后，Jenny进行了整理和分析，认为员工离职的原因主要有以下几点。

第一，工资水平不合理。据员工反映，VT公司每年工资的涨幅大概在5%～8%，也就是说，如果刚刚大学毕业的应届生进入公司时的工资为2500元，那么两年后，他的工资最高只能是3000元。但是，如果跳槽到同行业的其他公司，工资可以达到4000元。由此可见，VT公司现有的工资水平在市场中完全没有竞争力。如今，物价不断上涨，迫于生活的压力，很多员工不得不选择工资待遇更高的公司。

第二，工作压力大，无法找到工作和生活的平衡点。为了节约成本，即使业务部门经常加班到晚上10点，公司也不愿意招聘更多的人来缓解业务压力。员工们每天超负荷地工作，生活完全被工作占据，没有一点私人空间。偶尔业务量不多的时候，也不能按时下班，迫于Nakamura的工作习惯，员工们不得不留在办公室里假装学习业务。由于无法拥有足够的私人时间放松心情，面对每天的高标准服务质量要求时，员工们变得情绪更加紧张。

第三，工作缺少成就感。大部分工作不满两年就选择离职的员工表示工作内容缺乏挑战性，每天只是像机器一样，重复着同样内容的工作。他们更喜欢能够发挥自己优势、更具挑战性的工作。

第四，公司等级观念严重。很多离职员工反映，开始之所以加入 VT 公司，其中一个很重要的原因是 VT 集团"以人为本"的管理理念。但是他们来之后发现，VT 公司太过注重等级观念，甚至感受不到上司对下属的尊重，员工即使有意见也只能私下里抱怨。

第五，日本人对服务质量要求极高。很多离职员工提到，日本分公司的同事和客户对品质要求极高，员工们很难适应这种文化的冲突。

7. 尾声

已是深夜，此时的 Jenny 手里拿着离职访谈总结报告。且不提连续几个月员工流失率的飙升，就是这长长的离职访谈报告已经让 Jenny 身心俱疲。想到之前向老板承诺的降低 10% 离职率的目标，Jenny 陷入了沉思。工作缺乏成就感是 BPO 业务的共性，是无法改变的。可是工资结构、工作压力、个体尊重等问题都直接与公司的管理体制和管理文化有关。目前的业务是对日业务，公司的业务运营总监也是日本的 Nakamura 先生，引入日本的管理文化是必然的，然而面对中日文化的差异和冲突，人力资源部的道路应该何去何从呢？想到这里，Jenny 愈发茫然了……

思考问题：

1. 根据 Rajesh 在管理工作中的表现，你觉得他的管理风格是什么样的？根据 Nakamura 在管理工作中的表现，你觉得他的管理风格是什么样的？这两种管理风格是在什么样的环境和背景下形成的？你认为对于中国员工来说，选择什么管理风格更容易激发其工作热情？

2. 对于 Liz 的离职，你认为主要原因在哪里？如果你是 VT 公司的领导人，你会采取什么措施以避免这种情况的发生？

3. Norah 在 VT 公司入职以后先后经过了多次对公司情感的变化，请你分析一下 Norah 情感变化的原因在哪里？

4. Jenny 对离职员工进行了访谈，你觉得有必要吗？为什么？

分析要点：

1. 应用管理风格理论、文化冲突理论对第 1 个思考问题进行分析。

2. 应用文化价值模型对第 2 个思考问题进行分析。

3. 应用离职心理动因模型对第 3 个思考问题进行分析。

4. 应用离职心理动因模型对第 4 个思考问题进行分析。

案例 11

"以不变应万变"——记 X 会装公司组织结构的变迁

知识点：

组织结构设计、组织结构维度、组织结构影响因素

案例目的：

本案例通过对 X 会装公司组织结构变迁的分析，引导学生理解组织结构设计、组织结构维度及组织结构影响因素。

案例正文：

1. 引言

当一群人为了同一个目标在一起工作的时候，如何将这些人组织在一起，如何让群体工作变得更有效率，这些问题商业组织通常会通过建立组织结构来解决。组织结构并非千篇一律，组织管理实践中出现了各种各样的组织结构形态。哪种组织结构更加高效？哪种组织结构更适合本企业的需求？这些问题始终困扰着管理实践者，并激发着管理研究者的兴趣。本案例将讲述一家互联网公司的案例，从中可以组织结构的变迁过程。

2. 新创初期

X 会装公司是一家致力于提供房屋翻新和维修服务的互联网公司。公司的创始人王先生长期从事建材和家装行业，拥有一家小型的家装公司和一个售卖建材的商铺。在经营过程中，王先生发现传统家装行业存在很多局限和不足。一方面，很多消费者一生也就装修一两次新房，装修完成后，对于装修的需求变成了旧房的翻新和维修，但是很少有家装公司提供这类服务。消费者通常只能依靠物业和从事装修水电行业的亲戚朋友来进行维修工作，而旧房翻新通常只能依靠一些个体装修师傅或者小型的包工队。另一方面，由于利润率较高，家装公司对于新房装修业务非常重视，但是由于市场竞争激烈，获取新房装修的订单并不容易。而家装公司雇用的

设计师、水电工、木匠、油漆工等大多是以订单量为基础来获取报酬的，订单量的不足导致员工流失严重。而旧房翻新或者维修的业务订单总价较低，并且订单量也很不稳定，因此少有家装公司会开展这类业务。

王先生发现，如果能够将消费者维修和翻新的需求与家装公司对接，很可能会是一个巨大的商机。国内每年的装修业务量都是以千亿计的，虽然无法得知房屋翻新和维修的业务规模，但是保守估计也将是一个上百亿的巨大市场。为此，在2015年，王先生决定组建一家新的公司来开展房屋翻新和维修业务。有了这个想法后，王先生开始思考这个项目的细节。他很快发现，如果单独依靠自己的家装公司和建材店铺，是无法在房屋翻新和维修行业里翻出大的浪花的。本地的房屋翻新和维修的市场规模有限，就算通过自己的努力扩大业务地域，凭借现有的基础也只能覆盖一个城市内很小的一块区域，这与自己做大市场、影响整个行业面貌的最终目标差距很大。为此，他开始考虑借助互联网来实现自己梦想的可能。

2015年国内互联网行业已经蓬勃发展起来，人们生活的方方面面都受到互联网的深刻影响。王先生想借助淘宝的模式，将千千万万的家装公司与上亿的消费者联系起来。王先生将这个初步的设想与一位同样出身建材世家的年轻创业者钟先生进行了交流，发现他们的想法居然不谋而合。而且钟先生在学校先后参加了多次互联网相关的创业大赛，对于互联网技术及互联网创业的运作更加熟悉和精通。因此王先生果断地邀请钟先生加入，公司初创团队的核心基本形成。王先生和钟先生一起进一步细化了他们的商业计划，期望建立一个网络平台，将需要旧房翻新和维修的客户与家装公司和维修师傅联系在一起。消费者可以在平台上下单提出自己的需求，再由家装公司或维修师傅在平台上接单并在价格标准内达成协议。平台的主要收入则是订单的抽成。

想法细化后，王先生和钟先生决定继续扩大团队规模。一方面，他们没有信息技术相关背景，需要招聘专业的技术团队来负责应用的开发与平台的维护，并且还急需具备互联网运营经验的合伙人，以推进平台项目的顺利开展；另一方面，团队的资金积累并不充分，互联网项目需要在前期进行较大规模的投资，而仅凭两位现有的积累是无法满足未来的资金需求的。为此，他们开始招募技术团队和新的合伙人。经过一番努力，他们成功招聘到了一个技术团队来负责应用开发与平台维护，并且成功邀请技术团队的负责人作为合伙人加入核心团队，另外还成功引入了2位有互联网运营经验的创业者成为合伙人。至此，公司正式成为了以5位合伙人为核心，3位程序员为初创员工的创业公司。

在战略决定模式上，合伙人坚持共同协商的制度，要求任何重要决策都要所有核心成员达成一致才能通过，而不是根据股权的多少进行投票决策。在做出决策后，公司的核心成员进行简单的分工，分头开展融资、拓展市场、招聘员工、技术开发等工作。在初创阶段大家都很有干劲，不需要彼此的监督就能很快速地推进自己的工作。经过大家的努力，最初版本的App——X帮哥已经初步成型，并且公司还获得了50万人民币的种子轮融资，大大缓解了公司的资金压力。

3. 快速成长

在获得融资支持后，公司决定加快推进业务进展。当时有几家从事类似业务的公司也开始起步并获得了融资，所以公司需要更快地拓展自己的客户群体以占领市场。公司核心团队判断，获得最大份额市场，即拥有最多客户和服务提供商的公司，将在未来的行业竞争中占据主导地位；而发展滞后的公司，在行业同质化的前提下将很难再挑战领先者的市场地位。为此，公司决定招聘更多的员工在线下推广X帮哥App，一方面让更多的消费者了解和使用这个平台，另一方面让更多家装公司和维修师傅入驻，从而能够让消费者更快速和便利地寻找到服务提供者。所以公司首先招聘了几名新员工负责去各大城市线下接洽家装公司和装修师傅入驻平台，目的是让全国主要城市的消费者都能在平台上找到房屋翻新和维修的服务商。如果客户的服务无法得到有效满足，消费者将很快流失到其他平台。同时，公司也开始和很多网站和媒体合作，扩大App的知名度，让更多的消费者在平台上提出需求，从而让入驻平台的服务商能够获得更多的订单。随着公司的不断发展，原本的技术团队也开始变得繁忙。维护平台就耗费了大量的精力，导致他们无法腾出手来对App进行更新和完善。为此，公司又招聘了2名程序员来扩充公司的技术团队。

此外，随着公司的业务增长，一些具备资金、供应商等资源的创业者陆续加入了核心团队成为合伙人，核心团队扩充到了9人。至此，公司发展到了20人的规模，但问题也接踵而至。首先，合伙人变多后，大家的分工变得模糊了。各合伙人没有明确的职位，导致一些综合性工作，诸如财务、人事等都没有专人负责。原先由CEO钟先生来兼职这些工作，董事长王先生来负责统筹合伙人的工作。但是随着业务的增长，钟先生和王先生在融资和拓展业务上投入的时间越来越多，而人员的增长也让公司的综合性事务变得非常烦琐。这些都使两个人越来越力不从心。例如，原本公司的财务工作主要交由代账公司进行代账，钟先生负责监督。当时公司的业务量不大，钟先生可以比较轻松地处理。但是随着业务量的上升，代账缺乏及时性的问题日益凸显，而钟先生本人又不具备从事财务工作的资质和经验，这在一定程度上造成了公司财务数据的混乱。另外公司的决策效率也受到了挑战，原来公司一贯坚持合伙人集体决策和达成共识的制度，但是合伙人增加到9人后，在决策时达成共识变得更加困难，很多时候为了一项决策，核心团队甚至要开会讨论一两天，加起来十几个小时都无法彻底达成一致。有合伙人因为无法认同这一低效率的决策方式而退出，使得原本已经扩充到9人的核心团队缩减到了8人。

为了应对这些困难，公司招聘了一位新的员工负责财务和人事等综合事务，另外核心团队决定加强CEO和技术团队负责人的权力，大部分不涉及公司战略和方向的决策和事务被直接授权给CEO，而公司技术层面的事务大部分交由技术负责人全权负责。这些调整一方面加强了后勤保障，另一方面也减少了需要核心团队共同商议决策的事项，提升了效率。但公司业务的快速发展很快又让这个公司结构变得捉襟见肘。值得肯定的是，公司所瞄准的市场机会是很有前景的，旧房翻新和维修确实符合了很多消费者的需求，并且公司拓展线下服务商的举措也成效显著，平台的客户和服务商的注册数都上了新的台阶，同时平台上订单的成交量也大增。与之相应的，也需要更多的人来维护平台和处理客户投诉与纠纷，人员的增多和业务的增长也给财务和人力等后勤工作带来了更大的负担。为此，公司不得不进一步扩大规模。

公司首先成立了客服部来处理纠纷和加强与服务商的联系；其次招募了更多技术人员来充实技术团队，及时对平台进行维护和更新；最后还正式成立了综合部，来处理公司内部的财务、人事等后勤工作。新部门的成立和人员的扩充很快让公司的员工数量超过了50人，为了让这些部门能够有序运行，公司委派了团队的核心成员担任各部门的领导。但显然公司对管理的复杂程度缺乏准确的预估。

公司很快发现，虽然成立了综合部、技术部、客服部等部门，但是部门之间的界限却并不清晰。例如，向客服部反映的很多投诉意见都是由平台技术故障引起的；各个部门还经常把一些没有明确职责的问题推给综合部，导致综合部处理的问题变得非常复杂和多元化，很多工作内容都超出了综合部员工的能力范围。

这些问题给公司的运作造成了困难。第一，各部门由团队核心成员管理后，引发了团队核心成员间的矛盾。一些成员总是站在自己部门的立场上来思考问题和发表看法，为了减轻自己部门的工作量而推卸责任，忽视公司的整体利益。第二，各部门对于员工管理的许多基本问题缺乏共识。例如，一些部门常常需要加班到很晚，所以员工们第二天接近中午才上班，而另一些部门则坚持朝九晚六的上下班时间安排，导致很多工作因为人员不齐很难开展。第三，公司的薪酬体系和晋升机制都存在很大问题。规模比较小时，员工的奖励和晋升等比较简单，公司高层可以较为直接地观察员工的表现并直接给予一定的奖励或者提拔。而当规模变大后，公司高层对于很多员工的实际工作表现并不了解，需要更加完善的考核机制。

为此，公司决定进一步细化各部门间的分工和整体的规章制度。首先，公司明确了各部门的职责分工和工作范围，发布了由公司高层统一制订的组织结构图。由于部门间的职责界限难以完全通过分工来区分，公司还指定如果两个部门间出现分歧，由负责管理的公司高层负责协调，如未达成一致则由总经理介入。其次，公司完善了考核制度、薪酬体系和晋升机制。关于考核制度，原则上公司要求实施朝九晚六的工作时间，对于像技术部和客服部这样夜间工作量大的部门，可以弹性工作，但要在其他部门上班时段留员工值班。关于薪酬体系和晋升机制，公司将进行月度和半年度绩效考核，对半年以上表现优异的员工实施奖励和晋升。鉴于本身流动资金并不充裕，公司规定部分数额较大的奖励将以公司期权的方式发放，并且表现优异的员工有机会被提拔为公司的股东或合伙人。这些制度的出台大大减少了各部门间的冲突和员工的不满，提高了员工的工作积极性。

4. 发展壮大

得益于制度的规范化和翻新维修市场的扩大，公司业务规模进一步扩大。不到两年的时间，公司员工数量已经增长到 200 名。公司的办公场所也从创业孵化器内的四个隔间发展到了一层楼。公司的快速成长也得到了投资机构的关注，又先后获得了 1000 万人民币的种子轮投资，和高达 1 亿人民币的 A 轮投资。获得的高额投资给公司核心团队成员带来了更大的信心，他们希望进一步扩大公司在互联网旧房翻新和维修行业的市场份额。公司在互联网旧房翻新和维修业务上排名业内第三，在市场份额上与第二名的公司十分接近，但离业内第一名还有近 10% 的总市场占有率的差距。

此外，公司还在运作过程中发现国内互联网家装行业也存在比较诱人的市场机会。一方面，国内房地产市场持续火爆，消费者对装修有着很大的需求。但由于大多数消费者没有时间和相关专业知识，只能依托线下的家装公司来开展业务；而有些家装公司则为了追求利益在装修上偷工减料，或对装修材料以次充好。这种现象导致了消费者普遍对家装公司缺乏信任。另一方面，消费者的不信任也提升了家装公司的获客成本。由于消费者的不信任，成本较低的消费者介绍或直接上门等方式所能获取的订单完全无法满足家装公司的经营需求；为此，家装公司不得不投入大量的成本开展地推或者投放广告，并以较大的折扣优惠来吸引消费者。家装公司成本的上升又间接地增加了其采取不正当活动坑害消费者的可能，进而又强化了消费者对家装公司的不信任。这种恶性循环一直在国内家装行业内上演。对于公司而言，如果能够成为消费者和家装公司达成交易的平台，将会是一个很好的发展机会。一方面，消费者可以在平台上购买质量有保证的建材，确定装修方案，由平台落实建材配送，以及监督家装公司的装修质量；另一方面，家装公司可以在线上直接获得订单，大大降低了获客成本。为了抓住这个新发现的机会，公司决定开展互联网新房装修的这个新业务。

为了扩大市场份额和开拓新的业务，公司对员工进行了进一步的扩充。公司发展壮大的同时，也出现了一些问题。原先每个部门只有3～10名员工，工作安排都由负责人指派，基本能够做到井井有条。每个部门的员工数量激增后，部门负责人有些力不从心；加之部门内有很大比例的新入职员工，这也进一步地加大了部门负责人的管理难度。为了解决这一问题，一些部门负责人尝试通过任命组长、发布岗位职责说明书等方式来减轻自己的管理难度。这些做法一定程度上缓解了部门负责人的管理压力，但也存在一些隐患。在部门负责人下面设置组长分散了部门负责人的管理权力，导致部门负责人对于下属的掌控力降低。一些大的部门的负责人根本无法了解基层员工的工作状况，甚至一些工作经验较丰富的组长为了提升自己在部门中的地位架空了部门负责人，在部门负责人不知情的情况下做出了很多重要的决策。另外，给员工设置岗位职责说明书的尝试的确达到了很好的效果，很多新入职的员工通过说明书了解了基本的工作内容和要求，但是他们发现，所在岗位的实际工作时常和岗位职责说明书出现脱节的情况。毕竟作为一家迅速成长的公司，很多业务都在不断变化中，对于一个岗位的要求也在不停地改变，这些都使得岗位职责说明书渐渐变成了一纸空文，指导实际工作的作用已经微乎其微。

此外，公司开展新业务也并不顺利，维护和拓展旧房翻新和维修业务已经占据了公司的大部分人力物力，所以公司对于新业务的投入并不充足。更加致命的是，大家对于开展新的业务缺乏激情和动力。在公司核心团队成员方面，除了董事长和总经理，其他人对于开展新业务并不上心。一方面，多数核心团队的成员都已经成为公司某个部门的负责人，需要管理少则十几人，多则四五十人的下属，虽然他们对于公司开展新业务的尝试都表示支持和赞同，但是由于精力受限，实际工作中对于新业务的支持并不多。另一方面，在公司获得初步成功后，很多成员都表示想过相对稳定的生活，再为了一个新业务重新经历一遍初创时期的艰辛对于很多成员而言是难以接受的。但是新业务的发展已经到了迫在眉睫的地步，公司的互联网新房装修平台的发起并不是业内最早的，在公司开展这个新业务前已经有一些创业团队瞄准了这一市场，并获得了一定的投资；而新业务前几个月的相对停滞让公司已经处于不利的竞争地位，对于商业模式很容易被复制和追赶的互联网行业而言，速度和规模往往是获取竞争优势的"先手"，公司的新业务如果彻底失去了这一"先手"，将在后期的竞争中非常被动。

为了克服公司发展壮大后出现的一系列问题，公司高层决定再次寻求变革。

5. 化整为零

为了解决上述问题，公司展开了多轮商议。最后得出的结论是，公司目前问题的症结在于管理能力的不足。针对这一问题，大家提出两个方案。

一个方案是对公司进行"正规化"，即用各种规章制度来规范员工的行为，从而减少管理者的压力，将管理者的精力从日常的管理中解脱出来，依靠制订规章制度来实现管理目标。公司层面，需要进一步明确各部门的职责分工，完善部门间的协调机制；还需要建立员工的基本工作章程，规范员工的基本工作行为。部门层面，需要每个部门根据公司的战略需求进一步细化部门内的岗位职责和相应的工作程序，还需要在部门内建立信息汇报和传递的制度。但在讨论中，大家逐渐发现这一方案存在弊端。首先，互联网行业非常依赖快速的决策和反应，"正规化"虽然让员工的工作都变得有规可循，但同时也绑缚了员工的手脚，命令的上传下达阻滞了公司的行动，容易让公司变得僵化，即患上"大企业病"。其次，虽然公司已经达到了一定的规模，但是因为行业发展变化很快和自身经验不足，所以公司的许多业务和流程都在不断的适应和探索过程中。要想编制一套符合公司战略需求的规章制度变得非常困难，而且即使编制了出来，由于公司业务和战略的频繁变动，也需要不断地对规章制度进行更新，一个不断变动的制度很难让员工遵守并按照其指引来工作。这个方案的问题被指出后，越来越多的成员发现了该问题的严重性，所以这个方案不得不被搁置了。

另一个被成员戏称为"化整为零"的方案则得到了越来越多的支持。核心团队中有成员提出，既然各部门的领导者没有足够的能力和精力来驾驭规模扩大后的部门，那么就干脆把部门进一步拆分成小团队，由小团队作为基本的工作单元。大家很快发现，这一想法类似稻盛和夫的阿米巴经营模式。因此，公司结合阿米巴经营模式的思路对这一方案进行了细化。首先，将团队作为公司基本运作单元，原有的部门被拆分为一个个小型的团队；将部分决策权下放到团队层面，对于大部分具体业务层面的事项，团队均可以自行做出决策。其次，赋予团队领导更大的权力，公司除了基本的考核制度、薪酬体系和晋升机制，不再设置具体的工作流程和岗位要求。最后，明确各个团队的责任并完善团队间的协调机制。公司将整体战略和业务流程进行细分，交由各个团队负责；将一些规模较大的业务，交由几个团队合作完成，公司将派遣高管来协调团队间的合作。考虑到许多团队的业务都难以量化，公司没有明确要求像阿米巴经营模式那样对每个团队的投入产出进行核算，但每年都将对各个团队的绩效进行考评，并给予相应的奖励或惩罚。为了促进公司人才培养和管理能力的提升，公司还建立了每周管理教学和分享交流制度，由管理经验丰富的管理层、外部专家与团队领导、后备人才进行交流和解读。

在对待新业务上，公司延续"化整为零"这一思路，决定从总公司中分离出一个子公司来全权负责新房装修的业务。公司认为，与其让新业务在总公司中被"束手束脚"，还不如给予其更大的自主权让其"另立门户"。最终，公司决定让创业团队核心成员中最年轻和富有活力的两位成员负责这家子公司，以这两位成员为核心形成新的创业团队，推动新业务的发展。新公司在起步初期共享总公司的部分资源，正式运营后将逐渐脱离总公司的扶持和指导，自负盈亏、自行发展。

管理体制上的"化整为零"和新业务的"另立门户"使得公司从上到下经历了一次巨大的变革，而这一变革的影响也逐渐在企业后来的发展中显现出来。

6. 继续在"快车道"上疾驰

"化整为零"的组织变革实施后，公司的发展又重新进入了"快车道"。得益于运作效率的提升和对于市场变化的快速反应能力，总公司在未开展大规模和高成本的营销活动的情况下，依然在旧房翻新和维修市场上保持前三，并且相较于竞争对手，公司的现金流和盈利情况都非常健康。子公司也获得了快速的成长，实现了自给自足并获得了一定的收益，搬离总公司拥有了独立的办公地点，并很快发展到了接近200名员工的规模，在新房装修市场上也排名前十。接下来，如何更好地实现总公司和子公司的业务协同发展,将是摆在 X 会装公司面前的新课题。

思考问题:

1. X 会装公司的历次组织结构变革各是由哪些原因造成的?

2. X 会装公司的历次组织结构变革主要调整了组织结构的哪些要素?

3. 在成立子公司后,总公司如何在组织结构上实现新业务和原有业务的协同发展?

分析要点:

1. 应用组织结构设计和组织结构影响因素的相关知识对第 1 个思考问题进行分析。

2. 应用组织结构维度的相关知识对第 2 个思考问题进行分析。

3. 应用组织结构设计的相关知识对第 3 个思考问题进行分析。

案例 *12*

JNSP 物业中心的组织变革为何困难重重?

知识点：

组织变革、组织变革模型

案例目的：

本案例通过对 JNSP 物业中心的组织变革进行分析，引导学生理解组织变革、组织变革模型。

案例正文：

1. 引言

周总是 JNSP 物业中心的负责人，物业中心今天举办的会议让他倍感压力。在会议上，资深物业经理胡总对过去一年 JNSP 物业中心改革中存在的问题进行了总结和汇报，其他参会成员也纷纷表示赞同。

面对这些问题，周总明白，他现在需要冷静下来。首先是要保持管理的整体稳定，做好当前的工作；然后对问题进行分析并找出解决方法。

周总轻轻拉开窗帘，望着窗外的社区，回忆起这段时间的每一个细节，JNSP 物业中心改革过程中出现问题的原因究竟是什么？

2. 跨界携手

1999 年，上海 XYZJ 物业管理有限公司（以下简称"XYZJ 公司"）成立，率先发起"新居运动"。"新居运动"注重环保，崇尚自然，具有人文关怀，以房地产业为载体，已成为影响深远的创新运动。以此为契机，上海 XYZJ 公司专注于上海高端住宅物业的管理和服务，大胆引进成熟、先进的服务理念，结合上海地方特色，不断创新和完善住宅管理方法，受到业主、行业的高度赞扬，连续五年被评为上海市 50 强物业管理公司。

张总自接任 XYZJ 公司总经理以来，正式肩负起"新居运动"的重任。借助国际先进的物业管理理念，建立了"首都花园"，以"首都花园"为代表的住宅物业管理服务模式屡获殊荣，管理规模跃升了 50 倍。张总对这一成就感到满意，至少没有辜负前任总经理的期望。然而，以人文关怀为出发点的"新居运动"却成为了业主发泄不满的爆炸点。

为了更好地与业主沟通信息，提高服务能力，2013 年，XYZJ 公司联合京津科技公司推出了社区 App，并在 XYZJ 公司联合京津科技公司管理的社区全面推广，积极吸收用户反馈，不断改进。2014 年，XYZJ 公司联合京津科技公司创建了第一个 SaaS 社区平台，这是一个"温暖的微社区"，是发展基于云平台的社区物业管理和运营管理的关键一步。

2016 年，当 XYZJ 公司自信地认为可以将互联网应用程序成功应用于社区物业管理时，公司逐渐发现传统的社区物业管理与互联网的思维不兼容。社区应用程序的功能非常丰富且强大。但是传统的社区物业管理已难以适应互联网时代的步伐，转型势在必行。

周总是京津科技公司的创始人，张总和周总多次就双方合作的方向进行沟通。周总认为，先进技术在"温暖的微社区"运作中只是一个基本的服务平台，只有与真正的企业合作，才能拥有真正的未来。张总认为，对于物业管理公司来说，用互联网思维改造其传统基因是重中之重。如果京津科技公司和 XYZJ 公司合并，将是 XYZJ 公司创建新的物业管理机制的一个机会。因此 XYZJ 公司和京津科技公司决定进行跨界合作。

2016 年，XYZJ 公司收购了京津科技公司。周总任 XYZJ 公司副总经理，负责 JNSP 社区，肩负社区物业管理转型的重要任务。XYZJ 公司管理下的 JNSP 社区曾被评为上海物业管理优秀住宅小区。社区占地面积 20 万平方米，建筑面积 40 万平方米，主要为多层建筑，大约有 3000 户家庭和 10000 名居民。作为一名在互联网行业工作多年的 IT 人士，周总是一个典型的物业管理行业的"门外汉"。面对周总的担心，张总拍拍周总的肩膀说："你应该是门外的野蛮改革者。"

3. 暗流涌动

张总和周总选择 JNSP 社区作为试点，一方面是因为 JNSP 社区是 XYZJ 公司旗下第一个使用社区 App 的地方，周总对其情况比较熟悉；另一方面，JNSP 社区是 XYZJ 公司的旗舰和高端社区，可以发挥标杆作用。

作为一个典型的 IT 人士，周总的扁平化管理思想已经根深蒂固。上任之初，所有职能部门都被撤销，同时成立了四个管家小组，每个小组有一名管家，管家由原客服部客服经理担任。其他人员被平均分配到四个管家小组。根据地理位置，JNSP 社区分为四个区域，每个管家小组负责一个区域的物业运营。各管家小组财务独立，并对自己的损益自负。

然而，周总低估了传统物业管理行业对互联网思维的抵制。以胡总为代表的原管理层普遍反对取消职能部门，转型一直受到限制。

2016 年上半年，胡总到 XYZJ 公司汇报工作时，已经知道公司正在准备收购一家 IT 公司。

但胡总没有想到的是，周总担任 JNSP 物业中心负责人，全面负责物业管理转型，并将 JNSP 社区作为 XYZJ 公司物业管理转型的示范项目。

胡总和周总不同的背景使他们的想法往往不同，这给 JNSP 物业中心的转型带来了困难。尽管胡总的学历不高，但他在社会上所学到的人情世故绝非学校书本所能学到的。当周总决定撤销职能部门时，胡总强烈反对，并向 XYZJ 公司张总进行了汇报。然而，张总十分支持周总，所以胡总很失落。

管家小组的成立，确实打通了物业与业主之间的沟通渠道，提高了运营效率，但在过去的一年里，问题也层出不穷。

基于组织变革后的种种困难，周总决定召开一次会议，主要议题有两个：一是总结过去一年转型中存在的问题；二是集思广益，为下一步转型指明方向。令周总惊讶的是，这次会议上，大家都在抱怨和指责他的改革措施。

4. 冲突涌现

在会议上，周总要求所有人都畅所欲言的声音刚刚落下，就有人站了起来。

"周总，我是一名军人，我有话要说。自从保安部被撤销后，所有的保安都被分配到四个管家小组。但是保安工作有其特殊性，需要定期进行专业培训。现在人员分散在各个管家小组，难以统一管理。在最近的一年里，我们甚至没有进行过一次像样的培训。此外，我们还需要在公共安全、城市管理和消防检查方面与政府进行合作。过去，政府部门只需与我们联系。现在各个管家却都不太配合。我并不反对转型，但如果继续这样下去，会有问题。"前保安部负责人杨部长首先开始了一连串非常尖锐的批评。

"周总，在工程部被撤销前，它负责整个社区的维修工作，每年的维修备件都是按照标准采购的。现在，各管家小组财务独立，对自己的利润和成本负责。因此，四个管家组有四个采购订单，价格和质量参差不齐，业主觉得不公平就会来捣乱。一旦规划建设委员会发现，我们会非常被动。我们能尽快想出解决办法吗？"原工程部负责人边队长又说道。

"周总，保洁阿姨不止一次向我抱怨，现在每个管家小组的楼层都是按区域划分的，各小组保洁工作量大小不一，而且如果一个保洁阿姨生病或回家，就只能由其他人承担。但其他小组并不愿意帮忙。我以前没有遇到过这样的问题，因为我可以统一安排。现在保洁阿姨之间的关系并不比以前好。你认为这样的问题应该怎么解决？"这位原清洁部负责人紧随其后，发表了讲话。

"周总，社区绿化工作涉及两个方面内容：定期修剪和定期置换。过去定期修剪是统一安排的，但现在分为四组，各组安排不统一导致社区绿化不统一。此外，定期置换的问题类似于工程部。过去，苗木是统一购买的，现在采购工作委托给管家小组。有些经常更换，有些根本不更换。行业委员会的人多次提出意见，让我负责。现在绿化部都没了，你说我应该承担什么责任？"这位原绿化部负责人高声说道。

胡总喝了一口水，说道："让我也说几句话，当职能部门被撤销时，我不同意。职能部门不能轻易撤销，物业管理的目光不能只集中在社区，还有公安、城管、消防、行业委员会、社会工作委员会、规划建设委员会和各种社会组织，这是不可忽视的，必须有一个统一的管理。"

周总耐心地听取了大家的意见。虽然转型很难，但是他坚信在数字时代，传统物业管理行业应该顺应时代，为业主提供更好的服务和体验。

5. 路在何方

会议结束后，胡总和周总对转型进行了阶段性总结。表示 JNSP 社区应该立即终止转型。随后 XYZJ 公司决定暂停 JNSP 物业中心的转型和经验推广。

这年春节，管家小组的邢组长接到通知，JNSP 社区的供水将从晚上 9 点起暂停 8 小时。这是影响居民生活的重大事件，物业中心必须及时向领导汇报，并向社区发出通知，否则很有可能引发业主投诉。周总听了邢组长的汇报后，立即着手安排。他告诉邢组长要特别注意，停水通知不仅要在社区 App 上发布，还要在社区公告栏张贴，也要向行业委员会发出通知。周总还提出要让保安在社区巡逻时与业主交谈，通知大家提前做好蓄水准备，以免影响他们的生活。

汇报工作后，邢组长没有立即离开。虽然他犹豫了一下，但还是忍不住问："周总，这几天公司里有传言说元旦后你就要离开 JNSP 物业中心了，是真的吗？"周总让他不要担心，并告诉他好好工作。

邢组长于 2014 年大学毕业，通过校园招聘进入 XYZJ 公司，被分配到 JNSP 社区担任客户服务经理。他每天面对业主的投诉和咨询，然后将这些问题分类、反馈给各职能部门。这些工作并不复杂，但是很烦琐。在工作中，邢组长慢慢地看到了传统物业管理的弊端，职能部门各自为政，导致工作中有很多问题。他觉得传统物业管理模式转型是大势所趋，但他毕竟只是一名客户服务经理。幸运的是，2016 年下半年，周总来到 JNSP 物业中心，开始推动物业管理模式转型。

由于原有职能部门被撤销，所有职能人员被分配到各个管家小组，邢组长也升级为组长，带领管家小组负责社区 800 户左右的业主，这对他来说无疑是一个很大的肯定，当然也会有很大的压力。

近一年来，他不仅要处理日常烦琐的工作，还要管理小组。由于管家小组财务独立、自负盈亏，所以他需要时常关注小组的财务状况。同时，XYZJ公司一直在密切关注JNSP的社区转型，这也给了他很大的压力。虽然如此，他还是尽力把工作做到最好。然而，过去一年的转型，结果并不令人满意。确切地说，转型似乎失败了。最近公司内部的传言让他有一种不好的预感，XYZJ公司的张总会在国庆节访问社区，他担心社区的转型不能继续推进，一切又会回到原点。

原保安部负责人杨部长接到停水通知后，也陷入了沉思。他于2009年从军队退役，在XYZJ公司担任保安。他凭借出色的身体素质和严肃的军事作风，很快就崭露头角。2013年，他被任命为JNSP社区的保安部负责人。对于周总对社区进行的转型，杨部长内心是很矛盾的。一方面，他知道传统物业管理模式存在弊端，他钦佩周总这样大刀阔斧的转型，这很需要勇气。另一方面，他对周总推动的转型并不乐观。凭借直觉，他认为周总在对物业管理行业缺乏足够了解的情况下仓促实施转型，是非常危险的。

解决好停水问题后，唐大姐敲门走进了周总的办公室，给他递交上月财务核算表。

唐大姐看出周总脸上的烦难，询问他有没有什么可以帮忙的。周总抬起头来，叹了一口气，唐大姐是非常有经验的社区财务工作人员，他十分尊敬唐大姐，也想听听她对于过去一年社区转型的看法。

"我看您这一年来忙里忙外，是真想把这件事做好。但我觉得转型的方法有些问题，尤其是撤销所有职能部门。社区物业管理原有架构中的各类群体，无论保安部、工程部、绿化部还是清洁部，每一个部门都慢慢形成了自己无形的关系和格局。大刀阔斧的转型，会打破原有的关系和格局，令人难以接受。虽然转型能够提升服务效率，但也会有很大的阻力……"

6. 车到山前

在和唐大姐沟通后，周总又仔细调研了过去一年JNSP社区转型工作的细节。调研结果也证实了唐大姐的说法，甚至颠覆了周总的认知。周总不得不承认，员工们抱怨的这些问题确实存在。与此同时，周总也接到了张总的电话，表示想和周总谈谈，听听他的想法。周总也觉得是时候和张总一起制订一个新的计划了。

听了周总的讲述，张总感到震惊，但他也有些惊喜。转型虽然看起来并不成功，但却让他们真正了解到传统社区物业中心的内部利益关系。张总处于高位，没有足够的机会和精力去了解基层社区物业管理的内部利益关系。也正是这些导致了他们为转型所做的努力变得无效，这直接阻碍了管理转型的进程。

"此外，我注意到，社区物业管理的员工没有足够的激励机制，社区被视为一个资源市场，员工都想为自己争取更多的利益。这种情况下，所谓的管理理念和服务意识是无从谈起的。"

"接下来你准备怎么做？"张总接着问道。

"我现在有两个想法。第一个是考虑适当保留职能部门，将职能部门与管家小组的模式相结合。回顾过去，我先入为主地认为直接撤销职能部门是更高效的，这是我认识上的偏差。在撤销职能部门后，管家小组需要同时兼顾管理和运营，对于他们的工作能力要求太高。所以我认为可以循序渐进地转型，适当保留职能部门。"周总说道。

"这个想法有意思，你接着说。"张总鼓励道。

"我的第二个想法是加强公司的内部员工培训。过去的培训主要侧重于工作技能，虽然也强调管理理念和服务意识，但效果很差。从实际情况来看，物业管理行业员工的整体教育水平较低，所以我们在人才培养方面应该改革培训体系。不过在此之前，我认为应暂停转型，先对这些内部乱象进行整治！"周总又说到，张总的眼睛也亮了起来。

2017年10月的一天下午，XYZJ公司人力资源部曹主任来到JNSP物业中心会议室。

"我是带着使命来到这里的。主要是宣布XYZJ公司的两项决定，一是从现在起，周总将全面负责JNSP物业中心的物业管理；二是胡总不再担任JNSP物业中心的物业经理，另有任命。张总反复强调JNSP社区是XYZJ公司的示范社区，代表XYZJ公司的形象，希望大家配合周总的工作，努力打造出一个标杆社区。"

周总随后发表了讲话,"感谢 XYZJ 公司的支持,也感谢各位同事在过去一年里的支持。JNSP 社区是 XYZJ 公司的示范社区,这意味着我们的一举一动是 XYZJ 公司未来的方向。数字化时代,传统物业的管理转型是总体趋势,也是 XYZJ 公司的战略选择。我真诚地希望大家能继续支持我的工作。"周总语气平静,眼睛明亮,真诚地看着大家。

7. 尾声

会议结束后,周总坐在椅子上,回忆起过去一段时间的烦恼。虽然他经历了风风雨雨,但他始终坚信数字时代下社区物业管理变革的必然性,互联网与社区物业管理的结合将开花结果,这也是他的梦想。

周总慢慢站起来,他心里非常清楚,张总的支持并不意味着他所做的一切都是正确的。目前,一切似乎都在好转,与其说是张总对他的信任,不如说是对自己变革理念的认可。然而,这并不意味着可以成功。JNSP 物业中心未来的所有管理变革必须经受住实践的考验。他必须努力,不辜负张总的信任,建设好心中的"理想家园"。

思考问题:

1. 针对张总和周总两人所推出的组织变革措施,你是如何看待和评价的?为什么 JNSP 物业中心要转型,其主要驱动因素是什么?

2. 从案例来看,JNSP 物业中心在转型中遇到了哪些问题?为什么会产生这些问题?

3. 案例中有许多人物,在转型过程中扮演了不同的角色。JNSP 物业中心的不同人物在面对转型时,都有什么样的态度和立场?请你分析一下背后的原因是什么。

4. JNSP 物业中心所开展的转型是成功了还是失败了?如果你是周总,会如何推进 JNSP 物业中心转型的下一步工作?

分析要点:

1. 应用组织变革的相关理论对第 1 个思考问题进行分析。

2. 应用组织变革的相关理论对第 2 个思考问题进行分析。

3. 应用组织变革模型的相关理论对第 3 个思考问题进行分析。

4. 应用组织变革的相关理论对第 4 个思考问题进行分析。

案例 13

ZL 公司的组织变革之路

知识点：

组织变革的相关理论

案例目的：

本案例通过对 ZL 公司的组织变革进行分析，引导学生理解组织变革的相关理论。

案例正文：

1. 引言

从成立至今，ZL 公司已经走过了六十多个年头。虽然遭遇了 2008 年金融危机，但是在 2009—2013 年，ZL 公司的销售额获得了飞跃式的增长。公司成功化解了内外部危机，经营逐渐稳步发展。

2. 背景介绍

2.1 ZL 公司的现状简介

ZL 公司成立于 20 世纪 50 年代，总部设在北京，是一家以金属矿产的勘探开发、冶炼加工和贸易流通为核心业务，辅以金融服务、房地产建设、矿冶技术研发等新兴业务的大型跨国金属矿产企业集团。ZL 公司秉承"提炼百年不锈，打造绿色未来"的发展理念，致力于为全球提供优质服务。其业务范围覆盖全球 40 多个国家和地区，拥有近 20 万名员工，控制着 13 家国内外上市公司。改革开放前，ZL 公司是国内金属矿产资源进口的主要渠道；改革开放后，ZL 公司在全球近 40 个国家和地区开展业务，是较早"走出去"开展国际化经营的企业。2000 年，ZL 公司聘请国际知名咨询公司，制订了第一份发展规划，明确了 7 个业务板块和 2 个单元的"7+2"业务架构，其中，7 个业务板块分别为原材料、钢铁、有色、综合、金融、地产、教育，2 个单元分别为货运、招标。

2.2 ZL公司的历史沿革

2.2.1 政策专营期的发展脉络

ZL公司是中国第一批大型国有外贸专业公司，专门从事国家五金矿产的进出口贸易。20世纪50年代，在高度集中的计划经济体制下，公司拥有绝对垄断权，在全国范围内经营矿产品出口和钢材采购，这种情况一直持续到改革开放以后。从公司成立到20世纪80年代中期，公司营业额保持了良好的增长势头。1985年，ZL公司的营业额达到75亿美元，创造了公司发展史上的最高记录。

2.2.2 市场转型期的发展脉络

随着改革开放的深入，外贸体制改革也在深化。ZL公司在五金矿产进出口贸易领域的垄断局面一去不复返。1985年，外贸进出口权被下放给地方政府。中央企业的省级和市级分支机构已与总部完全脱钩，中央有关部委和各省市先后成立了自己的外贸公司，取得了五金矿产的外贸经营权。这给ZL公司带来了巨大的冲击，同时，许多外贸公司的多渠道经营也极大地影响了ZL公司可持续经营的品种。钢材进口代理制全面实施后，各省市经营钢材进口的外贸公司数量逐渐增多，ZL公司钢材进口量占全国的比重逐年下降，从1979年前的100%下降到1990年的60.2%。

为了应对市场变化，1988—1999年，ZL公司进入了市场转型期。1988年，ZL公司根据其主要业务情况将13个部门合并，成立了二级公司，包括有色金属贸易公司、稀有矿产品进出口公司、工业发展公司、ZL贸易有限公司，这些新成立的二级公司独立经营，独立核算，自负盈亏。与此同时，ZL公司在沿海和经济特区设立分支机构，并开始尝试多元化经营，投资项目涉及多个领域。在此期间，尽管ZL公司进行了一系列的探索和变革，但由于投资分散、战线长、管理薄弱，大多数项目都失败了。1999年，ZL公司的出口额降至14.8亿美元，为改革开放以来的最低水平。

2.2.3 战略形成期的发展脉络

2000年，ZL公司进入了战略形成期。ZL公司以战略为导向，通过内部资源整合，形成了清晰的"7+2"业务模式，确定了延伸金属矿产产业链、控制上游矿产资源、发展下游分销网络的发展方向。这一阶段的重点是全面实施新的发展战略，深化战略转型和内部改革。2000—2004年，ZL公司业务规模开始持续快速增长，营业收入年复合增长率达到45%，总利润年复合增长率达到62%，总资产年复合增长率达到26%，综合实力明显增强。

随着改革开放的进一步深入，经济全球化趋势日益明显，矿产资源竞争日趋激烈，国际金属市场持续升温，世界贸易流通格局发生重大变化，ZL公司的内部运作也面临着前所未有的严峻挑战。对于ZL公司来说，制约发展方式转变的体制和结构性矛盾没有得到根本解决，自主创新能力薄弱，与兄弟央企相比，发展速度和盈利水平存在较大差距。

2004年12月27日，李总接任ZL公司总经理职务。上任伊始，李总提出继续坚持战略转型，加强资源金属矿产项目管控和全球营销网络建设。

2005年，ZL公司与多个省、直辖市、自治区签署了战略合作协议或专项协议，初步完成了西部、中部、东北、环渤海经济圈区域经济合作的战略布局。随着区域经济合作的大力推进，ZL公司收购了中部地区的冶金集团，进入冶金工程建设领域，实现了产业链的新延伸。

2007年，ZL公司首次提出发展6大主营业务，形成了特色鲜明、脉络清晰的包含黑色金属、有色金属、金融、物流、房地产建设、教育的6大主营业务发展格局。

2009年，ZL公司抓住金融危机带来的产业调整机遇，先后收购重组了一批工矿企业和科研院所，完善了科工贸一体化的大产业链布局；控制了8家国内外上市公司；调整了战略愿景，将"国际领先的金属矿产企业集团"调整为"具有国际竞争力的金属矿产企业集团"，更加突出竞争力建设；提出了"大矿业""大流通""协同多元化"的商业体系结构，指导未来三年的改革与发展，为后续的组织变革奠定了战略基础。

3. ZL公司进行组织变革的动因

ZL公司实施组织变革的动因源于公司战略的变化，即ZL公司实施了战略转型。

3.1 战略转型的背景

2005年，ZL公司制订了2006—2010年五年发展规划，确定了"五年建成新ZL公司"的中期战略发展目标。经过三年的发展，ZL公司的战略转型已初见成效，2008年，公司业务规模和效益提前实现翻番。黑色金属业务初步建立了完整的钢铁产业链布局；有色金属业务已形成多金属、全产业链发展格局；拥有60多家工矿企业和24座矿山，掌握了铁矿石、钨矿石、铅锌矿等产品的开采能力和钢铁、氧化铝、钨制品、铁合金、锑、锡、铝等产品的冶炼加工能力。生产型业务对ZL公司收入的贡献占比从2005年的4%增加到2008年的26%，利润贡献率也持续增加。

然而，国际金融危机在2008年爆发，并蔓延到实体经济。随着危机的蔓延，ZL公司的主要业务在2009年开始受到严重影响，特别是黑色金属和有色金属这两大核心业务。2009年2月，ZL公司营业额同比下降50%以上。国际金融危机使行业经历了需求快速下降和流动性急剧收紧的双重打击，大部分金属矿产价格大幅下跌。在国际经济相对低迷的情况下，金属需求不会显著增加，金属周期处于相对低谷。与此同时，中国钢铁和有色金属长期能源过剩的矛盾逐渐暴露，市场由"资源为王"转向"订单为王"。如何充分发挥ZL公司的整体优势，如何调整经营战略，适应新形势的特点，已成为ZL公司保持行业竞争力面临的重要问题。

3.2 战略转型过程

在这种背景下，ZL公司运用科学发展观开展学习和实践活动，清楚地认识到公司在改革和发展中还存在许多深层次的矛盾和问题。2009年第二季度，ZL公司举办了几次战略研讨会，讨论公司的未来发展。集团目前面临的问题是业务规模和利润的急剧萎缩以及风险的急剧上升。这不仅是金融危机的结果，也是近年来在金属繁荣周期下公司的广泛经营没有得到完全改善的结果。

通过讨论和分析，ZL公司从发展模式、资源保障能力、业务结构布局、公司治理、人才保障、科技创新和基础管理等方面总结出9个问题，特别是在与国际领先的金属矿业企业的对标中发现，ZL公司仍存在较大差距。

因此ZL公司再次进行了自我转型——重新研究和调整了战略愿景，开始实施三年滚动规划。三年滚动规划改变了集团总部以往在原五年计划基础上简单修订的做法，采取上下结合、内外结合的方式，吸收二级公司从各自行业的角度提出的发展思路。ZL公司通过聘请外部咨询公司来论证公司最初战略愿景的可行性。经过几轮沟通，ZL公司确定了战略愿景，即"成为以贸易为基础、以资源为依托、具有国际竞争力的金属矿产企业集团"。

4. ZL公司正式启动组织变革

2009年4月14日，在部分中央企业学习实践活动座谈会上，ZL公司李总向中央企业领导汇报科学发展观学习实践活动，提出ZL公司将应对国际金融危机作为学习实践活动的重要组成部分，将"提高科学发展水平，实现三年新跨越"作为学习实践活动的指导理念，保持稳定发展，促进调整跨越。

李总认为，学习科学发展观要与实践相结合，在学习中推进实践，在实践中深化学习。ZL公司所在的金属矿产资源领域是国际金融危机影响下的"重灾区"。2009年，钢材和有色金属的价格比2008年下降了40%以上。市场交易疲软，业务增长受阻。李总认为应将国际金融危机视为一本罕见的"活"教科书，密切观察危机的演变趋势，重点了解危机的规律性和破坏性，深入分析危机中力量平衡的变化，重新认识全球经济一体化条件下的现代企业治理和经营管理，积极探索"化危机为机遇"的规律性特征和有效途径，为更高层次、更激烈的国际竞争做好准备。

李总的想法得到了国资委的积极响应。在国资委及相关部委领导的支持下，ZL公司开始了一步步的组织变革。2009年4月底，ZL公司正式启动整体重组，体制改革迈出重要一步；10月中旬，ZL公司将整体重组上市请示正式上报国资委；10月底，ZL公司审议通过了2009—2011年三年计划，提出了"大矿业""大流通""协同多元化"的商业体系结构；2010年1月，ZL公司调整主营业务，增加金属矿产工程设计、技术研发及相关服务为主营业务；2月，ZL公司成立专门小组研究业务结构和管控模式，并赴宝钢、中粮、中建、中化等单位学习、借鉴经验，于3月底形成初步的总体思路；通过向公司领导汇报和沟通，吸收有关调整和改进意见和建议，于4月份形成了公司业务结构和管控模式调整的总体思路，并经公司审议通过。

5. 对 ZL 公司组织变革的问题开展分析和诊断

战略转型推动 ZL 公司走上了从传统外贸向资源型企业转型的发展道路。在十年的转型中，ZL 的业务规模和效益持续显著增长，营业收入从 247 亿元增加到 1853 亿元，利润从 3.8 亿元增加到 70 亿元；产业结构明显改善，25% 的收入和 50% 的利润来自生产企业；科技实力大大增强，科工贸一体化的大产业链布局初步形成。ZL 公司的快速发展有目共睹，令人振奋。

随着战略转型的不断推进，ZL 公司业务领域不断扩大，企业规模不断扩大。公司的业务结构、人员结构、企业构成、经营模式和产业布局都发生了翻天覆地的变化，但原有的组织结构越来越难以适应企业新的发展要求，导致公司的运营管理出现了一系列问题：在业务快速发展的过程中，公司面临着业务、职能、区域三条线的协同管理问题，管理跨度和复杂性迅速增加；公司基于各业务板块的整体战略转型具有阶段性的特点；部分业务板块之间经营业务重叠，造成公司内部直接竞争的问题；海外业务边缘化，传统优势未能充分发挥作用。这些问题可以总结为以下两点。

5.1 ZL 公司原有组织结构存在的问题

根据经典战略管理理论，战略决定组织结构。如果一个企业想要实现其战略目标，就必须有一个匹配的组织结构来实施。然而，截至 2009 年底，除物流外，ZL 公司的其他主营业务没有统一的管理机构，主营业务模式与组织结构不相适应。此外，勘探、科研等业务均在主营业务框架之外，需要明确这些业务与组织结构之间的对应关系。由于组织结构与战略目标不匹配，导致 ZL 公司内部出现较为严重的交叉经营现象，造成资源的浪费。

资源的浪费主要反映在客户和供应商的结构与区域布局的不合理上。ZL 公司的客户和供应商数量众多，区域布局分散，内部财务、人力资源分配不合理，不能实现资源的集约使用。供应商与客户均存在结构问题，随机客户占比过多，渠道的稳定性有待提升。

5.2　ZL 公司原有管控模式面临的问题

首先，ZL 公司通过调整业务结构，建立了 6 个业务中心，初步解决了公司管理范围过宽、管理链条过长的问题。但是，对于不同业务格式的业务中心，需要建立匹配的控制方法。

其次，ZL 公司的职能管理仍需改进。在职能管理分工方面，ZL 公司尚未形成规范、统一、清晰的管控体系，责任的重叠和错位导致责任主体的不明确。以二级公司的设立、变更或处置为例，多个部门发布二级公司的相关管理制度并参与工作。多头管理，制度体系不统一，造成责任划分混乱和管理空白，导致管控体系混乱。

最后，公司分级管理、分级授权制度不完善。总部职能管理权限高度集中，二级公司内部经营计划、投资、人力资源变动等核心管理决策需要总部审批，导致经营活动发展不畅，权责划分和运行机制有待优化。根据咨询公司对 ZL 公司总部各职能部门及下属单位 100 多名总经理、副总经理管控问卷的调查反馈，36% 的受访者认为 ZL 公司整体管控状况良好，61% 的受访者认为一般，3% 的受访者认为较差。

公司业务类型多，经营重叠，业务条线混乱，这些都成为制约公司整体上市的因素。

6. ZL 公司进一步实施组织变革

6.1　优化重构组织结构

为了建立清晰的组织结构，解决交叉经营和内部竞争问题，ZL 公司需要解决一系列重大问题。

针对组织结构设计问题，根据国资委批准的主营业务，参照国际金属矿业公司的管理模式，ZL 公司将勘探开采与分销流通分离、前端与后端分离，构建独立营销平台，紧密整合物流和贸易，建立集团内共享的科技研发平台，重组二级公司，整合交叉业务，将公司划分为有色业务、黑色矿业、黑色流通、金融、房地产建设、科技、教育 7 大业务中心。

在明确组织结构之后，需要确定各业务中心的定位和管控模式；详细设计各业务中心的业务和职能结构，制订具体的运营计划；制订人力资源、运营、财务等核心管理体系的业务流程；提出信息系统连接和后续建设方案，以支持新的架构和管理模式。

为此，ZL公司成立了专门的公司变革工作组，并分别为各中心成立了分工作组，推动变革，制订具体实施方案。工作组成立之初，从建立工作机制入手，建立相关的组织、规划和推进体系，制订ZL公司业务结构和管控模式调整的管理办法，明确总体目标、任务分工和沟通机制，建立周例会制度、工作简报、专题报告等工作制度。工作组每周召开例会，汇报变革进展情况，及时讨论、协调、解决各种问题。

交叉业务问题涉及各业务中心之间的利益划分，因此必须在集团层面进行协调。为此，公司变革工作组出面逐一划分有争议的资产和业务边界，协调相关业务中心，使各业务中心的资产和业务边界更加清晰，避免交叉作业。

在运行机制方面，制订了供应链协调的总体原则和各环节的运行机制。各环节的运行机制如下。

（1）生产企业根据购销计划，通过相关业务部门批量采购生产原材料，产品由相关业务部门和区域中心销售，并按市场价格结算。

（2）在同等条件下，生产企业应选择物流部提供的物流服务。

（3）所有进出口货运代理业务和仓储业务原则上由仓储部、物流部实施，并按市场价格结算；将进出口货运代理业务和仓储业务的集中度纳入中央业务协作专项考核范围；在同等条件下，将运输业务和保险业务分别移交给租船部、保险部等业务部门。

（4）招标业务方面，相关单位应及时提供招标信息，并提前通知招标业务部门介入；投标业务部门应积极跟进，提供优质服务，满足内外部客户的需求。

（5）海外企业是ZL公司在海外的销售组织，负责当地市场、客户和业务的发展。原则上，境内企业实体在海外的销售业务应通过当地海外企业开展，并以市场价格或约定价格结算；采购业务无法通过境外企业开展的，应及时通知；境外企业的采购业务和内销业务原则上通过境内事业部开展。

针对资金不能集中使用的问题，商务中心制订了资金集中统一管理制度。在资金安排上，规定资金由中心统一安排，各事业部有偿使用；在资本预算方面，规定资本预算具有刚性约束力，预算调整必须遵循审批程序；在外部融资担保方面，规定未经中心书面同意，不得提供外部融资和担保。

6.2 进一步强化企业管控模式

要建立与业务相匹配的管控模式，需要确定管理范围、管理深度和管理方法。由于各业务中心的业务范围不同，控制的重点和难点可能不同。公司应根据业务本身的特点，构建总部与业务中心的关系。由于管控模式高度专业化，涉及总部与各中心的权责划分，通过外部咨询设计具有较强的说服力。因此，ZL公司的管控模式方案设计主要由咨询公司完成。

考虑到ZL公司已经确定了多主营业务的发展方向，不同主营业务的运营模式和核心竞争力差异较大，各主营业务之间业务协同程度中等，咨询公司认为战略控制模式为适合ZL公司的管控模式。考虑到7大业务中心不同的运营模式和业务特点，有色业务、黑色矿业、黑色流通、科技这4个业务中心采用以运营为导向的战略控制模式，金融、房地产建设、教育这3个业务中心采用以财务为导向的战略控制模式。在运营导向的战略控制模式下，ZL公司总部重点控制业务中心的战略方向，监控业务中心的执行情况，确保ZL公司战略意图的全面落实；在财务导向的战略控制模式下，ZL公司总部重点控制业务中心的战略方向，给予更高的业务自主权、预算自主权和投资自主权。

在控制手段方面，ZL公司形成了战略规划、计划与预算、绩效考核、投资与资本运营、关键岗位管理、风险管理与审计6大核心控制手段。总部通过战略规划确保下属业务中心的战略方向和实施；通过计划与预算管理和监控下属业务中心的运营；通过绩效考核对下属业务中心运营效果进行监督；通过投资与资本运营掌握下属业务中心的主要投资审批权限，按照分级授权的原则下放一般投资审批权限；通过关键岗位管理对下属业务中心关键岗位进行管理；通过风险管理与审计对下属业务中心进行审计，统一制订风险管理制度。

在部门职能优化方面，引入了核心职能的概念，建立和完善了总部控制所需的所有核心职能，解决了职能交叉问题；通过部门间核心职能的横向对接，解决职能管理的错位和缺失，实现部门间的有机联系。例如，投资管理部门应主要负责投资项目的评审、跟踪和评估，但其原有职能还包括投资企业管理，导致投资管理部门"兼任裁判员和运动员"。ZL公司在职能优化后，取消了其投资企业管理的职能。

6.3 企业改制问题

2009年4月，ZL公司开始全面重组，并于2010年底成立了一家股份制公司。ZL公司整体改制后，职能部门基本整体平移至股份制公司，采用"一个班子，两块牌子"的模式运作。

7. 组织变革后的ZL公司运转情况

7.1 开展组织变革后ZL公司的收获

通过业务中心的建立，ZL公司的业务结构更加科学合理，公司经营专业化、一体化优势明显加强，战略转型的有利局面进一步得到巩固，未来发展的系统竞争力迈上新台阶。

从经营业绩来看，2010年，ZL公司经营业绩显著提升。营业额跃升至430亿美元；营业收入2550亿元，同比增长49.62%；利润总额70亿元，同比增长123.2%；总资产超过2000亿元，净资产超过500亿元，均同比增长50%以上；资产负债率进一步下降，资产质量较好。2011年，改革效果进一步显现，企业规模和经济效益大幅提升，均达到历史最高水平。营业收入3551.8亿元，同比增长39.7%；利润总额127.7亿元，同比增长98.5%。公司实现了跨越式发展。

7.2 组织变革后出现的新情况

在ZL公司改革组织结构后，总部的运营和管理权力被下放。根据新的管控模式，总部只管理各业务中心的战略、计划、预算和评估，各业务中心管理下属业务单元。这种管理关系运作了两年后，总部的管理人员逐渐感到离业务越来越远。ZL公司总部业务分析部吴经理感慨道："过去做业务分析基本上可以得到业务的第一手信息，现在我觉得很多信息都被屏蔽了。"

此外，由于各业务中心刚刚成立，许多职能部门的管理人员都是应届毕业生，管理经验缺乏，会给业务开展带来阻碍。

虽然 ZL 公司整体经营状况较好，财务业绩得到改善，但也存在许多需要进一步改善的新问题。作为组织变革的主要领导者，李总也听说了这些新问题。有些问题较小，可以通过协调解决；有些问题是需要全面思考的重大结构性问题。如何解决这些新问题？李总陷入了沉思……

思考问题：

1. ZL 公司在面临内外部环境变化的关键时间节点开始推进组织变革，并取得了卓有成效的结果。请你结合案例，分析 ZL 公司在组织变革过程中采取了什么样的变革策略。

2. 案例中，ZL 公司负责人李总认为外部环境虽然紧张，但是对于公司推进组织变革却是好的时机。请你分析背后的原因是什么，以及 ZL 公司组织变革过程中内部文化和价值观的作用。

3. ZL 公司在推进组织变革的过程中，大量方案都来自外部专业性的咨询机构。你如何看待 ZL 公司组织变革中咨询公司的角色。

4. ZL 公司在推进组织变革的过程中，公司高层领导的作用十分重要。请结合案例，分析组织变革过程中领导和沟通机制的作用。

分析要点：

1. 应用组织变革管理的相关理论对第 1 个思考问题进行分析。
2. 应用组织变革管理的相关理论对第 2 个思考问题进行分析。
3. 应用组织变革管理的相关理论对第 3 个思考问题进行分析。
4. 应用组织变革管理的相关理论对第 4 个思考问题进行分析。

Case 1

Challenges Faced by BE Company

Key Words:

Personality theory; capability theory; attitude theory; job satisfaction theory; motivation theory

Purpose:

By analyzing the situation faced by BE Company, the case is intended to guide the students to understand and apply the personality theory, capability theory, attitude theory, job satisfaction theory, and motivation theory.

Case:

1. Introduction

Established on January 9, 2007, Ningbo BE Company is mainly engaged in the processing and export of home textile products. At present, it has 180 employees and 6 departments covering R&D, marketing, finance, production, management, and operation. In terms of the domestic trade business, BE Company mainly supplies products to the customers on some E-commerce platforms, while in terms of the international trade business, it mainly exports to the developed countries including USA, Germany, and Canada. After nearly ten years of unremitting efforts, BE Company has gained a firm foothold in the Ningbo foreign trade market and obtained stable sales channels. From 2016 to 2017, the sales profit of BE Company showed a steady increase, and the overall sales situation was good. Today, BE Company has grown into a medium-sized manufacturer of home textile products. However, it is still making preparations for further investments. It plans to give full play to its advantages in production technology by expanding the scale and inputting more time and human resources in the development of new products.

2. Company Overview

The following sections will introduce BE Company from the perspective of its internal resources. Internal resources are the sum of resources at all stages owned by a company in the process of production and operation. It is the basis for a company to get output and compete with other companies. Internal resources are divided into tangible resources (including financial resources, physical resources, technical resources) and intangible resources (including organizational resources, reputation resources, innovation resources, human resources).

2.1 Tangible Resources

This section takes financial resources and physical resources as examples to introduce the tangible resources of BE company.

(1) Financial Resources

Financial resources refer to the flow and operation of company funds. Whether financial resources can be reasonably developed and utilized is directly related to the normal operation of the company and the survival and development of the company. Table 1-1 lists the main financial data of BE Company in 2014—2018, from which two features may be seen: ① although liabilities are relatively stable, they are generally on an upward trend; ② profits are stable but have not increased significantly, and the growth rate of sales revenue has declined in recent years. If there are no successful new attempts in production and marketing, BE Company's profit situation may not last long.

Table 1-1 Main Financial Data of BE Company in 2014—2018

Item	Year				
	2014	2015	2016	2017	2018
Total assets/RMB million	93.9	98.0	101.0	108.0	111.0
Growth rate of total assets/%		4.66	3.02	6.78	2.74
Owners' equity/RMB million	47.0	49.0	50.0	52.0	53.0
Liabilities/RMB million	40.0	38.0	44.0	43.0	45.0
Assets to liabilities ratio/%	43.29	39.45	43.22	39.89	40.58

continued

Item	Year				
	2014	2015	2016	2017	2018
Sales revenue/RMB million	92.1	93.2	94.2	95.4	97.2
Growth rate of sales revenue/%		1.51	1.82	1.14	0.81
Profit/RMB million	12.0	11.0	13.0	12.0	15.0

(2) Physical Resources

BE Company has beautiful and tidy production buildings, office buildings, staff dormitories, and standard workshops. It has advanced cotton wadding production line which is equipped with leading cellucotton carding and to enable automatic production. It also has domestically and internationally leading hardware facilities including computer-controlled multi-needle sewing machine, single-needle sewing machine, and computer-controlled embroidery machine, laying a solid foundation for the production of high-quality textile products. BE Company has production buildings, raw materials warehouse and finished product warehouse, as well as four workshops including carding workshop, quilting workshop, sewing workshop, packaging and inspection workshop. The company has one automatic carding production line and two ordinary carding machines which could produce 150000 cellucottons and 100000 cloud silk quilts; 50 high-speed sewing machines which could produce 200000 bedsheets and 200000 duvet covers; 2 computer-controlled sewing machines; 1 pillow filling machine.

2.2 Intangible Resources

This section takes organizational resources and reputation resources as examples to introduce the intangible resources of BE company.

(1) Organizational Resources

The management of BE Company implements a hierarchical responsibility system, with clear responsibilities and powers for each department, and the CEO is responsible for overall affairs. Each department has different levels of work and responsibilities. The Production Department is responsible for routine production and manages four workshops:

carding workshop, quilting workshop, sewing workshop, packaging and inspection workshop. The head of each workshop is responsible for the production links. The HR Department is in charge of the recruitment and training of employees, as well as the establishment of performance assessment mechanism. The Finance Department is responsible for the payment of salaries, as well as the operation of production-related and sales-related capital. The Marketing Department consists of Domestic Marketing Division and International Marketing Division, which are responsible for the development of domestic market and international market respectively. The R&D Department is responsible for the innovative research and development of production equipment and technology to improve the functions of products, besides of which it also introduces domestic and international advanced equipment to transform and upgrade the obsolete production equipment and technology. The Logistics Department is responsible for the dining and accommodation of employees. It also establishes the labor union to protect the rights and interests of employees, and sets up a clinic to ensure the health of employees.

(2) Reputation Resources

BE Company has always taken product quality as the highest priority and it has established a comprehensive service system. BE Company aims at "quality first, scientific operation, customer first"; adheres to the concept of "care about the product, be considerate to customers, care about employees, and be responsible to society"; pursues the development vision of "be civilized employees, create good products, build a harmonious company"; and establishes the BE image of "quality optimization, good reputation, beautiful environment, and excellent order", striving to make the company stronger and better.

3. Problems with BE Company

(1) Weak R&D and Technical Innovation Capabilities

Weak R&D and technical innovation capabilities have seriously affected the development of BE Company, resulting in the company's primary production and sales of mid-to-low-end products, which significantly reduces the company's competitiveness. Due to the lack of design R&D capabilities, the company's products are hardly differentiated from those of other companies. The products tend to be homogenous, lack brand characteristics, and have little competitive advantage. The lack of production technology innovation ability makes it difficult for the company to improve product quality and technical level. Firstly, the company does not have its own design and R&D team, and the investment in this area is severely insufficient. Well-known large home textile companies invest a lot of manpower and financial resources into design and R&D, which directly leads to a gap in competitiveness with other companies. Secondly, the textile operation equipment is outdated, and no new equipment has been introduced, so there are no innovative products and lack of technology content. Thirdly, there are no personnel with professional technical skills. All these factors have limited the development of BE Company.

(2) Low Level of HR Management

BE Company is a family business, about 60% of the management members come from the family and friends of the members. The proportion of the management team recruited from outside is very small, which is not conducive to attracting excellent human resources from society, and limits the range of employment. This nepotism management method leads to the company's lack of treatment for violations by family members, and the execution ability is lacking. The emergence of this unfair phenomenon not only directly leads to a decrease in company profits but also causes other employees to have complaints, which is not conducive to unity within the company. To improve the level of human resource management, the company can analyze the allocation and composition of employees in the production process, and combine work demands according to the abilities of the employees to maximize resource integration. They can establish a clear process of training, selection, rewards, and feedback, thereby minimizing costs and optimizing product production and delivering the most suitable employees for each department. BE Company must abandon this outdated management team building method, accelerate adjustments and upgrades, strengthen internal management, select and train high-level excellent professionals through public recruitment, and only then can the company's human resource management level be improved.

(3) Imperfect Performance Assessment System

The HR Department of BE Company has only established a simple performance assessment system and has not linked employees' performance appraisals with salaries, nor has it combined performance goals with company goals, which is not conducive to the company's development. Firstly, this leads to a high turnover rate among frontline workers, which not only directly reduces the production rate and product quality but also increases the workload and corresponding financial input of the HR Department in recruiting new employees, leading to an increase in costs. Home textile companies have high requirements for the operation proficiency of frontline workers. Frequent replacement of operators will greatly affect production efficiency and quality. New employees need systematic training before they start work, which not only delays the working time of old employees but also leads to the waste of production materials. Secondly, since the assessment results do not affect the income of employees, employees do not value performance appraisals, and they lack a sense of responsibility and enthusiasm for work.

(4) Low Employee Satisfaction

Despite the financial statements showing that BE Company's total assets are growing at a rate of about 10% per year, both domestic and international markets are expanding to different extents, production orders are full, and the company's prospects are very optimistic. However, the results of the company's employee satisfaction survey are disappointing. The survey is divided into three parts: employee satisfaction with salary and benefits, satisfaction with personal career development, and satisfaction with the working environment and corporate culture. The survey results show that, out of a total score of 100, employee satisfaction with salary and benefits is 52, satisfaction with personal career development is 27, and satisfaction with the working environment and corporate culture is 40. In the past two years, BE Company's talent turnover rate has been 38%, which also indicates that there are some problems in talent motivation, employee salary and benefits, and corporate culture.

(5) High Turnover Rate

In the past two years, 38% of the company's employees have left and joined competitors in the same industry, especially many new college graduates. Once they complete their training and gain key management experience or project development experience, they are attracted by competitors with salaries higher than those of this company.

It can be found from the HR Department's survey that employee satisfaction is not high. Therefore, many employees are job-hopping, and most employees within the company lack enthusiasm for work and are not as proactive as they used to be.

This dilemma can be reflected in some departments. In the HR Department, the manager has absolute authority. In actual operation, all team leaders are directly responsible to the manager, so to a large extent, the supervisor has become a figurehead. HR Manager Wang Hao, who joined the company in 2016 after leaving a university, has always been very demanding on his subordinates. He inquires about everything in detail. When assigning work tasks, he not only requires new employees to operate according to the work process he set, but also the work methods and procedures of old employees must be approved by him before they can be implemented. He believes that this can avoid unnecessary exploration processes and improve work efficiency. His obsession with controlling the process not only makes subordinates feel suppressed, often worrying about making mistakes in detail and being reprimanded, but also the work of the subordinates lacks creativity and autonomy, and the achievements seem to be all the manager's merit, and the subordinates have no sense of accomplishment. In addition, when he criticizes his subordinates, he never allows them to argue. He believes that the primary duty of subordinates is obedience, and arguing is just looking for excuses for failure, and such employees will not seriously improve their work. Once an employee's work makes a mistake, it is often reprimanded at the least and punished at worst. When an employee's work achieves results, Wang Hao rarely praises them in person because he feels that doing well is their duty. Subordinates can hardly get promoted and raise their salary unless they make outstanding contributions. For this reason, his subordinates are all afraid of him, but within the company, he has won praise from senior managers for his rigorous and capablework style.

Confronted with these challenges, how should BE Company formulate management plans? The company is preparing to hold a meeting of senior management to discuss how to solve the company's predicament.

Questions:

1. What are the reasons for the high turnover rate and low employee satisfaction of BE Company? How to solve these problems?

2. What problems does BE Company have in employee management? How to solve these problems as a manager?

Tips for Answering the Questions:

1. Apply job satisfaction theory and motivation theory to analyze the first question.

2. Apply attitude theory, motivation theory, personality theory, and capability theory to analyze the second question.

Case 2

Emotional Labor—Flight Attendants of AC Airlines

Key Words:

Emotional labor and emotion management related theories

Purpose:

By making an analysis on the flight attendants of AC Airlines, this case is intended to guide the students to understand and apply the theories related to emotional labor and emotion management.

Case:

1. Introduction

As an airline mainly engaged in passenger transportation, AC Airlines has always been concerned about how to provide good experience to the passengers. The flight attendants undoubtedly bear the responsibility of accomplishing this task. Generally speaking, flight attendants refer to cabin service staff, including the chief attendant and cabin attendants. In order to improve aviation service quality, AC Airlines has formulated many performance and appraisal methods for flight attendants.

However, these assessments were not so effective. On the one hand, the assessment criteria are not closely related to the actual work and part of the work content could not be properly quantified. On the other hand, using these assessment methods will only increase work pressure and will not help flight attendants to provide better services. Instead, it further consumes their service enthusiasm.

Ali is an attentive chief attendant who is used to making records of her tasks at the end of each flight. In her five years of work as a flight attendant, she has completed dozens of flight logs. There is a special section in her flight log, that is, what kind of labor her workmates have to put in to deliver their services.

2. Emotional Labor Under Special Work Requirements

Ali recalls her experience as a flight attendant in the past five years. Before she started working, she thought her job as a flight attendant was decent and glamorous. However, after she really started working, she found that behind the glamorous facade, there were many hardships and difficulties that outsiders didn't know about. The average age of flight attendants is around twenty. However, even for such young people, high-intensity flight tasks have brought a great burden to their physical and mental health.

In addition to standing for long periods, frequent takeoffs and landings on popular domestic routes and flights make their work and rest extremely irregular. At the same time, in order to maintain their image, their weight is also strictly controlled, which accelerates the overdraw of these young flight attendants' health.

Although the company has issued a series of protective measures and policies to protect the basic physical health of flight attendants, such as stipulating that the total flight time of flight attendants cannot exceed 1200 hours per year; the crew of the same flight can fly a maximum of 4 takeoffs and landings in a day, and at least 2 hours of continuous rest is guaranteed between takeoffs and landings; the average weekly working hours do not exceed 40 hours. However, these measures only guarantee the basic health of the flight attendants, but they cannot solve their fatigue from the inside out.

Ali thought carefully about the reasons behind this and even sought advice from friends in the fields of management and psychology. She found that the reason why flight attendants feel so tired is that the nature of their work requires them to put in more emotional labor than ordinary people. As we all know, flight attendants need to maintain sufficient etiquette and provide good service under any circumstances. In this process, their real emotions cannot be revealed. But Ali's psychology friend told her that people cannot always be in a good emotional state. Emotions will be affected by various internal and external factors, and if the workplace has expectations or requirements for the emotions expressed, it will have to provide corresponding emotional labor.

After such consultation and thinking, Ali believed that she had found the key to the problem. In her subsequent working hours, she carefully experienced, observed, and recorded related events in her work process, hoping to find more information and clues from them.

3. Negative Examples

Ali recorded some negative examples in her flight log. A typical scenario involves new employees experiencing a significant gap between their expectations and the reality of the job, leading to difficulties in adapting to the work. Three years ago, when Ali was first promoted to a two-cabin flight attendant, she encountered a new member in her crew. This new member was very good at communication and expression, and she was very enthusiastic about her job at the beginning. However, not long after, she started to slack off. During a break, Ali had a chat with her and learned that the new member found the job to be much less glamorous than she had initially imagined. It was more about serving passengers, almost like being a waitress. She often complained, spreading negativity to the entire crew. In the end, this new member quit, and Ali was promoted to chief attendant and moved to another crew.

Ali could, to a certain extent, understand these complaints. The nature of the job of cabin crew requires them to serve all types of passengers. Some passengers respect their efforts, while others are demanding and haughty. When encountering rude passengers, the cabin crew still needs to respond with a positive and cheerful attitude, which is indeed a high demand. That's why Ali would always take special care of the new employees, trying to help them adapt to these job requirements as much as possible. Ali had to console the crew members who were reduced to tears by rude passengers on more than one occasion. She recalled one flight attendant who had only been on the job for two months. She was verbally abused by a passenger for several minutes but maintained a smile throughout, trying to pacify and reassure the passenger. Although the situation was eventually resolved, Ali could see the exhaustion in her eyes. Even though she had done her best, she was reported by a passenger for a fake smile during the second take-off and landing due to her fatigue. This complaint was the "last straw", and she couldn't help but shed a few tears. However, after crying, she still had to pull herself together to serve the next batch of passengers.

The most memorable incident for Ali was when her colleague had a severe argument with a passenger. This argument took place during the Spring Festival period on a flight from Beijing to Harbin. Due to weather conditions, the flight was delayed. The most crucial job for the cabin crew at this time was to continually reassure the passengers who were stuck in their seats. Despite their efforts, as the delay grew longer, the passengers' dissatisfaction increased. However, no matter how tired they were, the cabin crew still had to be patient, keep smiling, and tirelessly explain the situation to the passengers. In domestic flights, pilots are usually in charge, so they are usually the first to know and deal with any flight delays. However, for various reasons, they often can't share this information with the cabin crew. Yet, the ones facing the pressure from passengers are not the pilots but the cabin crew. This situation leads to the cabin crew needing to constantly reassure passengers without providing any valuable updates, which puts them under double pressure from air traffic control and passengers. Under these circumstances, even the slightest mishap, combined with inexperienced crew members or work mistakes, can easily lead to serious disputes. Due to a mistake, Ali's colleague failed to attend to a passenger's need in time. Another colleague went to remedy the situation but was unreasonably harassed and insulted by the passenger. Unable to bear it, the colleague ended up in a physical scuffle with the passenger, which resulted in a severe impact.

Ali reviewed the dispute afterwards. She felt that the dispute was the inevitable result of a confluence of several factors. (1) Due to prolonged delays and efforts to appease passengers, the cabin crew members were physically and mentally exhausted. (2) Resignation of some flight attendants at that time had negative impact on the working atmosphere and job satisfaction. (3) It was during the peak travel season, with a large number of passengers of varying qualities and a strong desire to return home, which intensified the dissatisfaction with the delays. (4) The chief attendant should have intervened promptly to prevent disputes and effectively manage the relationship between the crew and cabin crew, maintaining effective communication with the crew. (5) Most importantly, Ali thought that the chief attendant was excessively harsh on the cabin crew members, constantly using company performance evaluations to suppress everyone, resulting in the inability to establish a good team atmosphere, lack of motivation, and even a hostile and tense atmosphere.

4. Positive Examples

Ali also documented several positive examples in her logs.

She summarized that the situations that required the most emotional labor often occurred when dealing with flight delays or unexpected incidents on the aircraft. Among them, flight delays were the most common. Flight delays are a common occurrence due to various reasons. Ali not only reviewed various incidents she had experienced herself but also specifically searched for relevant reference cases shared internally by the company, hoping to find content related to emotional labor.

The first incident that came to her mind was a flight trouble she encountered when she was just promoted to the chief attendant of the Golden Flight. The Golden Flight was a round-trip flight between Beijing and Shanghai, which was the busiest domestic route. Therefore, the Golden Flight rarely had many vacant seats. However, on one occasion, there was a sudden incident where a malfunction occurred in another AC Airlines aircraft, causing some passengers to be transferred to the Golden Flight. This posed many challenges for Ali's work. On one hand, due to the flight issue, passengers were already extremely dissatisfied with the airline. On the other hand, many business class or first class passengers had to be accommodated in economy class after the transfer. As a result, some passengers intentionally created difficulties for the cabin crew. At this time, Ali promptly stepped forward. She believed it was necessary to fully consider the emotional instability of these passengers, so instead of retaliating, she sought solutions to their problems, aiming to earn their respect fundamentally. Ali took care of the needs of all passengers as much as possible, setting an example for other cabin crew members, inspiring their enthusiasm for service, and ultimately avoiding the escalation of conflicts.

In addition to her personal experience, Ali also found some cases shared within the company. One of them was also about a delayed flight. The chief attendant Zhou Lijia had worked for the flight from Beijing to Guangzhou for more than five years, a popular route of AC Airlines that was widely selected by business people. During a delay caused by air traffic control, Zhou Lijia successfully defused a potential conflict between flight attendants and a passenger. During the wait, a passenger repeatedly asked about the departure time, and Zhou Lijia patiently provided answers and maintained good communication with the crew, promptly relaying any information she obtained to the passenger. However, as the passenger needed to attend a meeting in Guangzhou and was concerned about being late, he became increasingly dissatisfied and used the threat of deplaning as leverage. With calm composure, Zhou Lijia handled the situation, respecting the passenger's concerns while providing proactive service and continuing to monitor the passenger's subsequent travel arrangements. She ultimately succeeded in calming the passenger and resolving any potential issues that could have arisen.

Encountering unexpected incidents during a flight is something nobody wants to see. However, cabin crew members must possess the ability to handle such situations. On a flight from Beijing to Nanchang, shortly after takeoff, the cabin crew received a notification from the cockpit that the aircraft had encountered a severe mechanical failure and needed to return immediately. The chief attendant forced herself to stay calm and quickly gathered the cabin crew for a brief meeting, explaining the situation to everyone and arranging necessary measures, showcasing the psychological resilience and job skills required of an outstanding chief attendant. While informing the passengers about the situation, the chief attendant utilized her professional expertise and sincere attitude, successfully calming the passengers' anxieties. During the return flight, the chief attendant maintained continuous communication with the cockpit and promptly relayed information from the flight crew to the passengers, earning the passengers' complete trust. This enabled the passengers to remain calm throughout the return process. Ultimately, with the collaborative efforts of the entire crew and passengers, the aircraft safely returned and landed at Beijing Capital International Airport, successfully resolving the crisis.

Although encountering unexpected incidents during a flight is undesirable, these examples demonstrate the importance of emotional labor for cabin crew members. Ali not only reflected on her own experiences but also sought valuable references within the company. By learning from these positive cases, Ali aimed to improve her own emotional labor skills and create a more harmonious and efficient working environment for the cabin crew.

Another memorable example for Ali was her colleague Liu Man, a recognized star chief flight attendant of AC Airlines. She has many qualities that other cabin crew members could learn from.

On a flight from Chongqing to Shanghai, Liu Man encountered a family rushing to Shanghai for a surgery. The little girl in the family suffered from bone cancer and had just undergone a chemotherapy surgery. But her condition did not improve, and she needed to undergo an amputation surgery in Shanghai. Upon learning about their situation, Liu Man coordinated with other passengers to arrange better seating for the family. Considering their difficult circumstances, Liu Man also organized a fundraising activity during the flight. When the plane arrived in Shanghai, the cabin crew led by Liu Man gained the respect of all passengers.

5. Closing Remarks

After a period of careful documentation and deep contemplation, Ali had gained a deeper understanding on emotional labor. She also realized that performance evaluations and assessments for cabin crew members could not truly address the various issues caused by emotional labor. Ali found herself pondering whether there might be better ways to fundamentally solve these problems. She believed that solutions could be found.

Questions:

1. Based on the cases, what factors do you think can influence emotional labor?

2. Based on the cases, how should the flight attendants provide emotional labor more effectively when dealing with dissatisfied passengers?

3. What capabilities should the flight attendants possess in order to improve the quality of service and the effectiveness of emotional labor?

4. What effects does emotional labor have on employees and customers respectively?

5. From the company's perspective, what measures should be adopted to protect the emotional resources of employees?

Tips for Answering the Questions:

1. Analyze the first question by applying the theory of emotional labor.

2. Analyze the second question by applying the theory of emotional labor.

3. Analyze the third question by applying the theory of emotion management.

4. Analyze the fourth question by applying the theory of emotion management.

5. Analyze the fifth question by applying the theory of emotion management.

Case 3

To Make Friends with the Teachers and Students

Key Words:

Personality theory, capability theory, attitude theory, motivation theory, emotion management theory, leadership theory

Purpose:

By making analysis on RA Experimental Middle School, this case is intended to guide the students to understand how the personality theory, capability theory, attitude theory, motivation theory, emotion management theory and leadership theory apply to individuals.

Case:

1. Introduction

Zhou Mei began working at RA Experimental Middle School in 2004 and has been serving as the principal since 2014. As a veteran of the RA Experimental Middle School, she witnessed the development of the school and the growth of numerous students. Her consistent management approach has been to be a friend to both teachers and students. At the outset, RA Experimental Middle School had a small scale and weak foundation. The teachers were recruited from more than 20 provinces across the country, with the majority being young teachers lacking teaching experience. Some teachers were even looking for opportunities to leave the school. The team of teachers was instable. Faced with this situation, Zhou Mei, as the principal, dared to reform and innovate. Leading by example, she created a well-qualified and relatively stable teaching staff, laying the foundation for the school's excellent performance in the college entrance examination in recent years.

2. General Information of the School

RA Experimental Middle School is a full-time private school funded by RA Group and directly under Ningbo Education Bureau. It is the practice base and also the leading organization for theoretical research on "experimental education", a national key research project on education and research. It is recognized as one of the outstanding private schools in China, outstanding performer of integrity brand in Zhejiang, and 5A-level safe campus in Ningbo. The school has more than 1500 students and 172 faculty members, including 130 full-time teachers.

The school takes the small-class teaching mechanism. Each class has about 40 students, and multimedia facilities and advanced modern teaching methods are used in the teaching. The school emphasizes the education and management of middle school students, which plays a crucial role in improving the quality of education. The school advocates self-esteem featuring "self-respect" and "self-discipline" to foster selfesteem in every student and promote their personal development. The school also advocates the educational concept of "being an upright person", guiding students to overcome their various bad habits and integrate into civilized society. Besides, the school adopts a combination of closed management and open operation systems.

3. Being Friends with Students

3.1 Interacting with Students on Equality and Respect

"All our work is centered around the progress and growth of students. Because parents' choice of RA Experimental Middle School is a trust in us, we must not let parents down." When saying these words, the gentle Zhou Mei appeared particularly firm and resolute.

When interacting with students, Zhou Mei emphasizes equality and respect. She believes that equality allows teachers to see the real students, while respect can stimulate their unique potential and personalities, helping them grow.

She remembered there was one student named Wu Hao in her class when she was still a class administrator. Wu Hao was very outgoing, active, and curious. He was easily distracted and often talked to others in class, disturbing the teacher and other students. But Zhou Mei never directly criticized him publicly. Instead, Zhou Mei paid more attention to him and often talked with him about his interests and hobbies. During class, if she asked questions to students, Zhou Mei sometimes called on Wu Hao to answer. After he responded, she would provide appropriate affirmation and praise. Later, she developed a harmonious relationship with Wu Hao and could chat with him like a friend. In the classroom, Wu Hao listened attentively, actively answered questions, and could control himself from talking. If there were classmates chatting around him, he would remind them not to disturb the teacher's class.

3.2 Focus more on Students' Difficulties and Less on Their Problems

In addition to class administrators, RA Experimental Middle School also implements a mentorship system, where each mentor is responsible for 3 to 5 students. The mentors provide guidance in terms of students' thoughts, academic tutoring, psychological support, and life guidance. Zhou Mei is also one of the mentors.

Zhou Mei's approach in dealing with student issues is to focus more on their difficulties rather than their problems. Once a student spent a lot of money on an online lending platform App and wanted to run away from home after being criticized by his parents. Concerned about the extreme actions the student might take, the parents approached Zhou Mei for help. Without hesitation, Zhou Mei contacted the student and carefully inquired about the reasons behind his action. It turned out that when the student went out with friends over the weekend, he felt frustrated seeing everyone wearing branded sports shoes and wanted to buy a few pairs online to alleviate his sense of imbalance. However, he couldn't control himself and ended up buying many other things, resulting in an exorbitant bill. The harsh criticism from his parents made him feel extremely upset. After understanding the situation, Zhou Mei gently counseled the student, and he soon realized his mistake.

"If you want to manage students, you must respect them and make them feel warm. They will willingly allow you to guide them, which saves a lot of effort." Zhou Mei said.

Wang Gang was one of the students whom Zhou Mei mentored. He had a strong personality and liked to challenge and argue with everyone. Once, Zhou Mei attended a poetry recitation rehearsal for the whole school, and Wang Gang happened to be standing at the center.

After the rehearsal, Zhou Mei quietly approached him and said, "You can lower the folder with the poems a bit so that the audience can see your facial expressions. It will enhance the effect of your recitation. From up there, you may not feel it, but from down here, it looks different." The student was surprised to realize that the principal wasn't just going through the motions but could notice details that others overlooked. The student followed Zhou Mei's advice and tried it again, and indeed, the effect was different. He secretly glanced at Zhou Mei in the audience and stuck out his tongue, showing a happy smile.

"During the process of growing up, the experiences students have with the outside world are essential, especially during their middle school years when they are psychologically sensitive. As teachers, we must pay special attention to the psychological characteristics of adolescents." Zhou Mei said.

Over the years, classroom is always Zhou Mei's favorite place. "The classroom is where the heart is at peace." This has been Zhou Mei's unwavering educational philosophy for over a decade. Whenever she has free time, she enters a classroom, sits at the back or squeezes in with the students to listen to the lesson attentively and learn together.

Zhou Mei's classroom visits are not just a formality. After listening to the class, she carefully summarizes and takes detailed notes. After the class, she asks students about their difficulties in learning.

Many students, even years after graduation, still remember the principal who was both a teacher and a friend, who helped them solve various problems.

3.3 Unleashing Students' Potential

Each student has their own preferences and strengths, but not everyone has enough opportunities to showcase them. This is an issue of unfair resource allocation and a dilemma in modern education. If students lack opportunities for experimentation, their chances of success are diminished, and over time, their potential gets suppressed. How can we unlock the potential of every child? The education field has various attempts.

"We insist on letting students try things first, rather than teachers imposing their knowledge. The classroom should revolve around learning, with guidance as the key." Zhou Mei said.

Guided by this educational philosophy, RA Experimental Middle School continuously adjusts and reforms its teaching methods based on the school's actual situation, ultimately forming the "Three Guidances, Four Learning" classroom teaching principles. The three guidances refer to guidance, supervision, and instruction, while the four learning methods include self-directed learning, cooperative learning, inquiry-based learning, and experiential learning. Taking a single class as an example, the "Three Guidances, Four Learning" approach advocates practice before explanation, emphasizing thorough explanations and ample practice. Students are encouraged to discover and raise questions based on their pre-lesson preparation. The teacher adjusts the teaching objectives based on the feedback received from students' questions and continuously adapts the class. "Our classrooms are based on teaching that fully understands the students' situation. We would rather slightly reduce the content of a class if it means ensuring that students grasp the core concepts. Additionally, we employ in-class assessments and individualized tutoring. By focusing on the starting point and the destination, the entrance and the exit, the effectiveness gradually becomes evident." Zhou Mei explained.

4. Becoming Friends with Teachers

4.1 Empathetic Management

Regarding employee management, Zhou Mei believes that teachers' willingness to confide in her is the greatest form of trust. RA Experimental Middle School currently has 172 employees including 130 full-time teachers, among which 106 teachers have intermediate and senior professional titles. The average age of teachers is 40. The school has gradually formed a relative stable team of competent teachers. However, prior to this, the stability of the teaching staff at RA Experimental Middle School faced significant challenges. Although it was the first private school in Ningbo as a legal entity of public institution, it could not match public schools in terms of teachers' job stability. In the previous years, many key teachers who had been cultivated for years left, which caused headaches for Zhou Mei.

In strengthening the teacher workforce, Zhou Mei places great emphasis on building relationships with each teacher. Firstly, she learns to listen. "Teachers confiding in me is the greatest form of trust. Whether it's about a student's learning problems or suggestions for daily management, I am always willing to listen." According to Zhou Mei, when teachers feel comfortable enough to speak openly with her, it signifies a strong and positive relationship.

Secondly, in addition to listening, Zhou Mei focuses on problem-solving. She approaches staff management from a humanistic care perspective. For example, if a middle-aged teacher at the school has a child facing the college entrance examination, the school will consider adjusting their work schedule and exempt them from certain duties. "Teachers can only invest themselves fully in their work when their mood is pleasant." Zhou Mei explains.

One teacher named Luo Hong, an English teacher, had been trying to conceive for several years due to habitual miscarriages. Recently, she joyfully discovered that she was pregnant. When Zhou Mei learned the news, she congratulated Luo Hong and advised her to take a rest at home, protecting her health and the baby. The school made arrangements for other teachers to substitute her classes. This considerate arrangement deeply moved Luo Hong, and after her maternity leave, she wholeheartedly devoted herself to her work. Today, Luo Hong has become a star teacher at the school.

Zhou Mei adopts different approaches in managing teachers based on individual needs. Gradually, a strong bond has formed within the teacher community at RA Experimental

Middle School, attracting the full dedication of all teachers and improving the overall teaching quality.

4.2 Remuneration Management

"Striving to secure teachers' welfare and addressing their concerns is an important way to enhance their happiness and strengthen their sense of belonging." Zhou Mei said.

In recent years, the school has reformed its remuneration system, implementing a combination of base salary and performance-based bonus. The base salary is based on the position and title of employees to guarantee the basic living needs of them, while the performance-based bonus is linked to workloads, motivating teachers to unleash their potential by teaching more classes and engaging in student guidance.

After the reform, the average annual income of teachers has consistently increased, and the social insurance base has doubled. The social insurance base for middle and senior-level teachers at the school has reached the average level of directly affiliated public schools in the city.

Additionally, before holidays and festivals, the school purchases different items as holiday benefits. For example, they distribute gift packages before the New Year, fruits during the Labor Day holiday, mooncakes and pastries during the National Day holiday, and so on. These gestures ensure that the staff feels cared for by the school.

4.3 Training Management

RA Experimental Middle School has always upheld the belief that training is the best gift for its staff. Therefore, training matters related to teachers are explicitly included in the school's management regulations.

The school organizes 4 types of training.
(1) New employee training. In July each year, the school recruits recent graduates and provides targeted training on various aspects, including an overview of the school, its mission, vision, values, working model and regulations, and its compensation and benefits

package. In addition to this, each new teacher is assigned a mentor to facilitate their quick familiarization with the school environment, adaptation to school life, and personal growth.

(2) Teaching skills training. The school regularly conducts teaching skills training for all teachers. Furthermore, specific subject-based teaching skills training is organized for different departments, inviting experienced teachers from within or outside the school to engage in research discussions and explore valuable teaching methods and instructional models.

(3) Technical contest training. The school encourages the teachers to take part in various technical contests to promote the improvement of teaching quality. Prior to such contests, the school invites experienced teachers to give lectures and training.

(4) External training. The school encourages the teachers to participate in various high-quality training programs during winter and summer vacations.

Over the past five years, the average training duration per teacher has reached 360 hours, and the professional titles of full-time teachers have significantly improved. While it is common for private schools to spend a large amount of money to hire external teachers, Zhou Mei believes that the school should invest time and effort in cultivating its own talent pool, as it creates a sense of belonging. In recent years, RA Experimental Middle School has produced many outstanding teachers dedicated to their profession and education, receiving honors such as "Municipal Excellent Teacher" "Municipal Excellent Class Administrator" "First Prize in Politics Class Contest" "First Prize in Mathematics Teaching Contest" "Special Award and Provincial Award of the Instructor of 19th Chinese Language News Cup National Composition Competition for Middle School Students".

4.4 Leading by Example

Zhou Mei has spent most of her weekends at the school. "As someone in charge of teaching, I need to be present when students are in class so that teachers can find someone to handle any situations." Zhou Mei said.

The summer vacation is a prime time for school development. With increased investment in education, RA Experimental Middle School has undertaken numerous construction projects during the summer vacation in recent years. Therefore, even during the holidays, Zhou Mei continues her usual routine, dividing her time between family and school. When it's her duty week, Zhou Mei typically arrives at the school at 6:30 in the morning to organize and guide the morning exercises for boarding students. In the evening, she conducts inspections during the evening self-study period, visiting all 36 classrooms from the first to the fifth floor, and only then returns home after inspecting the boys' and the girls' dormitories.

Due to her responsibilities during her duty week, when Zhou Mei returns home, she can only look at her sleeping child's face without the opportunity to speak with him. "It's impossible for my son not to complain. There was a time when he didn't pay much attention to me and said that I didn't communicate with him. I told him that he has things he needs to do, and Mom has things she needs to do. We each have to do our own things well." Zhou Mei said.

Later, the son of Zhou Mei was enrolled into a key middle school, which was also a boarding school. Although they met less, their relationships became more harmonious. In the afternoon of every Sunday, Zhou Mei takes her son to the school and chats with him during such a valuable time.

Zhou Mei was very gratified when her son said, "Mom, I realize now that teachers have so many things to take care of. I used to blame you, but you have so many students to manage."

5. Making New Achievements

In the past two years, RA Experimental Middle School has achieved a 100% college entrance rate, with a 45% rate of admission to undergraduate programs. Some classes have achieved a college admission rate of over 90%, with at least five students from each class being admitted to top-tier universities. These achievements are a result of the school's continuous improvement in teaching quality in recent years. Although there is still some gap compared to key high schools, RA Experimental Middle School stands out among private high schools, instilling strong confidence in its students.

Questions:

1. Analyze Zhou Mei's characteristics in terms of personality, attitude, emotion management, and capability, based on the concepts of organizational behavior.

2. Analyze the leadership style of Zhou Mei based on the case study.

3. Discuss how Zhou Mei enhances employee job satisfaction and engagement based on the case study.

4. Analyze why both students and teachers enjoy communicating with Zhou Mei, applying theories of motivation and leadership.

Tips for Answering the Questions:

1. Analyze the first question by applying the personality theory, attitude theory, capability theory, and emotion management theory.

2. Analyze the second question by applying the leadership theory.

3. Analyze the third question by applying the motivation theory and leadership theory.

4. Analyze the fourth question by applying the motivation theory and leadership theory.

Case 4

Management Dilemma Faced by the HR Department of L Company

Key Words:

Perception theory, emotional intelligence theory, motivation theory, job satisfaction theory, capability theory

Purpose:

Based on the analysis on L Company, this case is intended to guide the students to understand and apply the perception theory, emotional intelligence theory, motivation theory, job satisfaction theory, and capability theory.

Case:

1. Introduction

In today's rapidly developing economy, various industries are prospering, and competition has become fierce. While Company L is expanding, it continuously innovates its management practices, accelerates talent development, achieves standardized project management, actively expands its business scope, and gains a larger market share. The company has multiple branches across different locations, each operating independently. However, according to industry regulations, qualifications and personnel must be managed centrally by the head office.

Zheng Haitao, CEO of L Company, sits in his office, contemplating the recent issues faced by the company, and sends a message to Zheng Ling, HR manager, asking her to join him for a discussion.

2. Company Profile

L Company, located in Ningbo, was founded in 2003. It has supervision qualifications approved by the Ministry of Housing and Urban-Rural Development, including construction engineering, municipal engineering, water conservancy and hydropower engineering, mechanical and electrical installation engineering, civil defense engineering, and bidding agency for engineering projects. The company can undertake various types of construction supervision, project consulting and management throughout the process, and bidding agency services. The company's annual output value ranks among the top in the industry and is one of the major taxpayers known for its integrity. It has completed construction projects with a total floor area of over 20 million square meters, amounting to 45 billion yuan.

L Company follows a CEO responsibility system under the leadership of the board of directors. The company has over two hundred employees, the majority of whom are technical personnel. Among these technical personnel, there are multiple industry experts and elites, with more than 65% being intermediate-level or above professional and technical staff. Additionally, several experts have been selected for the industry expert pool, providing suggestions and advice for industry development. L Company currently requires a large number of highly skilled technical personnel. These personnel must meet the company's job requirements and possess the necessary knowledge structure. Precise positioning of talent needs is conducive to the implementation of recruitment activities, the selection of recruitment channels, and ultimately meeting the company's recruitment goals.

3. HR Manager's Dilemma

The HR Department of L Company is divided into Qualification Management Division and Personnel Management Division. The former is responsible for the management of qualifications of L Company and its employees, including occupational qualification certificates, professional title certificates, business qualification certificates, and documents about the industry associations, while the latter is mainly responsible for recruitment. The recruitment of each branch is carried out by the HR Department of the branch using the recruitment channels provided by and in collaboration with the head office.

Case 4 Management Dilemma Faced by the HR Department of L Company

3.1 Core Talent Attrition Issue

Recently, the HR manager, Zheng Ling, encountered a troublesome matter. Huang Bo, the project manager of the technical department, submitted his resignation. Huang Bo has always maintained excellent performance since childhood. He scored high on the college entrance examination and was admitted to a prestigious university. In college, he excelled academically and was a confident and ambitious student. After graduation, he smoothly entered L Company. Two years later, due to his outstanding work performance, he was appointed as the project manager of the technical department, responsible for developing a new project. He had 10 technicians under his supervision and believed that with hard work, they could successfully complete the new project.

Six months later, a new technical developer named Qiu Ming joined the project team of Huang Bo. Qiu Ming quickly immersed himself in the work and exhibited strong abilities, gradually making a name for himself.

A few days into the job, Qiu Ming shared his thoughts with the project team members and discussed related mathematical models and knowledge in artificial intelligence. The team members were impressed by Qiu Ming's capabilities and considered him highly competent. Throughout the day, Huang Bo felt increasingly frustrated, unable to explain why.

A month later, the project team held a project demonstration and discussion meeting. Huang Bo presented his own proposal, which received recognition from most members who provided some suggestions for improvement. Huang Bo felt delighted. However, when it was Qiu Ming's turn to speak, he presented a completely different proposal that was deemed unfeasible by the team. Qiu Ming was not discouraged by their reaction; instead, he enthusiastically explained the specific details of his proposal. His excellent communication skills and rigorous logical reasoning impressed everyone, making them see him as an exceptional talent. In the end, most members expressed their understanding and support for Qiu Ming's proposal.

L Company ultimately adopted Qiu Ming's proposal and planned to invite experts to the company to validate the new project in one week. As per usual, Huang Bo, as the project team leader, should have been the main spokesperson at the validation meeting. So he tentatively asked the CEO: "Qiu Ming is the main contributor to the new proposal and has research experience. Shouldn't we let him be the main spokesperson?" The CEO looked at him and happily said: "Your suggestion is good. Let's do as you said and let Qiu Ming be the main spokesperson." Huang Bo felt disappointed.

At the validation meeting, Qiu Ming's presentation was a great success. His clear thinking, insightful arguments, and outstanding communication skills left a deep impression on all the participants. Huang Bo admired Qiu Ming's abilities, but at the same time, he couldn't shake off an indescribable feeling of discomfort.

After the meeting, some project team members became distant towards Qiu Ming. They believed he was too eager to showcase himself. As a result, Qiu Ming started becoming more silent. Meanwhile, Huang Bo also felt a bit down. One month later, he submitted his resignation to the HR department. When Zheng Ling received the resignation, she fell into contemplation. Why did Huang Bo want to leave? How should the company retain talents? Additionally, were there any issues in the company's recruitment of new employees?

3.2 Team Coordination Management and Management Issues

In recent years, with the company's development, the number of project team members has increased, and there have been several coordination and management issues between teams.

Zheng Ming is a technician of the Customer Relations Maintenance Department. Although introverted, Zheng Ming is highly skilled and proactive. Recently, the company received complaints from several client leaders about Zheng Ming. This greatly affected his work morale and enthusiasm. The manager of the Customer Relations Maintenance Department learned that after receiving client requirements, Zheng Ming would start working without consulting them. The lack of effective communication led to repeated revisions and wasted time, affecting work efficiency.

Zheng Ming's work and character were generally recognized within the team, but some people believed that he had poor communication and problem-solving skills, average emotional intelligence, and occasionally caused negative impacts.

Another employee in the team, Hu Jun, is diligent, highly efficient, and never procrastinates. He also adheres to principles, and the company's CEO has shown interest in developing him. However, Hu Jun has a prominent issue—he speaks bluntly and lacks flexibility. He often argues with members of other teams, causing discontent among colleagues. As a result, he frequently receives complaints, with some perceiving him as evasive and inflexible. Although Hu Jun is diligent in his work, his performance remains average.

Huang Lei, a project leader of the Installation Department, is frequently absent from work, leaving early even when nearing project deadlines. Messages sent to him often go unread, and even if they are read, there is often no response. Moreover, he is frequently late for work, ranking first in the number of late arrivals within the technical department according to the HR department's statistics. Currently, the team is understaffed, and Huang Lei has decent technical skills, as he has the most experience in the department.

3.3 Ineffective Training Programs

Due to the impact of the COVID-19 pandemic, the company's performance has significantly declined. To improve the company's operational efficiency, the company's leadership decided to provide training for all employees to enhance their overall qualities. Ruan Ping, the head of the HR department, took charge of this training program. She invited several well-known trainers from outside the company to organize several training sessions, which included basic technical skills, communication abilities, and management skills. The training sessions were generally scheduled on weekends, but some employees always found excuses not to attend or left midway through the training sessions. After the training, there was no assessment system for the participants, and there was no evaluation system for the quality of the trainers' teaching. The employees' participation in the training was also lackluster. After several months of continuous training, the company's overall performance did not improve, but instead declined further, resulting in a significant expenditure on training costs. The company's leadership concluded that the training had no effect.

4. Closing Remarks

After the conversation between Zheng Haitao and Zheng Ling, a frown appeared on their faces, and there was no trace of a smile. They realized that the company was currently facing several challenges. Externally, they were uncertain about when the COVID-19 pandemic would end, while internally, more and more problems were arising.

Questions:

1. Why do you think Huang Bo wanted to resign? How should the company retain core talents?

2. Do you think Hu Jun is capable of handling the job? Why or why not?

3. Briefly describe the recruitment issues in L Company based on the case and provide your recommendations.

4. Based on the case, discuss the impact of emotional intelligence on job performance.

Tips for Answering the Questions:

1. Analyze the first question by applying the job satisfaction theory and motivation theory.

2. Analyze the second question by applying the capability theory and perception theory.

3. Analyze the third question by applying the perception theory.

4. Analyze the fourth question by applying the emotional intelligence theory.

Case 5

Knowledge Workers and Non-material Incentives in HC Company

Key Words:

Knowledge worker theory, corporate culture theory, motivation theory

Purpose:

This case is intended to guide the students to understand the knowledge worker theory, corporate culture theory, and motivation theory through an analysis of HC Company.

Case:

1. Introduction

Lin Li is the Director of HR Department at HC Company. She used to be the HR manager of a shoemaking factory in Wenzhou. A few years ago, her former boss started a new business and recently asked her to come and assist. Out of trust and gratitude towards her old boss, Lin Li resigned from the shoemaking factory without hesitation and joined the newly established HC Company.

2. Company Overview

HC Company is a technology manufacturing enterprise mainly engaged in the production of core parts for industrial robots, including servo motors, controllers, and reduction gears. These three components are crucial parts of industrial robots that were previously monopolized by foreign companies. HC Company decided to focus on this field and make breakthroughs, and its growth rate has been very fast. HC Company's products have gradually replaced some imported core components, while continuously improving product quality and technology.

At the beginning of its establishment, HC Company quickly formed an efficient team consisting of research and development, production, and sales, with strong support from the Quzhou Municipal Government and the influence of its founders. With the company's growth and rapid expansion, the team has grown from just over 100 people to nearly 800, with research and development personnel accounting for nearly 40%. The emphasis on research and development is one of the key reasons for HC Company's rapid rise. Currently, HC Company is undoubtedly the leader in the servo motor field domestically, and it is also rapidly developing in controllers and reducers, with the potential to become the industry leader in the next five years.

However, rapid growth and reliance on research and development have also brought some problems to the company. Firstly, although the Quzhou Municipal Government attaches great importance to HC Company and provides a lot of support and preferential policies, the company still lacks attractiveness for relatively high-level talents, which are greatly needed by HC Company. This has become a major concern for one of the founders of HC Company, Xu Dong. Secondly, with the rapid expansion of HC Company's workforce, the existing personnel management methods are no longer applicable and urgently need reform. Lin Li came to HC Company to solve the most pressing issue for Xu Dong: how to attract and retain high-level talents.

3. Lin Li's Challenge

Although Lin Li joined HC Company without hesitation, she still had some concerns after starting her work. She lacked confidence in solving the problems currently faced by HC Company. The work situation she is facing has indeed brought her great challenges.

Lin Li has received three resignation letters this month, all of which were from the R&D Department. The latest resignation application came from Mr. Xiao, a member of the R&D Department. Xiao has been working at HC Company since graduation, already three years. Lin Li has some understanding of Xiao's situation, so she pulled him aside and asked him many questions.

After communication, Lin Li found that Xiao is quite satisfied with the company's salary and work pace, and his resignation is more due to the relatively small platform in Quzhou. Xiao's explanation made Lin Li ponder. It reminded her of the two colleagues from the R&D Department, Mr. Zhao and Mr. Li, who resigned in the previous two months. They both had a common reason for leaving, which is that they believed Quzhou was a small platform.

Lin Li realized that the primary reason for talent attrition in HC Company is the location issue. The employees of HC Company come from all over the country, and they are generally younger. Most importantly, they all have higher education, with half of the research and development personnel having graduate degrees. Lin Li also understands that the issues they consider and value are completely different from those of the production department's operators. Lin Li looked at the resignation letters on her desk, lost in thought.

4. Knowledge Workers

After Xiao left, although everything seemed to have returned to normal, Lin Li's anxiety did not diminish. However, she lacked experience in this area and didn't know where to start. She thought of a high school classmate who is now a management professor at a university. So, Lin Li contacted this long-lost classmate, intending to seek advice from him.

Lin Li visited Zhang Xiang, her classmate who works at Ningbo University, and explained the problems she faced. After listening to Lin Li's description, Zhang Xiang pondered for a moment and then said, "In fact, the problem you're facing can be summed up in one sentence: how to retain knowledge workers."

It turns out that the R&D personnel at HC Company belong to a special type of employee known as knowledge workers. Knowledge workers are those who possess knowledge and apply it to their work. They engage in activities within the organization that involve producing, creating, and applying knowledge. They possess knowledge capital as a productive resource.

Lin Li gained a lot from her communication with Zhang Xiang. She decided that upon her return, she would summarize the characteristics of the knowledge workers and develop corresponding solutions based on her old classmate's guidance.

5. Analysis by Lin Li

The first step Lin Li took was to analyze the characteristics of the knowledge workers at HC Company. After a period of observation and understanding, she gained a deeper understanding of knowledge-based employees. The main characteristics of the knowledge workers are as follows.

5.1　High Individual Qualifications

Employees in the R&D Department all have bachelor's degrees or higher, which sets them apart in terms of educational level compared to employees in other departments. Furthermore, R&D employees at HC Company have a distinct advantage in terms of technical expertise. They primarily come from fields such as computer science and electronic information, many of them have their own patents, and some even have the ability and experience of publishing academic papers. These characteristics significantly differentiate them from employees in other departments.

5.2　Strong Autonomy

Lin Li also noticed that the knowledge workers are quite dynamic. Their work characteristics differ significantly from those of the Production Department's assembly line operators. Compared to assembly line operators in the Production Department who passively adapt to equipment operation, R&D Department employees are more proactive. They are willing to actively identify issues in their work and do not require strict supervision or discipline from leaders.

5.3　High-value Creative Labor

Most importantly, the work performed by R&D Department employees has high utility for the company. HC Company's rapid growth from a small technology company to a star enterprise in the field is clearly attributed to its strong R&D Department. These R&D personnel have not only broken the long-standing monopoly of foreign companies in the servo motor field but have also developed a series of competitive new technologies. This allows them to compete with foreign traditional advantage companies in terms of patents. These factors provide HC Company with the confidence to set the goal of becoming the industry leader in controllers and reducers within five years.

5.4 Difficulties in Monitoring the Labor Process

The performance assessment specialist responsible for the R&D Department has complained to Lin Li multiple times about the difficulty of their work. Lin Li discovered that the crux of the problem lies in the fact that the work outcomes of R&D Department employees are challenging to evaluate using a fixed performance assessment scheme. The department's leaders have also repeatedly informed Lin Li that after implementing performance evaluations at HC Company, many R&D Department employees expressed dissatisfaction. This is because their work is difficult to monitor, and some technical development work is not simply repetitive. The labor process is often intangible, and the results of their labor are challenging to measure. Using a general performance assessment scheme to evaluate R&D Department employees would be unfair.

5.5 Desire for Self-value Realization

What troubles Lin Li most is that the knowledge workers have a strong desire to realize their self-value. This desire is, of course, positive, but it also means a lot of challenges for managers. For example, the three colleagues from the R&D Department who resigned earlier had a common reason for leaving: they were dissatisfied with the current situation and had aspirations for higher-level development. These employees prefer challenging work and easily become bored with routine tasks. Leaving the company is not necessarily because of poor material benefits provided by the company, but rather because they feel that HC Company cannot offer them more challenges and fulfillment.

6. Response Strategies

From the characteristics of knowledge workers, the difficulty in monitoring the labor process and the desire for self-value realization add to the challenges of management. Lin Li believed that after gaining a more comprehensive understanding of these knowledge workers, it would be easier to develop corresponding strategies. So she dedicated another week to conducting interviews with all the employees in the R&D Department, hoping to understand their true needs. She believed that once she understood their genuine needs, motivating and retaining them would no longer be an issue.

Lin Li decided to start from the following aspects.

Firstly, reform the performance evaluation system in the R&D Department. Lin Li discovered that the current performance evaluation system was a major complaint among R&D Department employees. According to the existing system, employees in the R&D Department were expected to work towards the goals set by the HR Department. However, on one hand, the HR Department lacked understanding of R&D work, and on the other hand, the actual work process in R&D is difficult to monitor and measure, making the current evaluation method inappropriate. Lin Li believed that a personalized performance evaluation scheme should be implemented in the R&D Department. After conducting research, the company decided to adopt the widely used OKR (Objectives and Key Results) model common among Internet companies, which would provide the R&D Department with more independence and greater freedom to encourage exploration.

Secondly, provide more non-material incentives at the spiritual level. Lin Li discovered that R&D Department employees were generally satisfied with their current salary and compensation. However, material incentives were not the sole focus for them; they also valued non-material incentives at the spiritual level. In this regard, Lin Li developed various corresponding strategies: strengthening company culture to enhance the sense of belonging and identification among R&D personnel, elevating their status and level of respect within the company, actively conducting training and guidance on R&D career planning to provide clearer directions and paths for their growth within the company, and more. These strategies served as effective complements to the current material incentives.

Finally, adopt more targeted incentive plans. Lin Li believed that the biggest difference between knowledge workers and general employees lies in their diverse needs. Therefore, incentive plans should be tailored accordingly. Although this brought significant work pressure to the HR Department as real-time and dynamic understanding of the diverse needs of R&D Department employees required a substantial amount of time and effort, Lin Li believed it was all worthwhile. After all, these R&D employees were the company's greatest asset. Only with a stable R&D team could HC Company ensure significant development.

7. Closing Remarks

The strategies formulated by Lin Li have been implemented for some time and have yielded satisfactory results. However, for Lin Li, this is only the beginning of her work, and there are many challenges ahead. For example, the disadvantageous location of Quzhou still remains unresolved. Although the company can currently retain and motivate R&D Department employees well, future company growth will undoubtedly require more high-level knowledge workers to join. However, Quzhou lacks attractiveness for these high-level talents. So, what is the real solution? Lin Li found herself in a new line of thinking.

Questions:

1. What are knowledge workers? What characteristics do they have?

2. What problems did HC Company encounter? Why did these problems arise?

3. Which measures were taken by HC Company to motivate the knowledge workers?

4. What other measures do you think can be taken to motivate the knowledge workers?

5. What other measures do you think HC Company could take to attract more knowledge workers in the future?

Tips for Answering the Questions:

1. Analyze the first question by applying the knowledge worker theory.

2. Analyze the second question by applying the corporate culture theory.

3. Analyze the third question by applying the corporate culture theory.

4. Analyze the fourth question by applying the motivation theory.

5. Analyze the fifth question by applying the motivation theory and the corporate culture theory.

Case 6

Tortuous Experience of Natian · Handicraft Theme Homestay Entrepreneurial Team

Key Words:

Leadership style, team attributes, team decision-making, team conflict, five-stage development model, input-process-output model, punctuated-equilibrium model, power and political behavior

Purpose:

Based on the analysis of the team of Natian· Handicraft Theme Homestay, this case is intended to guide the students to understand and apply the leadership style, team attributes, team decision-making, team conflict, five-stage development model, input-process-output model, punctuated equilibrium model, power and political behavior.

Case:

1. Introduction

Entrepreneurship is a challenging process that involves limited resources and high uncertainty (McMullen and Shepherd, 2006). That's why most entrepreneurial activities are initiated and carried out by teams, using collective wisdom and resources to overcome difficulties in entrepreneurship (de Mol, Khapova, and Elfring, 2015; Lazar et al., 2020). While this approach is beneficial for overcoming challenges and limitations in entrepreneurial activities, it can also lead to new conflicts and crises within the team. This case will illustrate the hardships and twists and turns in the entrepreneurial journey through the real story of an entrepreneurial team.

2. Inception

Ms. Wang is a well-known handicraft artist in Hangzhou. She owned a cultural creation company that primarily sells her own handmade crafts, such as paintings, leather bags, ornaments, and notebooks. Due to limited office space and the booming homestay market in Hangzhou, Ms. Wang conceived the idea of opening a handicraft-themed homestay in 2014. The ground floor of the homestay could serve as a showcase and sales area for the company's handicrafts, while the second and third floors could be used for accommodation services. By combining handicrafts with homestay operations, it not only provides a sales venue for handicrafts but also showcases unique features distinct from other homestay hotels, attracting customers. With this idea in mind, Ms. Wang began searching for a suitable location to open the homestay. After inquiries and recommendations from various sources, she chose to open it in Baileqiao Village. Baileqiao Village is located at the foot of Lingyin Temple, by the West Lake, with a unique geographical advantage. It is backed by the Beigao Peak, and crossing a mountain leads to the Xixi Wetland. The village is abundant in vegetation, and a clear stream flows through the entire village, creating a pleasant landscape. Originally, Baileqiao Village was inhabited by tea farmers, and after the geographical advantages were discovered by homestay practitioners, many of the village's houses were already rented out for homestay operations. Baileqiao Village has now become an important gathering place for homestay hotels around West Lake.

3. Initial Team Formation

After selecting the location, in early 2015, Ms. Wang began preparations but encountered difficulties along the way.

On one hand, the capital required for opening the homestay hotel exceeded the budget. Firstly, although Baileqiao Village is a small village, its unique geographical advantage has led to rapid development in the homestay industry. Due to high demand and limited supply of houses in the village, the annual rent for a 300～500 square meter house has increased from 50000～60000RMB to 300000～400000RMB, and the rent needs to be paid every six months or even annually. Secondly, most of the houses that had been converted into homestay hotels in the village had already been rented out long-term by other homestay hotels, leaving only a few houses available for rent, which required extensive renovation to meet the needs of a homestay hotel. Thirdly, since Ms. Wang wanted to emphasize handicrafts as the theme, it further increased the workload for renovations. Preliminary estimates

Case 6 Tortuous Experience of Natian·Handicraft Theme Homestay Entrepreneurial Team

indicated that the cost of renovations would exceed 600000 RMB, bringing the total cost close to 1 million RMB, surpassing Ms. Wang's budget. On the other hand, opening a homestay hotel proved to be more complex than anticipated. Ms. Wang lacked experience in the necessary procedures and management involved in running a homestay hotel. As the project progressed, she realized that opening a homestay hotel not only required renting and renovating a property but also obtaining fire safety permits, business licenses, health certificates for employees, and various other procedures and documents. Additionally, she needed to determine the pricing, operation, and marketing strategies for the hotel, as well as learn about staff recruitment, management, and maintaining relationships with suppliers and customers. All of these tasks were unfamiliar to Ms. Wang, and the workload and required expertise exceeded her expectations.

Ms. Wang recognized that it would be difficult to smoothly proceed with the homestay project using only her own abilities and resources. She decided to recruit partners and leverage the power of a collective to compensate for her lack of funds and experience, thereby facilitating the successful implementation of the entrepreneurial project. Initially, she approached her past collaborators and friends to find a partner who was willing to join the project. Through recommendations, she found three additional partners who decided to invest. The addition of new team members not only provided additional funding for the homestay project but also brought important experience from the hotel industry, as one of the new members had experience in operating an economy hotel chain. With this, Ms. Wang formed a five-member entrepreneurial team, including herself, Mr. Huang, Ms. Liu, Mr. Bai, and Ms. Li. With the successful formation of the team, most of the funding needs were met, but there was still a shortage of cash and contingency funds. To address this, leveraging her influence in the handicraft community and among numerous clients, Ms. Wang initiated a crowdfunding campaign for the homestay project. She promised that all participants in the crowdfunding would receive a share of the hotel's profits based on their investment ratio. The crowdfunding project received support from many of Ms. Wang's relatives, friends, and clients, and the process went smoothly. With this, the entrepreneurial team essentially resolved the funding issue for the homestay project.

4. Difficulties Mounting

With the team in place and the funds secured, the team started to make rapid progress with the homestay project. By the end of 2015, they successfully leased a well-located villa situated in the center of Baileqiao Village. The villa was positioned next to the Qingxi, a stream that flowed down from Beigao Peak and formed a small waterfall on the side of the villa, creating a beautiful landscape. To ensure long-term operation, the team signed a long-term agreement with the property owner, with a "three-year lease with an option to renew for two years", and they paid the first year's rent in advance.

The team then began the renovation work on the villa, separating the renovation of the ground floor which would serve as Ms. Wang's workshop or the cultural and creative company's exhibition area from the renovation of the second and third floors. Ms. Wang was mainly responsible for the ground floor, while a decoration company and interior designer were hired to handle the design and construction of the second and third floors. However, as the team expected a smooth progress in the renovation work, a series of problems started to arise.

Firstly, the renovation and construction proved to be more challenging than anticipated. Although the villa had been used as a homestay before, the previous renovations were not comprehensive. The original design of the property did not consider the needs of accommodating guests, requiring an overall transformation. However, many design and construction plans were hindered by the limitations of the property's structure, and the design proposed by the interior designer did not fully satisfy the team's expectations. Secondly, the construction workers from the decoration company often seemed idle due to the delay in determining the start of construction. This left a negative impression on the team members, who began to criticize the decoration company for their lack of responsibility and the delay in the project timeline. As the progress of the renovation directly affected the cost recovery and profitability of the hotel, the conflict between the team and the decoration company escalated.

After nearly five months of renovation, intense verbal conflicts arose between the team members and the decoration company. The team members expressed strong dissatisfaction with the company's continuous delays in the construction schedule, while the decoration company claimed that the team had not effectively communicated the structural issues of the property in advance and had set overly high design and construction standards.

In this intensified conflict, the decoration company decided to keep only the portion of the advance payment received from the team and withdrew from the construction. After the decoration company's withdrawal, the team members held a collective meeting to discuss countermeasures for advancing the renovation. Considering the high cost of finding a new interior designer for the remaining work, the team unanimously decided that Ms. Wang, who had a certain level of craftsmanship experience and artistic taste, would take charge of the further hard and soft decoration of the homestay hotel. The other team members pledged their full cooperation.

5. Escalating Internal Conflict

To the team members' surprise, this arrangement gradually led to conflicts within the team. After the division of tasks, Ms. Wang swiftly carried out the related work, formulated a plan for the final stages of the renovation, and, with the help of the team members, contacted a construction team willing to take over the project. She started working on the finishing tasks. To expedite progress, Ms. Wang worked overtime and finalized a comprehensive soft decoration plan, including furniture, appliances, and decorations required for the entire hotel. To discuss and finalize the plan, she called for a team meeting. However, both the process and outcome of the meeting did not go as expected. During the meeting, except for Mr. Huang, the other three team members did not approve of Ms. Wang's soft decoration plan. Ms. Wang argued that the team had previously authorized her to make decisions regarding the soft decoration plan and opposing it contradicted past decisions. On the other hand, the other three members believed that Ms. Wang's plan was too costly and significantly deviated from the originally agreed-upon plan. Unable to reach a consensus, the dispute between the two sides intensified, eventually leading to a temporary suspension of the soft decoration plan.

After the meeting, cracks began to appear among the team members. Ms. Liu, Ms. Li, and Mr. Bai, who were already familiar with each other and had previous business experiences together, gradually formed a small faction. They sought to win over Ms. Wang, the main investor and initiator of the homestay project, and attempted to exclude Mr. Huang from the entrepreneurial team. They started questioning Mr. Huang's financial capabilities, attributing the high renovation costs to him. They even spread rumors to Ms. Wang, suggesting that Mr. Huang may have misappropriated some of the team's funds to repay his own loans. However, Ms. Wang did not believe these accusations. She had worked with Mr. Huang before the entrepreneurial venture and trusted his professionalism and integrity. Moreover, if Mr. Huang were to be pushed out of the team, Ms. Wang risked being marginalized by the other three members. Therefore, she frequently stood up to defend Mr. Huang whenever the small faction accused him. As a result, mistrust and animosity gradually emerged among the team members. The situation took an unexpected turn due to an administrative order issued by the government.

The G20 Summit was planned to be held in Hangzhou in early September 2016. It would be an important opportunity to improve the urban development of Hangzhou and showcase the city's charm to the world. However, it also placed high demands on the city's security and environmental improvements, which the Hangzhou municipal government took seriously. A five-star hotel located less than 500 meters from Baileqiao Village was booked exclusively by a delegation from a particular country. Although the G20 Summit was scheduled to begin in early September, advance teams from various delegations had already started to check in from late August. Considering safety and environmental factors, the municipal government ordered the suspension of road and renovation construction in the vicinity of the hotel. As a result, the renovation work for the homestay hotel would be delayed by at least one month. This was a significant blow to the entrepreneurial team, which was already time-constrained and in urgent need of cash flow.

Faced with this problem, the team members began to split further for their own interests. The small faction of three members contemplated leaving the team and pursuing alternative paths.

Coincidentally, there was an operational homestay hotel in Baileqiao Village seeking a transfer. They planned to withdraw their shares from the team and take over that hotel, enabling them to quickly recover costs and potentially generate profits. For Ms. Wang, the handicraft-themed homestay project was indispensable. On the one hand, it was a matter of her own ideals and aspirations. On the other hand, the project had received support through crowdfunding from her relatives and friends, abandoning or deviating from the handicrafts theme would breach trust and damage her longaccumulated reputation and network. Therefore, Ms. Wang wanted to join forces with Mr. Huang to retain the project. The team members were at odds, with the three members having contributed more than 40% of the total investment in the homestay project, and the significant expenses already incurred in the renovation. The demand for a full refund of their shares created an insurmountable financial gap. On the other side, the other three members lacked confidence in the progress of the project and had mistrust towards Ms. Wang and Mr. Huang, demanding control over financial management to continue the collaboration. Unable to find common ground, both sides reached an impasse.

6. Team Restructuring and New Beginnings

Given the delay in the hotel's opening, but with the art studio on the ground floor already mostly renovated, Ms. Wang decided to take on art-related projects to increase the hotel's visibility. Thus, her art studio took on the exhibition of a children's painting competition. However, when a significant amount of artwork and display stands arrived at the hotel, the lack of cooperation from the three-member faction led to a complete split within the team. After the exhibition materials were delivered, Ms. Wang invited the team members to help set up the exhibition hall. However, the three-member faction chose to remain indifferent and passive, making it impossible to proceed with the exhibition setup. Faced with no other choice, Ms. Wang decided to convene another meeting with all the team members. The three members expressed their intention of withdrawal resolutely again on the meeting. Ms. Wang and Mr. Huang had no choice but to accept their request and refunded most of the funds originally subscribed for by the three members after negotiation. The situation led to a complete breakdown within the entrepreneurial team.

After the departure, the three members quickly took over the transfer of the homestay. In fact, even before the team completely split, they had already negotiated and reached a preliminary agreement with the other party regarding the takeover details. Therefore, the process of taking over the homestay went very smoothly, and they started operations even before Ms. Wang and Mr. Huang's handicraft-themed homestay. Ms. Wang and Mr. Huang decided to continue promoting the handicraft-themed homestay project, which was closely related to Ms. Wang's career. Ms. Wang did not want to give up, and Mr. Huang expressed his support. After discussions, they divided the management and decision-making of the homestay project as follows: most operational decisions were made by Ms. Wang, with Mr. Huang providing suggestions; major decisions regarding operational strategies and new project investments were made jointly by both of them; other minority shareholders who obtained shares through crowdfunding would continue to have no operational power and only receive profit dividends. Thus, after the team split, Ms. Wang and Mr. Huang formed a new team to continue their entrepreneurial journey.

7. A Difficult Start

The reestablished team faced the initial problem of insufficient funds. After the three members withdrew their shares, the team's already limited funds became even tighter and could no longer support the subsequent renovation and operation of the homestay. There weren't many feasible solutions to address this issue. On one hand, the team had lost confidence in recruiting partners due to the previous failed experience. Investors interested in investing in the homestay with a higher share ratio generally demanded operational power, and based on past experience, finding investors who could trust each other and had a cooperative spirit was very difficult. Recruiting purely financial investors was also not viable as the profit margin of the homestay was not high enough to attract such investors. On the other hand, conducting another round of crowdfunding faced obstacles as well. Ms. Wang had already conducted crowdfunding for the homestay, and launching another crowdfunding campaign before the homestay had even started operating would greatly impact her reputation and potentially lead to questions about illegal fundraising. In the absence of viable options, Ms. Wang had to mortgage her own property to obtain precious funds to fill the funding gap of the entrepreneurial project. In terms of personnel, the exit of the three members also resulted in a shortage of staff for the homestay. Ms. Wang recruited a front desk staff and a cleaner for the homestay, which essentially solved this problem.

The next step was to wrap up the renovation of the homestay hotel.

After discussion, Ms. Wang and Mr. Huang reached a consensus: the team entrusted Ms. Wang with the full authority to finalize the subsequent renovation plans and other related matters. They finalized the specific construction details and determined the materials and furniture for the soft furnishings through communication between Ms. Wang and the renovation team during the G20 summit. After the conclusion of the G20 summit, the renovation of the homestay progressed very smoothly under the collaboration between Ms. Wang and the renovation team, and all subsequent work was completed in less than a month. In late October 2016, all the preparatory work was finally completed, and the "Natian • Handicraft Theme Homestay" officially opened to the public. Looking back, it took nearly a year from the start of founding the homestay to its official opening (Figure 6-1), with the renovation of the homestay alone taking almost eight months, while the original team had anticipated a renovation period of three months.

Figure 6–1　The exterior of the renovated homestay hotel

After the homestay hotel opened, the expected bustling scene did not materialize. There were only a few guests staying, and on weekdays, there were often no guests at all. This situation made the team members very anxious. Ms. Wang and Mr. Huang analyzed the reasons for the low number of guests to find a breakthrough. They discovered that, on one hand, due to the delay in renovation, the homestay missed the peak tourist season during the summer and October in Hangzhou, resulting in a lack of out-of-town customers and insufficient customer base. On the other hand, the villa had previously operated as a homestay two years ago. In order to facilitate registration and other aspects, the new homestay partially retained the name of the original homestay, "Natian", and added "Handicraft Theme Homestay" as a suffix to the name. On major travel websites, the homestay inherited the original homestay's account and the name "Natian". However, the original homestay had received low ratings and accumulated a large number of negative reviews, such as "unclean bedding" "insects in the room" "poor service attitude". In addition, the fact that very few customers had stayed at the new establishment made it difficult to quickly overcome the negative reputation accumulated in the past. These factors led to a challenging situation for the homestay right from the beginning.

The problem of how to attract customers and improve reputation was placed in front of the restructured entrepreneurial team. If this problem could not be solved quickly to realize profitability, the pressure of repayment of the loan and profit sharing to the minority shareholders would further threaten the survival of the homestay hotel.

8. Get on Track

In order to overcome the operational challenges, Ms. Wang and Mr. Huang started implementing various measures to attract customers. The core strategy of the team was to fully utilize the handicraft theme of the homestay, not just as an external style but as an experiential element for guests during their stay. The team realized that although the homestay had a handicraft theme, it hadn't effectively utilized this feature. The overall decoration of the homestay adopted the style of Jiangnan handicraft, with all beddings made of representative blue-printed fabrics produced using traditional tie-dyeing techniques in the Jiangnan region.

The furniture, furnishings, and decorations in the homestay all reflected the poetic charm of the ink painting of Jiangnan (south of the Yangtze River) (Figure 6-2). Unfortunately, apart from visiting the homestay directly, customers found it difficult to experience its uniqueness. Advertising on major online hotel platforms was also expensive and not affordable for the struggling team. Just when the team was at a loss, an opportunity came with a promotional activity from a well-known online hotel platform. By participating in the activity and providing discounts or gifts to customers from the platform for Sunday to Thursday stays, they could gain free traffic and publicity. The team saw this as an important opportunity to attract customers and, as such, committed to offering an 80% discount for all customers staying from Sunday to Thursday, along with a small handicraft gift for all guests.

Figure 6-2 Room layout

This measure had an immediate effect, significantly increasing the online reservations for the homestay. As the number of guests increased, the Jiangnan handicraft style of the homestay gained popularity and recommendations from many customers. Some guests even purchased the same bedding sets used in the hotel, while others. expressed great appreciation for the received handicraft gifts and requested to buy more as souvenirs for their friends and family. From this, the team gradually discovered the business opportunities for Jiangnan-themed handicrafts. As a result, they repositioned and transformed Ms. Wang's handicraft workshop on the first floor, retaining its function as a craft exhibition and sales space while increasing customer participation. Guests staying at the homestay could personally engage in crafting activities such as making headbands, ornaments, notebooks, and mouse pads at the craft workshop on the first floor, as well as participate in the dyeing process of the distinctive blue-printed fabrics of Jiangnan.

This measure had a positive impact, with the majority of guests participating in the craft activities at the workshop on the first floor, significantly increasing the overall revenue of the homestay. Additionally, it attracted a large number of customers interested in experiencing the handicraft activities. Many parents wanted to bring their children to the homestay to participate in the craft-making experience, and even small tour groups began choosing the homestay for their accommodation. The business situation of the homestay greatly improved, and it often faced high demand on weekends, with a significant increase in occupancy rates during non-weekend periods, typically maintaining occupancy levels above 80%. At the same time, customer reviews of the homestay improved significantly. Despite being burdened by a large number of low ratings accumulated by the previous establishment, the homestay's overall rating showed a noticeable improvement on mainstream hotel and travel platforms.

From then on, the operation of their homestay hotel entered a stable track.

Figure 6–3　Ornaments in the homestay hotel

9. Closing Remarks

After more than three years of formal operation, "Natian • Handicraft Theme Homestay Hotel" has become one of the most representative and popular homestays in Baileqiao Village. It has become a preferred accommodation choice for many tourists who want to experience the Jiangnan atmosphere during their trip to Hangzhou. Customers have given high praise to the homestay's service and taste. Now, it is not only a homestay hotel, but also a bridge and witness of friendship. Many tourists who have stayed at "Natian • Handicraft Theme Homestay Hotel" are reluctant to leave, and they often arrange gatherings and reunions there. Some customers have even established friendships with the operators and staff of "Natian • Handicraft Theme Homestay Hotel." They ask Ms. Wang to purchase the most authentic West Lake Longjing tea for them, and some out-of-town visitors send local specialties and small souvenirs to Ms. Wang after returning home. The homestay is no longer limited to accommodation and craft-making experiences. It has also launched an online store to sell clothing and accessories created by Ms. Wang's handicraft workshop, which combine Jiangnan characteristics with modern aesthetics. Due to their handmade nature and unique designs, these products have gained popularity among both homestay guests and non-guests, and once a product is launched, it tends to sell out quickly.

This case study tells the story about an entrepreneurial team, from which we can see that even for a "small business" like starting a homestay hotel, there are still various difficulties to be faced. Internal conflicts within the team and changes in the external environment can have a significant impact on the entrepreneurial process and outcomes. How to deal with uncertainty and various constraints in the entrepreneurial process, and how to build and develop an efficient entrepreneurial team, are all worth exploring for researchers and entrepreneurs.

Questions:

1. Based on this case, how many stages can the development of a team or group be divided into?

2. What factors led to the disagreements and divisions within the entrepreneurial team?

3. Based on this case study, how do you think an effective entrepreneurial team should be constructed?

Tips for Answering the Questions:

1. Use the punctuated-equilibrium model and the five-stage development model to describe and analyze the stages of team development and their characteristics.

2. Based on the knowledge of team conflict, team attributes, and team decision-making, analyze the factors that are likely to trigger conflicts among team members.

3. Based on the knowledge of leadership style, input-process-output model, power and political behavior, analyze the factors that may influence team processes and team effectiveness.

Case 7

Employee Management Dilemma of B Company

Key Words:

Competence model, self-efficacy theory, job satisfaction theory, motivation theory, leadership theory

Purpose:

Based on the analysis of B Company, this case is intended to guide the students to understand the competence model, self-efficacy theory, job satisfaction theory, motivation theory, and leadership theory within an organization.

Case:

1. Introduction

B Company was established in December 2010 with a registered capital of RMB5 million and an investment scale of RMB50 million. B Company has an independent laboratory building of more than 4000 m^2 and over 300 sets of advanced testing equipment to provide testing services covering the entire production process of electronic and electrical products, including measuring calibration, data analysis, software test and evaluation, quality testing, reliability analysis and other technical services. B Company holds multiple national qualifications. Since its establishment, B Company has won the trust and support of clients by delivering professional expertise and high-quality services. It serves more than one thousand enterprises every year, and its business area covers East China. In addition to serving enterprises, B Company also provides technical support to the industry and local governments, contributing to the healthy development of the testing industry and the improvement of product quality in the covered regions.

Over the years, B Company has maintained a good momentum of development, with continuous and stable business performance, gradual expansion of the workforce, and increasing brand influence. Currently, B Company has 297 employees and 13 departments, including 5 functional departments and 8 business departments.

2. A Busy Chairman

One night in December 2020, the senior executives of B Company were holding a yearend department performance discussion meeting. Due to the impact of COVID-19 epidemic, the sales dropped by 30% compared to the same period in 2019. Although KPIs were set up for all departments, the actual implementation was complex, requiring significant efforts from the HR Department to follow up. Moreover, employees had a negative attitude towards the assessments and were not very cooperative. After the meeting, the Chairman Zhang Jun stayed in the office alone, reflecting on the original intention of starting the business and the journey he had gone through, sinking into deep contemplation.

After graduating from Zhejiang University, Zhang Jun worked as a civil servant in a government agency for two years. In 2010, he led a technology team to establish B Company, which has since grown from an initial team of 20 employees to the current 297. Zhang Jun has always emphasized his own learning and the improvement of his management abilities, holding an MBA from a business school. However, recently, he felt trapped in a dilemma.

Sometimes, Zhang Jun would complain about the hardships of entrepreneurship. He liked to be hands-on, personally involving himself in the company's material and equipment procurement by contacting suppliers, negotiating product models, specifications, and prices. When it came to selling products, he would also personally guide employees on how to promote and communicate with clients, offering many suggestions. Even during the company's holiday gift purchases for employees, he would take charge and provide many procurement recommendations. All of this made him feel exhausted, with no personal or family leisure time, and sometimes he felt overwhelmed.

Recently, due to the management chaos in the company, the senior management hired Li Hongmei from a professional consulting firm with extensive experience in consulting for many large companies. Li Hongmei conducted in-depth research upon joining the company.

3. Problems Arise Successively in the Technical Department

To add insult to injury, the Chief Technical Engineer Chen Hai submitted his resignation. Soon after, Zhang Jun received resignations from four other department managers, including the Advertising Department and the Marketing Department. Surprisingly, the reasons for their resignations were astonishingly similar: aside from a few individuals who wanted to pursue further education or were dissatisfied with their salary, everyone expressed difficulty in managing the newly recruited employees in recent years. Astonished, Zhang Jun decided to have a conversation with his old friend, Chen Hai.

Chen Hai expressed his reluctance to leave the job as well but felt helpless due to the difficulties encountered with the newly hired employees in the past two years. He advised Zhang Jun to get to know these employees.

Following Chen Hai's advice, Zhang Jun visited the Technical Department for a discreet observation. Coincidentally, he witnessed a heated argument among four or five individuals in a meeting room. They were engrossed in the argument to the extent that they didn't notice Zhang Jun quietly standing near the open door, observing them as they shifted blame onto each other.

Zhang Jun left quietly. He realized that the situation was worse than he had imagined. As he walked away, he heard another voice of criticism. Upon careful listening, he recognized the voice. Chen Hai was at his desk, explaining fundamental professional knowledge to a new employee. Chen Hai seemed a bit angry due to the employee's basic and obvious mistakes.

Zhang Jun returned to his office and fell into deep thought. In Zhang Jun's impression, Chen Hai, the Chief Technical Engineer, always had a cheerful demeanor and had never had any conflicts with anyone. During the early days of entrepreneurship, Chen Hai would often share his vision of the future with Zhang Jun, eagerly anticipating leading his core team to achieve greater technological accomplishments. However, now he maintained his habit of continuous learning, while the department's employees lacked even the most basic professional skills.

Considering the current situation, Zhang Jun logged into his corporate mailbox and sent a mail to the HR Department to approve the resignation application of Chen Hai. Then he logged into his personal mailbox and sent a message to Chen Hai: "Farewell, may everything go well for you. I await your return after furthering your education."

4. HR Department's Numerous Challenges

4.1 Formalistic Recruitment Process

Zhang Jun suddenly remembered the argument he overheard outside the Technical Department's meeting room, along with the resignation letters from several department managers. A thought began to emerge in his mind. He called the HR Manager, Cai Lei, and thoroughly questioned the company's recruitment process over the past two years. He also had individual discussions with some newly hired employees.

Wang Hongli, a recent joiner in the Technical Department during the spring, recalled the first round of group non-structured interviews. During the discussion, they collectively shared their opinions, and Mr. Chen summarized and reported on the discussion. However, Mr. Chen took credit for most of the discussion outcomes, causing other members to resentfully argue, leading to a heated dispute that briefly spiraled out of control. In the end, when someone pointed out that one of Mr. Chen's conclusions from the report was not accurate, Mr. Chen directly responded to the interviewee who raised that point, saying: "It's because of your wrong argument that I was criticized!"

What surprised Wang Hongli was that Mr. Chen also advanced to the second round of interviews. The second round was a personal interview, but the interviewer avoided discussing her professional skills that would be suited for the Technical Department, only asking irrelevant questions, and hastily concluded the interview. In the end, both Wang Hongli and Mr. Chen received acceptance notices. Zhang Jun called Mr. Chen into his office. As Mr. Chen entered, Zhang Jun immediately recognized him as the young man who was shirking responsibility in the meeting room that day.

4.2 Rigid Performance Management Mechanism

In January of this year, as the new quarter began, the Sales Department initiated a new round of performance management. The performance management process consisted of four steps: goal setting, performance evaluation, performance review, and improvement.

(1) Goal setting. As usual, Zhang Ming, the head of the Sales Department received the target assigned by top management: a 10% increase in sales for the quarter. Without conducting careful research, he spontaneously set a higher goal for his subordinates: a 20% increase in sales for the quarter. He thought that setting higher goals might inspire employees' enthusiasm for work and, in turn, improve sales. He sent this target to each employee's email and loudly announced it in the employee workspace, even writing it on the blackboard in the Sales Department office. Of course, there were objections in the past, with employees attempting to discuss goal setting with Zhang Ming. However, he always refused and stated that, as the leader, his word was final. Over time, nobody dared to question goal setting anymore.

(2) Performance evaluation. The performance evaluation started when the first quarter ended. The company did not have clear assessment guidelines, only simple rules. Employees' assessments were based on two aspects: sales figures and daily performance, each accounting for 50% of the total score. Sales figures were objective and ranked to determine the scores. However, daily performance was highly subjective. Zhang Ming would assign scores as he pleased. Generally, employees who had a good relationship with Zhang Ming received high scores for their daily performance, regardless of whether they had behaviors such as tardiness or early departure.

(3) Performance review. Zhang Ming usually opted for phone communication. Occasionally, he had face-to-face meetings, but he found them to be inconvenient. During the reviews,

senior employees would raise questions and concerns. However, Zhang Ming believed that what mattered was expressing his own thoughts clearly, not receiving feedback from employees. Phone communication was not only convenient but also saved time. If employees asked questions, he could easily respond with a few words before ending the call. Dealing with such situations would be more challenging in face-to-face meetings. Therefore, most of the time, Zhang Ming chose phone communication.

During performance evaluations, when Zhang Ming encounters employees with high ratings, he simply says: "You're doing well. Keep up the good work next quarter." Then he hangs up the phone without mentioning any substantial rewards, only providing brief verbal praise. When he talks to employees with low ratings, he adopts a simplistic method of scolding. He always says: "What's wrong with you? Your rating is so low. Reflect on yourself and do better next quarter. The Sales Department's performance is not improving because of all of you." If an employee wants to express their thoughts, Zhang Ming would say: "Stop making so many excuses. Go back and think about it yourself." Li Jun, whose performance evaluation score is relatively high, tries to work harder every day to increase sales and achieve high performance in order to receive rewards. However, Zhang Ming only gives him simple verbal praise, which makes him dissatisfied. As a result, Li Jun becomes increasingly lazy at work and has even submitted a transfer request. On the other hand, Chen Xin used to be hardworking, but due to a lack of guidance and average relationship with Zhang Ming, his performance rating is very low. During performance evaluations, Zhang Ming usually only blames him without questioning the reasons or taking measures to help him. Chen Xin also becomes increasingly disengaged from his work.

(4) Improvement. For employees with average or poor performance, Zhang Ming, during performance evaluations, not only criticizes and blames them but also fails to analyze the reasons for their poor performance, the gaps in reaching targets, and the forms and processes that should be adopted in order to improve work performance. He also shows no concern for whether employees need support or resources to help them achieve performance goals in the future.

4.3 Lack of Passion in Team Management

Through research, it was also found that the team lacks cohesion and there is no standardized employee incentive system. For example, if a project earns the company one million, the team would only receive a reward of ten thousand. This insufficient performance reward compared to the contribution leads to a lack of motivation among employees, who only focus on performing their assigned tasks.

Moreover, the distribution of project rewards takes a long time, usually one year after project completion. More and more employees express dissatisfaction because of the long settlement period. If members leave the project team, they often do not receive a share or receive very little.

4.4 Unclear Job Responsibilities and Performance Objectives

During the evaluations, Li Hongmei found that nearly 80% of the management team is unclear about their job responsibilities. Mr. Chen, a senior employee who has been with the company for ten years, is well-liked and familiar with all departments. Sometimes, when other staff members are overwhelmed, they also rely on him for assistance with tasks such as delivering goods to nearby stores. According to him, it's difficult to refuse when colleagues ask for help. In the conversations, many employees mentioned that meetings were the most painful aspect of daily management operations. The main reasons cited were long meeting durations, excessive instructions, and a lack of employee involvement. If managers want employees to think about solutions during meetings, they may need to make changes.

Deng Ming, the Manager of the Quality Control Department, also noticed several instances where an employee was browsing social media or online shopping during work hours. Initially, Deng Ming attributed it to work stress and allowed the employee to relax for a while. However, even after a few reminders, the employee, Song Yi, continued this behavior, which eventually affected their work. The number and rate of product inspections did not meet the company's requirements.

5. Closing Remarks

After Li Hongmei spent a month in the company, collecting all the interview and research data, she summarized the company's current situation and identified the problems. She formally submitted the report to Zhang Jun, who looked at it with a myriad of thoughts. He immediately called the HR Manager and asked him to arrange a meeting for the company's senior management to discuss future development strategies.

Questions:

1. Why has the CEO become the busiest salesman and employee of the company?

2. Discuss the recruitment problems faced by the company and how to solve them.

3. Discuss the performance management problems faced by the company and how to solve them.

4. Based on the case, what are the reasons for employees' lack of motivation at work?

5. What is efficient team management? Based on the case, discuss how to improve the leadership in team management.

Tips for Answering the Questions:

1. Analyze the first question by applying the motivation theory and leadership theory.

2. Analyze the second question by applying the competency model.

3. Analyze the third question by applying the motivation theory.

4. Analyze the fourth question by applying the job satisfaction theory and motivation theory.

5. Analyze the fifth question by applying the self-efficacy theory and leadership theory.

Case 8

How to Deal with the Post-90s Employees

Key Words:

Personality theory, values theory, attitude theory, motivation theory, communication theory, leadership theory

Purpose:

Based on the analysis of ZS Bank, this case is intended to guide the students to understand and apply the personality theory, values theory, attitude theory, motivation theory, communication theory, and leadership theory in an integrated manner.

Case:

1. Introduction

Liu Dan is a manager in the Customer Service Department of ZS Bank's Credit Card Center. She has just finished a busy day of work, handling several customer complaints and conducting performance reviews with several subordinates. The continuous work has left her feeling exhausted. Sitting on the subway on her way home, she opens her phone and browses her WeChat Moments, one of the few moments she can relax. Her favorite posts to read are those from the young employees in her department. Liu Dan, a person born in the 1970s, currently manages a department of about 40 employees, most of whom are "post-90s" (people who were born in the 1990s).

Liu Dan has been working for nearly twenty years, and as more and more post-90s join the company, the generation gap becomes apparent for managers like Liu Dan. In recent years, ZS Bank's credit card business has grown larger, with increasing demands for product and service quality. Liu Dan's department also faces greater work pressure. This often worries Liu Dan. Can her young employees handle such responsibilities?

2. New Force in the Credit Card Center of ZS Bank

The Credit Card Center is an important first-level division of ZS Bank. The Customer Service Department is primarily responsible for handling customer complaints and providing follow-up services. Among the various departments in the Credit Card Center, the Customer Service Department has one of the closest relationships with customers.

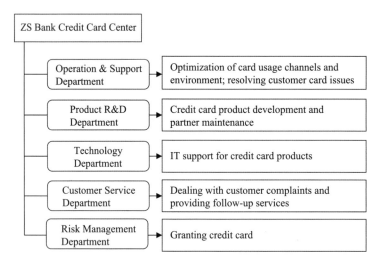

Figure 8–1　Organizational structure of ZS Bank Credit Card Center

Since 2013, an increasing number of post-90s have entered the workforce. This period also coincided with the rapid development of ZS Bank's Credit Card Center, resulting in a large number of post-90s joining the center. Taking Liu Dan's Customer Service Department as an example, there are a total of 45 employees, with 38 post-90s, and nearly half of these 38 employees are post-95s. The same situation exists in other departments of the Credit Card Center, with a higher proportion of post-90s as young employees join the bank. Therefore, there is a practical question facing managers like Liu Dan: How can they effectively communicate and interact with these post-90s to ensure smooth workflow?

3. Worries about Post-90s

In Liu Dan's view, although post-90s have entered society and some have gained several years of work experience, many times their behavior still resembles that of immature children. They are generally only children and have been spoiled by the whole family.

Their behavior makes Liu Dan feel that these post-90s have not fully embraced their roles at work. Instead of being capable and independent employees, they resemble helpless fledglings. It seems that they expect someone to take care of them and help them, considering it as something that should naturally happen.

What particularly perplexes Liu Dan and some other department leaders is that the young people of this new era are described as "having little competence but a big temper" and "lacking significant abilities but having high aspirations". Liu Dan recalls a case involving a young woman who graduated from a prestigious university and had outstanding qualifications. She joined the Product R&D Department. This young woman, whose surname is Zhao, had impressive capabilities in various aspects and received significant attention from department leaders. However, during a communication with a cooperative partner regarding certain requirements, Zhao couldn't accept the partner's demands and ended up in conflict. When the department leaders became aware of the situation, they criticized Zhao. Unexpectedly, the usually gentle Zhao became furious, feeling deeply wronged and even escalated the matter to the Human Resources Department, making it difficult to resolve. In the end, Zhao submitted her resignation letter and left ZS Bank.

Furthermore, Liu Dan encountered another headache. She had devoted a lot of effort to nurturing a group of newly hired young employees. However, not long after, two of them submitted their resignations. Liu Dan spent a long time communicating with them to understand the reasons for their resignations. She was extremely worried that her own shortcomings in her work or giving them too much work pressure had caused dissatisfaction among these young people or made it difficult for them to adapt. However, the results were somewhat unexpected. After working for a while, these young people felt that they didn't actually like the job, not because they were dissatisfied with the salary or had doubts about their career plans. In fact, since the department began accepting a large number of post-90s, Liu Dan has faced similar headaches, but it has become more noticeable in recent years. The post-90s seem to have more courage, simply resigning without considering their future or having a backup plan, unlike Liu Dan and her generation.

In Liu Dan's view, the environment in which the 1990s generation grew up is completely different from her own. Not only does she find it difficult to understand them, but she also believes it's challenging for them to understand her. Liu Dan often doubts whether these individuals can handle the responsibilities of their jobs. And can ZS Bank really rely on these young people for its development?

4. Is It Prejudice?

Liu Dan approached her colleagues in the Human Resources Department to learn about the reasons for the resignations of the post-90s. In the Credit Card Center, there are over 400 employees, with more than 50% of them being post-90s. However, their turnover rate is alarmingly high compared to non-post-90s, with the turnover rate of post-90s being approximately 20% higher, and it has been increasing in recent years.

However, Liu Dan's colleagues in the Human Resources Department provided her with additional data. One of their responsibilities is to retain employees who express an intention to leave or submit their resignations. Through one-on-one conversations, they aim to understand the true reasons behind their resignations. The data in front of Liu Dan shows that, in comparison, the post-90s are not particularly concerned about salary. They value aspects such as job satisfaction, a sense of belonging to the team, and other factors. Liu Dan attributes this to the fact that the post-90s are less "pragmatic" compared to her generation.

It made Liu Dan feel even more puzzled by these young people. She was worried that she may have biases towards the 1990s generation, affecting her judgment and work. Therefore, she decided to have a good conversation with several other department managers.

5. The Post-90s with Strong Personalities

Taking advantage of the almost end-of-work time, Liu Dan visited the Product R&D Department. Feng Tian, the head of the department, joined ZS Bank at a similar time as Liu Dan and is also from the 1970s generation. The Product R&D Department has nearly 100 employees and is a truly large department. Liu Dan believed that Feng Tian had valuable experience in dealing with post-90s employees.

When Feng Tian learned about Liu Dan's purpose, a trace of helplessness appeared on his face, and then he started talking. It turned out that Feng Tian wanted to share his grievances with Liu Dan.

"The biggest problem with post-90s employees is that they can't stand criticism!" Feng Tian found this aspect particularly difficult to accept. He believed that criticism was beneficial for improvement and should be accepted humbly. However, now he was afraid of upsetting the employees and causing them to resign.

Hearing Feng Tian's complaints, Liu Dan didn't know what she should say. While she understood Feng Tian's perspective, she also felt that this issue could possibly be avoided. Liu Dan realized that she might not gain any valuable insights from Feng Tian. So she took her leave, deciding to have a chat with the head of the Operations & Support Department the next day.

At the lunchtime next day, Liu Dan sat next to Li Ran, manager of the Operation & Support Department. Li Ran was transferred to the Credit Card Center a few years ago as the manager of the Operation & Support Department. As a post-80s, Li Ran is younger than Liu Dan, but he is highly competent in his work. Moreover, due to frequent work interactions, they have become acquainted. Liu Dan explained the purpose of her visit, and Li Ran smiled, saying: "I'm younger than both of you, so I don't have as many difficulties in dealing with the post-90s employees." Liu Dan quickly asked him to share some of his experiences.

Li Ran believed that the biggest characteristic of post-90s employees was their strong individuality. In their work, if they had a dispute with their superiors, they wouldn't tolerate it and would boldly refuse to do the work if they didn't want to, and if they felt their superiors were wrong, they would clearly point it out. Many times, these behaviors made their superiors feel somewhat embarrassed, but the post-90s employees seemed completely unconcerned about it.

However, over time, Li Ran realized that these young people had no ill intentions; it was just a habit they had developed. After understanding this point, communication with them became much easier. Additionally, they were particularly concerned about whether they were being respected. Li Ran gave an example from before he was transferred to the Credit Card Center. At that time, due to work reasons, he was hosting a client who asked for a young girl from their department to have a drink. However, the girl firmly refused to drink, which made the client lose face. In the end, Li Ran, as a leader, had to step in and mediate the situation to avoid it becoming too embarrassing. Li Ran told Liu Dan that young people today have strong personalities and also care a lot about whether they are being respected. Fortunately, he supported the girl in that situation and didn't blame her for not giving face to the client; otherwise, she would have definitely quit.

In addition, Li Ran noticed that these young people had a strong sense of boundaries. They generally didn't like to talk about personal matters in the workplace, and excessive care from colleagues would make them particularly resentful. This sense of boundaries was also evident in their clear distinction between working hours and non-working hours. Li Ran mentioned a young person from the Technology Department who had strong technical abilities but despised working overtime and being disturbed by their superiors about work matters during non-working hours. After making these observations, Li Ran was particularly cautious when chatting with young people and never asked questions that crossed the line. Furthermore, when arranging training or organizing departmental activities, he tried not to take up their rest time. By using these simple methods, Li Ran became the most popular department heads in the Credit Card Center among young people.

Liu Dan learnt a lot from Li Ran's sharing. She had some biases against the post-90s generation before. Rather than saying that the post-90s generation was not trustworthy, it was more accurate to say that managers did not understand their ways.

6. The Trustworthy Post-90s Employees

Liu Dan had to admit that although her post-90s employees had caused her trouble and their work was not always satisfactory, they also had many shining moments. One time, the department encountered an unexpected event involving a complaint from a key client. This client was a platinum credit card customer who experienced multiple transaction failures when purchasing international flight tickets using the credit card. The transaction failures were attributed to insufficient credit limit. The client was extremely angry, stating that there was no issue with their credit limit and demanded an explanation from the credit card center. Upon receiving the complaint, Liu Dan and her team went to the backend to investigate but couldn't find the exact cause.

At that moment, several post-90s employees of her department stepped forward. They contacted the airline company, made active communication with the Technology Department and the Operation & Support Department, and calmly and systematically resolved the issue. It turned out that the reason for the transaction failures was an error in the way the client entered their name when purchasing the tickets. Of course, the more significant problem was the lack of meticulous attribution of transaction failures by the Credit Card Center.

Through the collaborative efforts of several departments, the problem was successfully resolved. This incident gave Liu Dan a new understanding of the post-90s employees. They were indeed trustworthy.

7. Closing Remarks

A young employee who had recently submitted his resignation returned to his position after some serious consideration. He realized that he had been impulsive and felt that Liu Dan respected his thoughts. He also experienced the joy the work brought in this environment. Subsequently, he became a reserve talent of the Customer Service Department and worked even harder.

Liu Dan gradually learned the methods and approaches to communicate with the post-90s employees and quickly established a good relationship with them within the department. She began to ponder new questions, such as how to lead this young team better and help these young employees grow.

Questions:

1. What are the characteristics of the post-90s employees described in the case? What are the reasons behind these characteristics?

2. What are the potential impact of these characteristics on the work performance of the post-90s employees?

3. What are the fundamental differences between the post-70s employees and the post-90s employees?

4. What are the characteristics of communication with the post-90s employees as reflected in the case? What are their communication preferences?

5. What are the strengths and weaknesses of Feng Tian's and Li Ran's leadership styles, and which leadership style do the post-90s employees prefer?

6. Based on the case study, provide suggestions for effectively communicating with post-90s employees.

Tips for Answering the Questions:

1. Analyze the first question by applying the personality theory.

2. Analyze the second question by applying the values theory and the attitude theory.

3. Analyze the third question by applying the communication theory.

4. Analyze the fourth question by applying the communication theory.

5. Analyze the fifth question by applying the motivation theory and the leadership theory.

6. Analyze the sixth question by applying the communication theory.

Case 9

How a Start-up Realizes Digital Innovation in the Traditional Industry: The Entrepreneurial Story of Zebra Warehouse

Key Words:

Creativity theory, innovation theory, leadership style theory, team attributes theory, organizational structure theory, corporate culture theory

Purpose:

Based on the analysis of Hangzhou Bancai Technology Company, this case is intended to guide the students to understand the creativity theory, innovation theory, leadership style theory, team attributes theory, organizational structure theory, and corporate culture theory.

Case:

1. Introduction

Digital innovation refers to the creation of new products or services using digital technology. Digital innovation has had a tremendous impact on China's economic development and people's lives. It is not only an important means for businesses to gain competitive advantage but also plays a crucial role in promoting industrial transformation and improving industry quality, efficiency, and management. Surprisingly, in many industries, it is not the large and established companies that dominate the industry that take the primary responsibility for digital innovation but rather small-scale start-ups. Examples of such start-ups include Alibaba, which has reshaped the retail industry, Meituan and Ele.me, which have significantly influenced the operating models of the catering industry, and Didi, which has brought profound changes to the taxi industry. These start-ups often face challenges of limited resources, insufficient capabilities, and resistance due to their lack of influence in the industry. How do these start-ups achieve digital innovation and drive business growth under such unfavorable conditions?

Currently, research on digital innovation is still in its early stages. Existing studies mainly focus on the impact brought by digital technology but fail to provide a clear description and explanation of how startups achieve digital innovation. This case will focus on Hangzhou Bancai Technology Company (Zebra Warehouse) and investigate the process and mechanisms of its digital innovation in the home decoration industry.

2. Industry Background and Company Overview
2.1 Traditional Home Decoration Industry

In the traditional home decoration industry, both customers and home decoration companies face inherent difficulties and pressures, commonly referred to as "pain points" in the field of management practice. The "pain points" in the traditional home decoration industry mainly include the following aspects.

(1) "Pain points" from the perspective of consumers

① Inconsistent quotations among different companies without standardized references.

② Many companies deliberately omit items in their quotations to attract customers with lower prices and then charge additional fees during the construction process.

③ Lack of a unified project management system, resulting in a lack of guarantee for the quality of decoration.

④ Uncertain construction timelines, often resulting in losses borne by customers due to project delays.

⑤ Lack of quantification and transparency in decoration costs, especially in electrical and plumbing renovation costs, which easily exceed customers' budgets.

⑥ Loose cooperation between project managers and home decoration companies, often resulting in an inability to promptly resolve issues and protect customers' legitimate rights and interests.

(2) "Pain points" from the perspective of home decoration companies

① High costs of acquiring customers, inhibiting the industry's healthy development. Due to information asymmetry, customers lack effective methods to select and evaluate home decoration companies and can only rely on market reputation to make their choices. As a result, small companies without financial strength are unable to engage in advertising and end up losing most customers attracted by the advertising efforts of larger companies, leading to a vicious cycle of price wars. Price wars also result in a decline in the quality of decoration, ultimately trapping small companies in a difficult operational cycle.

② High turnover rate and difficulty in managing talents. The remuneration of decoration personnel in home decoration companies is mostly based on order volume, which exhibits significant seasonal and intermittent fluctuations. As a result, decoration workers frequently switch jobs or change professions, making it challenging for home decoration companies to manage their workforce effectively. This indirectly affects the quality and progress of decoration projects.

③ Limited ways to acquire orders and high marketing costs. Home decoration companies lack effective channels to acquire consumers' decoration needs, which forces them to invest heavily in advertising and incur high marketing costs.

2.2 Internet Home Decoration Industry

Currently, the market share of the Internet home decoration industry is relatively small compared to the overall home decoration industry. However, Internet home decoration aligns better with people's increasingly Internet-driven consumer habits. Internet home decoration offers the advantage of information transparency, allowing people to complete negotiation, design, material purchase, and other processes online. Furthermore, Internet home decoration can fulfill personalized customization, leading to an overall improvement in product and service quality. With the rise of Internet home decoration giants, transparent corporate management and innovative business models are expected to continue expanding the market space for the Internet home decoration industry, posing a challenge to the traditional home decoration industry.

As shown in Figure 9-1, in 2014, the market scale of China's Internet home decoration industry exceeded RMB100 billion, and in 2017, it reached RMB246.1 billion at a year-on-year growth rate of 25.7%, and had kept a high growth rate over 25% since 2015. In 2018, this figure reached RMB295.6 billion. However, compared to the overall market size of the home decoration industry, the penetration rate of Internet home decoration remains relatively low, indicating vast development prospects.

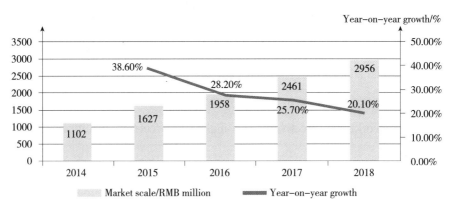

Figure 9-1 Market scale of China's Internet home decoration industry 2014—2018

In the context of the increasingly advanced Internet technology and the promising prospects of Internet home decoration, the startup company, Zebra Warehouse, has gradually emerged with its efficient and innovative operational model.

2.3 Company Overview

Zebra Warehouse was founded in 2017 with a registered capital of RMB5 million. In September 2019, it was recognized as a high-tech enterprise in Hangzhou and included in Hangzhou Eagle Program, making it a potential unicorn enterprise valued at 100 million US dollars in the future technology city. Zebra Warehouse is located in Hangzhou, Zhejiang Province, which is at the forefront of Internet technology in China. Zebra Warehouse integrates the Internet with traditional building materials, creating an industry router model

Case 9 How a Start-up Realizes Digital Innovation in the Traditional Industry: The Entrepreneurial Story of Zebra Warehouse

in the home furnishing field. Through advanced technologies such as big data, cloud computing, blockchain, AR, VR, and SaaS systems, the company integrates core resources in the home furnishing field, addressing pain points in the home decoration industry's supply chain. Zebra Warehouse is committed to building an S2B2C one-stop home decoration supply chain platform that integrates products, sales, logistics, and services.

While initially focusing on the Zhejiang regional market, Zebra Warehouse has expanded its service area to more than 400 districts, cities, and counties in over 20 provinces nationwide.

3. The Success of Zebra Warehouse
3.1 Digital Innovation Process

Through the case study on Zebra Warehouse, we found that the digital innovation process can be divided into five stages: ① identifying opportunities through external environmental observation, ② addressing customer and company needs through the migration of digital business models, ③ optimizing services and empowering the platform through the migration of digital technology, ④ integrating and adapting business models based on the effects of opportunity utilization, ⑤ continuously iterating and applying digital technology. Additionally, the background of the a startup company influences the opportunity identification process, and the obstacles and new discoveries encountered during opportunity utilization stimulate the integration and adaptation of the business model. The digital innovation process is summarized in Figure 9-2 below.

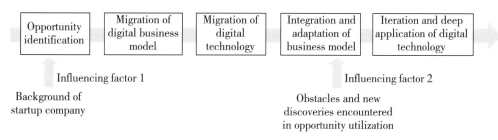

Figure 9-2 Digital innovation process

3.2 Opportunity Identification

In the home decoration industry, traditional business models have limitations and are challenging to address. From rough housing to fully decorated houses, the decoration process involves numerous steps, including material selection, design, construction, and acceptance. Each step has its inherent mode of operation. For inexperienced consumers, it is a real challenge to complete the entire decoration process smoothly.

As the era progresses, there are increasing numbers of renovation models, such as semi-package and full-package. However, both models have their challenges, causing headaches for consumers and industry professionals.

In the semi-package model, consumers need to purchase materials themselves and then find home decoration companies or construction teams for the actual renovation work. While it saves costs to some extent, consumers have to invest a significant amount of time and effort in material selection and finding suitable renovation teams, often resulting in lengthy project timelines. Additionally, once the renovation is completed, if any issues arise, there is often a blame game between material suppliers and renovation teams, making it difficult to safeguard consumer rights.

In the full-package model, home decoration companies are responsible for both material procurement and construction, saving consumers time and effort. Furthermore, in case of quality issues, consumers can hold the home decoration companies accountable. However, in recent years, problems and contradictions within the full-package model have started to surface. Home decoration companies often compromise on quality and prolong project timelines, aiming to make extra profits. Moreover, due to consumers' limited understanding of specific renovation details, many companies inflate material prices, and in some cases, collude with material suppliers for illegal gains, leading to inflated overall renovation costs. These practices significantly harm consumer interests and undermine trust in home decoration companies.

To a certain extent, the existence of these situations has also contributed to the current dilemma in the supply side. The lack of consumer trust in home decoration companies and concerns about the protection of consumer rights have made it increasingly challenging for these companies to acquire customers. As a result, they often need to invest more in marketing costs. Additionally, since traditional home decoration designs cannot provide a clear visualization of the expected outcomes, and customer demands are highly uncertain, there is a frequent need for design changes during the construction process, leading to complex and prolonged projects and increased difficulties and costs. The challenges in customer acquisition and increased costs have sown the seeds of market chaos, while the chaotic market environment further erodes consumer trust, creating a vicious cycle. The supply side and the demand side exhibit inconsistencies, and the contradictions between the two continue to escalate, resulting in a challenging development situation for traditional home decoration models.

Mr. Lin, the founder of Zebra Warehouse, comes from a family with a background in building materials and has a deep understanding of the home decoration industry. After attending university, he actively participated in entrepreneurial activities and won numerous awards in various entrepreneurial competitions as a college student. Even after graduating from undergraduate studies and successfully entering a master's program, Mr. Lin did not give up his dream of entrepreneurship. Together with a partner who had years of experience in the renovation industry, he co-founded "e Xiuge", an Internet platform specializing in the renovation and repair of old houses.

After two years of hard work, the company became one of the leading companies in the industry. With his keen insight and Internet thinking, Mr. Lin identified an excellent business opportunity in the new house Internet home decoration sector. If a platform could be established to act as a bridge between the demand and supply sides, many problems could be effectively addressed. Firstly, the platform would carefully select and certify building materials and provide quality assurance for consumers in their interactions with home decoration companies. Simultaneously, home decoration companies and material suppliers could obtain orders through the platform, facilitating the connection between supply and demand. Secondly, the platform would hold the renovation payment in escrow and only release it to the renovation company once the desired results meet the consumer's expectations. This would greatly reduce consumer concerns and lower the acquisition costs for home decoration companies and material suppliers, effectively reducing transaction costs in the home decoration industry. It would also contribute to the standardization of the market and promote the healthy development of the industry.

In terms of China's overall home decoration industry market size, this presents a tremendous business opportunity. In recent years, homeownership has become a fundamental need, and discussions about house decoration have been on the rise accordingly. With the shift in the age demographic of homebuyers, the younger generation has become the main consumer group in the renovation industry. The fastpaced lifestyle of the young consumers often leads to "renovation anxiety" due to the many cumbersome processes involved in renovation. As a result, whole-package renovation has become the preferred choice for the majority of people, especially in first-tier cities. As early as 2017, the acceptance rate of whole-package renovation exceeded 60% among consumers in first-tier cities, and this number continues to rise. In the future, the scale of whole-package renovation is expected to continue expanding, becoming the mainstream in the renovation industry, leaving ample room for development in China's whole-package renovation market. Seizing this opportunity, e Xiuge, a unicorn startup that has received hundreds of millions of RMB in investment, decided to establish Zebra Warehouse to focus on the new house decoration market. Mr. Lin, the general manager of e Xiuge, took on the role of CEO in Zebra Warehouse. In the early stages, the company's organizational structure mainly consisted of departments such as personnel, administration, finance, marketing, operations, and technology. As the business lines continued to evolve, additional departments were established, such as social e-commerce and order dispatch, to better empower customer acquisition. The team size has grown from dozens of people initially to over a hundred. As the business expanded and roles became more specialized, the company's organizational structure underwent further adjustments and updates, aimed at better addressing the pain points of both the supply and demand sides, adapting to the development of the Internet era, and facilitating the upgrading of the home decoration industry.

3.3 Migration of Digital Business Model

Unlike the self-managed business mode of traditional home decoration companies, Zebra Warehouse introduces the digital business mode featuring "Meituan+ JD" into the home decoration industry. With the aim of delivering a highly cost effective supply chain of main materials, it takes the all-category strategic cooperation mode to integrate numerous first-tier brands by relying upon the resources of e Xiuge. Furthermore, it carries out multi-channel operation and in-depth cooperation with 20000 decoration companies free of charge to pool the consumers on line and distribute the consumers off line. Table 9-1 shows the advantages of "Meituan" model and "JD" model.

Table 9-1 The advantages of "Meituan" model and "JD" model

"Meituan" model	"JD" model
1. Provides order resources and meets customer demands	1. Provides a one-stop, cost-effective solution for materials
2. Reduces the cost of promotion and publicity	2. Save consumers' time and energy
3. Realize "shared construction and joint development" in the home decoration industry.	3. Addresses customer trust issues

On the one hand, the "Meituan" model provides a platform for home decoration companies to acquire orders online. Through this platform, home decoration companies can access valuable order resources and understand customer demands, greatly reducing the costs of customer acquisition, promotion, and advertising. The general process of the "Meituan" model is as follows. ①Customers place orders on the Zebra Warehouse platform, providing their basic information, as well as their ideas, requirements, and budget for the renovation. ②After receiving the customer's order, the platform communicates with the customer to understand their needs and assigns an interior designer to create a suitable design. The design is presented to the customer for feedback and modification. ③Once the final renovation plan is confirmed, the platform allocates the necessary materials and connects the customer with a home decoration company. This new model not only provides a wide customer base for Zebra Warehouse but also enables precise positioning by matching customers with their preferred home decoration companies. Home decoration companies can acquire customers at lower costs, obtain consumer data from the platform to understand the latest decoration preferences and demands, and develop new design solutions and adopt new decoration technologies and materials.

On the other hand, the "JD" model provides customers with a one-stop, cost-effective package of renovation materials. Through strict auditing and bulk purchasing, customers can acquire high-quality materials at a lower cost, saving time and effort, and addressing their distrust of materials provided by home decoration companies. The "JD" model provides a quality-assured one-stop platform, where customers can trust the purchases they make. If there are any dissatisfaction, after-sales support is provided. Meanwhile, material suppliers can sell their products through the Zebra Warehouse platform at a lower cost, reducing their reliance on offline showrooms and distribution channels, and significantly lowering marketing and channel costs. Additionally, with the support of platform data, material suppliers can obtain customer feedback and reviews in real-time, facilitating product updates and upgrades.

The combination of these two models significantly reduces transaction costs and improves transaction efficiency for both the supply and demand sides. Zebra Warehouse follows the concept of "co-construction and sharing", introduces the "JD + Meituan" business model, connects consumer demands with suppliers, and enhances the integration and utilization of resources, ultimately creating a digital business platform that matches supply and demand. This model effectively addresses the difficulties faced by consumers, home decoration companies, and material suppliers.

3.4 Migration of Digital Technology

After establishing the new business model, Zebra Warehouse further enhances its services to consumers and businesses (home decoration companies and material suppliers) through the application of digital technology. Zebra Warehouse leverages digital technology to improve consumer experience and enhance efficiency while reducing costs for home decoration companies.

At the consumer level, Zebra Warehouse utilizes technologies such as Smart Cloud Eyes and 3D Cloud Design to greatly upgrade the consumer experience and increase satisfaction with the services. Smart Cloud Eyes uses facial recognition and intelligent big data analysis to recommend suitable tags to customers, allowing them to filter and add tags based on their preferences. Based on these tags, the platform recommends suitable decoration styles and presents panoramic VR images for customers to visualize the expected results. Once customers make their selections, the system provides budget estimates, project timelines, and recommendations, ensuring transparency throughout the process and allowing all procedures to be completed with just a few clicks. This improves customer stickiness and dependence by providing a transparent and efficient experience. On the other hand, 3D Cloud Design enables customers to become the designers of their own homes, creating high-quality, customized designs based on their preferences and quickly generating visual representations. This "what you see is what you get" approach eliminates discrepancies between customer expectations and actual results. This innovative design method facilitates customer interaction and collaborative design with designers, maximally satisfying individual customer needs, and reducing the difficulty of design and communication between designers and customers. The technology has become a powerful tool for generating orders, benefiting manufacturers and designers alike. The introduction of 3D Cloud Design allows customers to have an intuitive experience of the renovation effects in virtual scenes, actively participate in the process, and foster a sense of ownership. The continuous improvement of customer satisfaction greatly increases the number of successful orders while reducing the costs and pressures associated with frequent design changes for both customers and home decoration companies.

At the business level, Zebra Warehouse provides home decoration companies with management platforms and tools such as Customer Relationship Management (CRM) and Enterprise Resource Planning (ERP), enabling better understanding and analysis of customer needs and more efficient management of internal resources and external suppliers. CRM utilizes information technology and the Internet to coordinate the interaction between enterprises and customers in marketing, sales, and service, automatically matching customers with the most suitable products and services, thereby helping companies improve management practices and enhance efficiency. The CRM client offers a range of customer services, including automatic customer profile creation, tag retrieval, immediate understanding of customer requirements, automated telephone communication, real-time chat via WeChat, and follow-up on signed contracts. This allows Zebra Warehouse to establish long-term relationships of mutual trust with customers, solidify existing customer relationships, attract new customers, continuously integrate customer resources, improve management systems, and enhance overall competitive advantage. On the other hand, ERP is a management platform based on information technology that provides decision-making and operational tools for the management team and employees. Zebra Warehouse utilizes ERP to comprehensively track the entire construction process, monitor in real-time, and ensure project progress and quality. By effectively managing customer information and matching resources, Zebra Warehouse shares this information and data with home decoration companies operating on the platform, allowing them to better understand customer needs and continuously improve work efficiency and competitiveness.

3.5 Integration and Adaptation of Business Modes

Zebra Warehouse entered the home decoration industry through digital business models and continuously improves its services to consumers and businesses through the application of digital technologies. It has received positive feedback in the home decoration industry and experienced rapid growth in order volume. However, after a period of operation, Zebra Warehouse realized that relying solely on digital technology and digital business models in the home decoration industry still faced some resistance and shortcomings.

On the one hand, customers' offline consumption habits in the decoration industry are deeply ingrained, and many consumers still prefer to physically touch and view decoration materials and experience the sample room effects on-site. In the traditional business model of home decoration, customers can see physical building material displays and decoration effects, resulting in a more intuitive perception and experience. On the other hand, the business operations of home decoration companies and material suppliers on the platform still rely on offline activities and participation. After customers purchase decoration materials on the platform, the delivery of these materials still requires the involvement of offline material suppliers to complete the final steps of the process. Similarly, decoration contracts reached on the platform need to be coordinated and implemented by offline home decoration companies, as the platform cannot directly participate in the specific construction process. Furthermore, according to market survey questionnaire data, a considerable number of respondents are still unwilling to try Internet-based home decoration and still feel more at ease with offline traditional decoration. Most respondents choose a combination of online and offline decoration methods, and no respondents are willing to use purely online decoration services.

Taking into account customers' concerns about online decoration and their actual need for offline experiences, Zebra Warehouse has developed an "online + offline" model. In addition to its existing online platform, Zebra Warehouse has set up offline showrooms in major cities across the country, as shown in Figure 9-3. These showrooms allow customers to experience digital home decoration services such as 3D Cloud Design, as well as traditional offline exhibition elements such as sample designs and physical decoration materials. This provides home decoration companies and material suppliers with exhibition and sales venues, while also offering consumers a more intuitive space to learn about Zebra Warehouse's services, and observe and experience decoration materials and sample designs. This new initiative not only alleviates customers' concerns about Internet-based home decoration but also provides material suppliers with an offline platform to showcase their products.

Figure 9–3 Real picture of an offline showroom

3.6 Iteration and Deep Application of Digital Technology

After the establishment of the "online + offline" model, Zebra Warehouse continues to innovate its technological services and applies new digital technologies to provide better services to consumers and businesses. Through the comprehensive application of SaaS systems, Smart Magic Mirror, CRM, VR, AR, ERP, as well as the feedback from customers and home decoration companies' big data, Zebra Warehouse iterates and updates the relevant digital technologies, laying a foundation for tapping into a broader potential market.

Firstly, Zebra Warehouse upgraded its core SaaS system platform and CRM system. The upgraded SaaS system platform allows for more precise analysis of customer needs and effective integration of resources among consumers, material suppliers, and home decoration companies. The structured upgrade of this platform combines the SaaS system with product, sales, service, storage logistics, and other platforms, enabling accurate and efficient analysis and utilization of platform data. This fundamentally helps home decoration companies improve their management and application capabilities, facilitating Zebra Warehouse in providing better services to consumers. Additionally, to assist managers in connecting with customers, identifying and maintaining valuable customers, Zebra Warehouse also upgraded and improved its CRM system. The combined and deep application of the upgraded SaaS system platform and CRM system enables better customer acquisition, deeper understanding and fulfillment of customer needs, real-time data updates, and provides customers with cost-effective personalized decoration design solutions, enhancing the overall benefits and competitive advantages of Zebra Warehouse. The accelerated iteration and deep application of Zebra Warehouse's SaaS system platform and CRM system have greatly advantaged the all-round improvement of management and operational efficiency, as well as the development of target customers.

Secondly, Zebra Warehouse applied VR and AR technologies in its offline showrooms, enhancing the authenticity of the on-site experience for customers. Through the operation of versatile digital technologies, the integration of VR and AR technologies provides an immersive and interactive decoration experience for offline customers. Simultaneously, the combination of VR and AR technologies not only allows for the application of scenes and the tactile sensation of material selection but also enables the customization of various high-quality sample rooms, offering customers a new and convenient experience. This series of digital technology applications make customers' design plans more specific and adjustable, increasing their willingness to engage in decoration and better satisfying their basic needs. It also allows for on-site adjustment of pre-designed decoration plans based on customers' personalized requirements. The updated and applied VR and AR technologies inject vitality into Zebra Warehouse's offline experience, continually attracting new customers to try its services.

Finally, Zebra Warehouse launched Banji App for the consumers to access the services of

Zebra Warehouse more conveniently. In the current era of challenging customer acquisition and high customer acquisition costs, the Banji App designed for consumers was launched shortly after the platform was established. It aims to provide consumers with high-quality and cost-effective home building materials services, while promoting brand awareness for home building material merchants, gaining consumer traffic, and facilitating building material transactions online.

The all-round update of digital technologies by Zebra Warehouse has been well-received by consumers, and its significant potential market has attracted numerous high-quality home building material brands and emerging building material and decoration small enterprises. This has achieved a virtuous cycle for the company's business, driving the digital transformation and deep application of the entire industry.

Prior to this, Zebra Warehouse mainly obtained consumer demand information by scanning with the smart cloud eyes in shared and co-built showrooms. Now, Banji App can assist in the information collection in this link. Based on the concept of ecommerce, it can obtain more consumer information, which is conducive to better empowering the development of enterprises. In this process, Zebra Warehouse coordinates enterprise development resources through the information platform and data platform, attracts traffic and locks customers, and introduces high-quality brand merchants, which improves the efficiency of the entire industrial chain and the utilization of resources. Through the offline application of VR and AR technologies and the development of Banji App, Zebra Warehouse has fundamentally solved the initial pain points of the home decoration industry. Focusing on the business. development model with the orientation of digital transformation and upgrading, Zebra Warehouse has accelerated its iteration and deep application of digital technology and formed a good trend of sharing and co-building, providing correct guidance and a healthy competition cycle for the future direction of the industry. Throughout this process, innovation, development, and updates have never ceased, and Zebra Warehouse's digital technology updates and iterations are ongoing.

Questions:

1. What insights does this case offer for breaking through industry barriers for start-ups?

2. Based on this case, what do you think is the difference between innovation and creativity?

3. Following the success of Zebra Warehouse, what measures should organizations take to foster innovation?

Tips for Answering the Questions:

1. Analyze the first question by applying the creativity theory and the innovation theory.

2. Analyze the second question by applying the creativity theory and the innovation theory.

3. Analyze the third question by applying the leadership style theory, organizational structure theory, team attributes theory, and corporate culture theory.

Case 10

Brain Drain of VT Company Caused by Cultural Conflicts

Key Words:

Management style theory, cultural conflict theory, cultural value model, psychological motivation model of employee turnover

Purpose:

Based on the analysis of VT Company, this case is intended to guide the students to understand the management style theory, cultural conflict theory, cultural value model, and psychological motivation model of employee turnover.

Case:

1. Introduction

On the evening of November 29, 2013, at 10 o'clock, Jenny, the Manager of Human Resources Department at VT Company, finally finished her day's work and walked out of the office building with weary steps. Looking back, the entire office building was dimly lit, with only the emergency exit lights still on. Jenny couldn't help but sigh deeply. Today was a long-awaited Friday, and she should have finished her work early, closed her computer as soon as it was time to leave, rushed out of the office, and started enjoying the weekend. However, for Jenny, all of this could only be a beautiful wish. This year has been a difficult year for VT Company's Human Resources Department. The employee turnover rate of the company continues to rise, reaching 32% from 12.19% three years ago. In the recent conference call, when the 32% turnover rate was mentioned, Jenny could clearly sense the dissatisfaction from her boss regarding this number. Although Jenny listed various objective reasons that contribute to employee turnover, her boss considered them as excuses because, compared to the process, most bosses tend to focus more on the results. Therefore, in her report, Jenny set the goal of trying to control next year's turnover rate within 25%. However, the boss was still dissatisfied with this number and further made a demand. After negotiation, both parties finally reached an agreement to keep next year's turnover rate below 22%. Faced with this goal, Jenny furrowed her brow....

2. Basic Information about VT Company

2.1 Company Profile

VT Company was established in 2005 and is a subsidiary of the well-known VT Group, a Fortune 500 company based in the United States. VT Group's business scope covers information technology, audio-visual imaging, management consulting, and other areas, with branch offices in various countries around the world. Since its establishment, VT Group has adhered to core values of "Customer First, Results-Oriented, Precision Work, Striving for Progress, and Collaborative Development", a mission and vision of "Making the world flatter with innovative technology and services", and a management philosophy of "People-Oriented". By the end of 2013, the company had a total of 625 employees. Among them, 603 employees were directly involved in the BPO (Business Process Outsourcing) operational business, accounting for approximately 96% of the total workforce. Other employees were distributed in functional departments such as administration, finance, and human resources, mainly providing services to the core business departments of the company.

With the rise of the BPO industry, VT Group set up outsourcing service centers in India, Russia and other countries since the 1990s. As the importance of Japan in the Asia-Pacific region increased, after extensive research and evaluation, the group's relevant departments decided to establish VT Company, an outsourcing service center for Japan, in Dalian. VT Company was founded in 2005 and initially focused on standardized and processable businesses related to the Japanese market. Although well-known companies such as GE (now Genpact), Accenture and IBM had already established a presence in Dalian, VT Company, due to its promising prospects, competitive salary levels, and benefits, was once considered the best foreign company in Dalian by university students. From 2005 to 2013,

VT Company experienced eight extraordinary years of development. It surpassed other internal outsourcing centers of the group in terms of quality control and customer satisfaction. In 2009 and 2010, it was awarded the title of "Top 10 Employers in Dalian". Since its establishment, VT Company has rapidly expanded its scale and continuously broadened its business scope.

In 2012, all standardized and processable businesses of VT Group's Japan branch were transferred to Dalian. Among the companies engaged in BPO business in China, VT Company stood out and became a professional outsourcing service company with an annual transaction volume exceeding RMB100 million.

2.2 Organizational Structure of VT Company

Although the organizational size of VT Company has been expanding constantly in the past eight years and the number of staff reached 625, it still primarily adopts a linear functional organizational structure (Figure 10-1).

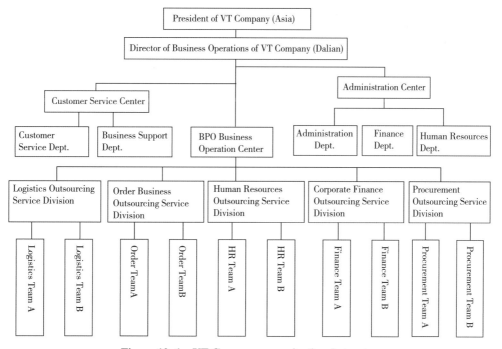

Figure 10–1 VT Company organizational structure

In the organizational structure of VT Company, the highest-level executive is the President, and below the President is the Director of Business Operations. The Director of Business Operations manages three business units: Customer Service Center, BPO Business Operation Center, and Administration Center. The Customer Service Center consists of the Customer Service Department and the Business Support Department, while the Administration Center consists of the Administrative Department, Finance Department, and Human Resources Department. The BOP Business Operation Center in charge of the first-line operations is divided into Logistics Outsourcing Service Division, Order Business Outsourcing Service Division, Human Resources Outsourcing Service Division, Corporate Finance Outsourcing Service Division, and Procurement Outsourcing Service Division.

In terms of organizational hierarchy, team members are the actual operators of specific tasks, primarily following established operating procedures. Assistant Managers and Team Leaders, who are more experienced employees, are the most knowledgeable individuals in terms of business knowledge within their respective teams. They not only need to be familiar with basic operations but also have a deep understanding of the business background, making them a crucial guarantee for the continuous operation of the business. Employees at the Manager level are primarily responsible for team management and do not require in-depth knowledge of specific business operations. Therefore, within the entire Business Operations Department, the key individuals involved in specific business operations are team members, team leaders, and assistant managers.

2.3 Industry Background of VT Company

When VT Company was established, the BPO industry was just beginning to emerge. Being part of a new and promising industry, the company attracted many talents with competitive salary levels and benefits. However, as the BPO industry rapidly developed, more new companies entered the market in Dalian. To compete for talent, companies spared no effort in offering higher salary packages. As a result, VT Company's previously competitive salary and benefits became less attractive. The initial starting salary, although slightly adjusted due to rising prices, couldn't match other companies. At the same time, a peculiar phenomenon emerged in various companies. Employees hired from other companies within the same industry, due to their relevant work experience, were offered much higher salaries than the existing employees, even if their positions were the same. In this situation, employee loyalty gradually declined. Due to the wage gap, many people changed jobs for better salaries, and some even returned to their original company after working at another company for a period of time. To some extent, the entire industry has entered an unhealthy development state.

3. Unexpected Personnel Changes in VT Company

3.1 "People-Oriented" Leadership of Rajesh

Rajesh has been serving as the Director of Business Operations at VT Company since its establishment. He was specifically transferred from the outsourcing center in India by the group headquarters for the development of BPO business in Dalian. Although Rajesh is of Indian descent, his international experience has deeply influenced his leadership style with American culture. Rajesh not only has extensive experience in process management but is also an expert in quality control, holding a black belt in Six Sigma. Even though the target market shifted from India to Japan, Rajesh, with his wealth of experience, effectively managed the department's operations. In dealing with employees, Rajesh always adheres to a humanized management philosophy. He emphasizes that employees are the owners of the company and that without teamwork and the relentless efforts of the employees, VT Company wouldn't be where it is today. To facilitate open communication with every employee, Rajesh replaced all the windows in his office with transparent glass. Rajesh believes that managers should lead by example, and while supervising employees, they should also be open to being supervised by employees and work together with them. Rajesh's management style fully embodies the "people-oriented" company culture and management philosophy, and it has been recognized by the entire company. By the end of 2012, when Rajesh retired, VT Company had successfully transferred three projects, logistics, orders, and finance, from Japan to Dalian.

3.2 "Unwanted" Retirement of Rajesh

Although VT Company did not officially announce Rajesh's retirement, the news had already spread throughout the company, and almost everyone knew about it. Many people believed that Rajesh should not retire at this time. Rajesh had been in office for 7 years, and under his leadership, VT Company successfully transferred projects from Japan.

Rajesh had led everyone through the most difficult times, and now the company's various businesses were steadily developing, but he was retiring, which everyone felt was a pity. Without Rajesh, VT Company would not be able to function. Employees collectively wrote a letter to the group headquarters requesting Rajesh to continue his role. Although Rajesh was deeply moved by this request, he did not want his personal feelings to affect the overall planning of the company. The company also hoped that Rajesh could provide a reasonable explanation to all employees publicly, in order to avoid any adverse effects on the company.

As one of the veterans in the group, it was the group's mission for Rajesh to lead the new company onto the right track, and this task had now been successfully completed. Under Rajesh's leadership, VT Company had grown from a small and fragile sapling into a towering tree, so it was time for him to leave. After much consideration from his perspective as well as for the employees and the company's development, Rajesh made a statement to everyone. In the end, everyone reluctantly immersed themselves in the next phase of work.

3.3 A Different Management style of Nakamura

Regarding the selection of a successor, the VT Group carefully considered various factors. In the end, considering that all standardized and processable businesses in Japan had been transferred to Dalian, the group believed it would be better for a Japanese manager to directly lead the entire team. Therefore, Nakamura from the Japan branch was assigned to

Dalian to take over Rajesh's work. Nakamura served as a Business Manager in the Japan business department, and under his leadership, the performance of the Japan branch was among the top in the group. Moreover, Nakamura had a serious and meticulous work attitude. The group believed that he could streamline the scattered state of the Operations Department after Rajesh's retirement and motivate employees to face the current intense competitive environment together. Since joining VT Company as the Director of Business Operations, Nakamura has adhered to a typical "Japanese-style" management style, focusing on details, hierarchical concepts, and a strong sense of time. Nakamura believed that strict rewards and punishments could make employees actively engage in organizational work. Since Nakamura arrived in Dalian, the working atmosphere at VT Company had changed. Nakamura's strict leadership style and strong hierarchical concepts have attracted dissatisfaction from many people, and more and more people began to miss the working atmosphere under Rajesh's leadership.

4. Departure of New Employees

4.1 Induction Training at VT Company

Liz, a university graduate, joined the company in 2012 when VT Company was gradually flourishing under Rajesh's leadership. After joining VT Company, Liz was assigned to the Order Processing team. During her initial period in the team, Liz received training from experienced colleagues responsible for training new employees. Liz learned very quickly, the colleagues in charge of training believed Liz would become an excellent staff in the future. Liz was also confident in her work.

After about a month of training, Liz attended a meeting hosted by Rajesh for the first time. "I believe that during the onboarding training, everyone has gained a certain understanding of VT Company's basic situation. So, the main purpose of gathering everyone here today is twofold: to express gratitude for joining and to understand everyone's level of recognition of the company." Upon hearing this, Liz, who had been nervous all along, finally breathed a sigh of relief. She secretly felt that the director seemed approachable. Rajesh went on to share his own work experience within the group, saying: "Today, I want to share my journey with all of you to make you understand that opportunities are always in your hands. The company will not give up on any employee unless you give up on yourself! We are a family here at VT Company. In this big family, everyone has equal opportunities for development, and I will pay attention to the development of each and every one of you newcomers. So, I hope we can help each other and progress together." The company could provide a platform for employees, but Liz knew that she also had to put in the effort.

In the end, Rajesh said: "We've had a long day. Let's wrap it up here and go rest! My office is right next to the training room, so if you encounter any work-related problems, feel free to come find me. And of course, you can also consult me for any personal matters." Although the meeting wasn't long, Liz felt the company's care and Rajesh's warmth.

4.2 Controversy over Operation Manual Modifications

By December 2012, Liz had been with VT Company for over six months and had performed exceptionally well in her work. However, since Nakamura's arrival, Liz found herself under increasing pressure.

Not long before, there was an operational error in Liz's Order Team. Upon learning of the mistake, the responsible person from the Japan team not only required the Dalian team to write a report explaining the causes, process, results, and countermeasures, but also demanded the creation of a detailed operation manual to prevent similar issues in the future. Unfortunately, Liz was tasked with this responsibility. Liz quickly completed the operation manual, but the responsible person from the Japan team was not satisfied. Due to differences in work style and culture, what should have been a simple task turned into multiple rounds of revisions for Liz, leaving her physically and mentally exhausted.

4.3 Liz Decided to Leave

Later, an incident became the final straw that made Liz determined to leave. It happened on a Monday morning when everyone in the office was busy with their tasks. Nakamura stormed out of his office and went straight to Todd, and started yelling and berating him without regard for his own position. The office fell into complete silence, except for Nakamura's continuous shouting and insults. Everyone was shocked, and no one dared to look in Nakamura's direction, instead pretending to continue working with their heads down.

Liz was also stunned, her heart pounding, unable to regain her composure for a while. She had never experienced anything like this before, and she believed that even as a leader, one should not yell at subordinates in such a manner. Eventually, Nakamura seemed to realize the impact of his actions and took Todd into his office, but the shouting and harsh tone continued. It later emerged that Nakamura had exploded in anger because Todd had not reported a problem to him promptly, as Todd was busy handling the urgent matter and had planned to provide a detailed report afterward.

Liz couldn't imagine how she would handle such a situation if it happened to her. Liz felt even more lost, questioning if this was the kind of work she wanted. With that thought in mind, Liz decided to quit her current job and explore opportunities outside.

5. Loss of Key Personnel in the Company

5.1 Norah's Journey in VT Company

In February 2014, a significant event occurred at VT Company. Norah from the Logistics Team A resigned! Norah was an assistant manager in the Logistics Team A, known for her strong business capabilities and effective team management. She had earned a good reputation within VT Company and among the Japanese clients. As news of Norah's resignation spread, it immediately caused a stir. Norah had joined VT Company as a fresh graduate in 2006, and through her hard work and dedication, she became the youngest assistant manager in the company by June 2012.

But the new position wasn't as easy as Norah thought it would be, and challenges came one after another. The Japan branch was planning to launch a new logistics business system, which meant that Norah's team had to adapt their entire workflow to the new system. With the new system already developed, Norah had to study how to operate it, create new operation manuals, and provide training within the team. With only two months until the new system's implementation, Norah had no choice but to work overtime, studying tirelessly with two team leaders. Two months later, the new system was successfully launched, and Norah's team received high praise from the Japan branch, commending the deep understanding of business knowledge and reliability among the Dalian employees.

Hard work doesn't go unnoticed, and efforts are rewarded. One day in December, Norah learned that her salary had been exceptionally increased to RMB 4200 yuan per month. During the salary adjustment in February 2013, Norah, recognized as an outstanding employee, received another raise to RMB 5000 yuan per month based on the standards for outstanding employees. At VT Company, Norah had become a shining star.

Norah felt very happy. She believed that despite the hard work and even tears shed in her job, all her efforts and contributions were acknowledged by Nakamura and other company leaders. Norah once again felt the greatness of VT Company and was determined to work there for a lifetime.

5.2 Norah's Change in Attitude Towards VT Company

The Logistics Outsourcing Service Division was divided into two teams, Logistics Team A and Logistics Team B, based on specific business areas, and Norah belonged to Logistics Team A. In August 2013, Logistics Team B experienced a surge in workload, and employees had to work overtime until after 10 pm every day. Although the company provided overtime pay and corresponding allowances, some employees couldn't handle the heavy workload and started submitting their resignations. The departure of employees from Logistics Team B created a shortage of manpower, leading Nakamura to decide to borrow two employees from Norah's Logistics team A to support Logistics Team B. Nakamura's leadership style was taskoriented, prioritizing the smooth operation of business. Although Norah was not enthusiastic about the decision, she knew that in Nakamura's view, every team had to support each other when facing difficulties to ensure the smooth progress of work. Consequently, Norah selected two outstanding members from her team to temporarily support Logistics Team B, resulting in a shortage of two capable employees in her own team. Norah had to find ways to improve the efficiency of Logistics Team A's work, hoping that Logistics Team B could overcome the challenges soon and that her borrowed employees would return as soon as possible.

However, after two months, Logistics Team B seemed to show no improvement. According to feedback from the employees assigned to Logistics Team B, despite an increase in workload, the team's efficiency was severely lacking. The employees were not putting in their best efforts and were seen browsing unrelated websites when Nakamura was not around. Norah, having noticed this behavior, decided to bring up the issue with Nakamura in a tentative manner. To her surprise, Nakamura vehemently assured her that the employees of Logistics Team B were giving their all. Norah felt a sense of unfairness but couldn't express her dissatisfaction directly to Nakamura.

To Norah's disappointment, during the quarterly recognition ceremony, Logistics Team B was awarded the title of "Outstanding Team" for successfully overcoming challenges despite the increased workload and limited staff. However, Logistics Team A, despite lending support to Logistics Team B under Nakamura's pressure, received no recognition or appreciation. Norah felt disheartened that despite her team's diligent efforts, the company failed to acknowledge their contributions. It seemed that those who were merely going through the motions were being rewarded while dedicated employees like herself were overlooked. Additionally, Nakamura seemed oblivious to the disappointment felt by his subordinates.

5.3 Norah's Resignation

In the annual performance evaluation, Norah was rated as excellent again, which meant salary increase. In recent years, the company emphasized reduction of cost and expenses, so the salary increase rate was not as high as that in previous years. Norah thought that she could get an increase of 5% at least. But at last, she received only a 1% raise.

Norah started doubting Nakamura's initial gesture of a salary raise and felt that it was merely a superficial move to assert his authority rather than a genuine recognition of her contributions. Norah believed that challenging Nakamura regarding her salary would be futile due to his strong adherence to hierarchical norms, realizing that her dissatisfaction would not lead to any meaningful change. After much contemplation, Norah made the difficult decision to leave the company she had loved and dedicated eight years of her life to.

6. Employee Turnover Survey at VT Company

6.1 Jenny's Analysis and Statistics

To address the issue of talent loss, Jenny, the head of the Human Resources Department, gathered the entire team to discuss countermeasures. They decided to conduct an exit survey and collect data on the departing employees' future plans, satisfaction with salary, management style, work pressure, and sense of achievement. The survey aimed to provide insights for better problem-solving.

(1) Survey and statistics on the plan after leaving (Figure 10-2)

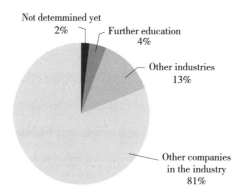

Figure 10-2 Survey and statistics on the plan after leaving

(2) Survey and statistics on salary satisfaction (Table 10-1)

Table 10-1 Survey and statistics on salary satisfaction

Are you satisfied with the salary	Reasons for dissatisfaction	Survey results	
		Number of participants	Proportion
Yes	–	7	8.86%
No	Lower than the salaries of other companies in the same industry	43	54.43%
	Lower than the salaries of other industries	11	13.92%
	Lower than the efforts	18	22.79%
	Lower than the salaries of other colleagues	0	0.00%

(3) Survey and statistics on management style satisfaction (Table 10-2)

Table 10-2 Survey and statistics on management style satisfaction

Are you satisfied with the management style	Reasons for dissatisfaction	Survey results	
		Number of participants	Proportion
Yes	–	14	17.72%
No	Lack of communication between managers and employees	9	11.39%
	The management style is not in line with the company culture	9	11.39%
	Managers are demanding and fault-finding	16	20.26%
	Managers are lack of respect for employees	26	32.91%
Not sure	–	5	6.33%

(4) Survey and statistics on work pressure (Table 10-3)

Table 10-3 Survey and statistics on working pressure

Degree of work pressure	Reasons for very high work pressure	Survey Results	
		Number of participants	Proportion
General	–	12	15.19%
Very high	Stringent service requirements	20	25.32%
	Imbalance between work and life	35	44.30%
	Managers impose high requirements	9	11.39%
	Tense work atmosphere	3	3.80%
No pressure	–	0	0.00%

(5) Survey and statistics on sense of achievement (Table 10-4)

Table 10-4 Survey and statistics on sense of achievement

Sense of achievement	Reasons for no sense of achievement	Survey results	
		Number of participants	Proportion
Strong	–	3	3.80%
No	Repeated work	26	32.91%
	Low degree of participation	17	21.52%
	Less challenging	13	16.46%
	Less innovative	15	18.99%
General	–	5	6.32%

After two consecutive weeks of hard work, the HR Department completed the preliminary survey and statistics on the employees who left VT Company. But the results were just for reference and could not address the high turnover issue. To gain a deeper understanding of the true reasons behind employee departures, Jenny believed it was necessary to conduct interviews with some of the employees who had already submitted their resignation.

6.2 Interviews with the Employees Intending to Leave VT Company

The HR Department organized a collective interview, convening 30 employees who had applied for resignation for the next round of exit reason investigations. After the interviews, Jenny conducted sorting and analysis, identifying the following main reasons for employee resignations.

① Unreasonable salary structure. According to employees' feedback, the annual salary increase rate at VT Company is about 5%～8%. This means that if a recent college graduate joins the company with a salary of 2500 yuan, after two years, their highest salary can only reach 3000 yuan. However, if they switch to another company in the same industry, the salary can reach 4000 yuan. Thus, it is evident that VT Company's current salary level is completely non-competitive in the market. With the constant rise in prices, many employees are compelled to choose companies that offer higher salary packages due to the pressures of life.

② High work pressure causes imbalance between work and life. In order to save costs, even though the business department often works until 10 pm, the company is unwilling to hire more people to alleviate the workload. Employees work overloaded every day, and their lives are completely occupied by work, leaving no personal space. Even during periods of low workload, they are unable to leave on time. Due to Nakamura's work habits, employees have to stay in the office pretending to study business. Since they cannot have enough personal time to relax, they become more emotionally tense when facing the daily demands for high-quality service.

③ There is a lack of job satisfaction. Many employees who choose to resign within two years express that their work lacks challenges and they simply repeat the same tasks every day, feeling like machines. They prefer jobs that allow them to utilize their strengths and offer more challenges.

④ There is a severe hierarchy concept within the company. Many resigning employees report that one of the important reasons they joined VT Company was its "people-oriented" management philosophy. However, after joining, they found that the company placed too much emphasis on the hierarchy concept, and they couldn't even sense their superiors' respect for subordinates. Even if they had opinions, they could only complain privately.

⑤ Japanese colleagues and clients in the Japanese branch have extremely high expectations for service quality. Many resigning employees mention the difficulty of adapting to this cultural conflict.

7. Closing Remarks

It was late at night, and Jenny held the summary report of the exit interviews in her hands. Not to mention the skyrocketing employee turnover rate over the past few months, just this lengthy exit interview report had already exhausted Jenny physically and mentally. Thinking about the goal she had promised her boss to reduce the turnover rate by 10%, Jenny fell into contemplation. The lack of job satisfaction is common in the BPO industry and cannot be changed. However, issues such as salary structure, work pressure, and individual respect are directly related to the company's management system and culture. The current business focuses on Japanese operations, and Nakamura is from Japan. It is inevitable to introduce Japanese management culture. However, faced with the differences and conflicts between Chinese and Japanese cultures, where should the Human Resources Department go? Thinking about this, Jenny became even more confused...

Questions:

1. Based on the performance of Rajesh and Nakamura, what do you think of their management styles respectively? Under what circumstances and background did these two management styles form? In your opinion, which management style would be more likely to stimulate the enthusiasm of Chinese employees?

2. What do you think is the root cause for Liz's resignation? If you were the leader of VT Company, what measures would you take to avoid this situation?

3. Norah experienced several changes in her emotional attachment to the company after joining VT Company. Please analyze the reasons for such changes.

4. Do you think it is necessary for Jenny to conduct interviews with the employees who left VT Company? Why?

Tips for Answering the Questions:

1. Analyze the first question by applying the management style theory and the cultural conflict theory.

2. Analyze the second question by applying the cultural value model.

3. Analyze the third question by applying the psychological motivation model of employee turnover.

4. Analyze the fourth question by applying the psychological motivation model of employee turnover.

Case 11

"Response to Change" —Changes in the Organizational Structure of X Decoration Company

Key Words:

Organizational structure design, organizational structure dimensions, influencing factors of organizational structure

Purpose:

Based on the analysis of the changes in the organizational structure of X Decoration Company, this case is intended to guide the students to understand organizational structure design, organizational structure dimensions, and influencing factors of organizational structure.

Case:

1. Introduction

When a group of people work together towards a common goal, how to organize them and make their collective work more efficient are questions that business organizations typically address through establishing organizational structures. Organizational structures are not one-size-fits-all; various forms of organizational structures have emerged in organizational management practices. Which organizational structure is more effective? Which organizational structure is more suitable for the needs of a specific company? These questions have always troubled practitioners in management and have sparked the interest of management researchers. This case will narrate a case of an Internet company, where we can observe the process of organizational structure changes in the company.

2. Initial Stage

X Decoration Company is an Internet company dedicated to providing house renovation and repair services. Mr. Wang, the founder of the company, has been engaged in the building materials and home decoration industry for a long time, owning a small-scale decoration company and a building materials store. During the operation, Mr. Wang noticed many limitations and deficiencies in the traditional home decoration industry. On the one hand, many consumers only renovate their houses once or twice in their lifetime, and after the completion of the renovation, their needs shift towards renovation and repairs for old houses. However, few decoration companies provide such services. Consumers usually have to rely on property management or friends and relatives in the plumbing and electrical industry for repair work, while old house renovation is typically carried out by individual craftsmen or small-scale construction teams. On the other hand, due to high profit margins, decoration companies prioritize new house decoration, but obtaining new house decoration orders is not easy due to fierce market competition. The designers, plumbers, carpenters, painters, and other employees hired by decoration companies rely on order volume for remuneration, and the insufficient number of orders leads to significant employee turnover. Furthermore, the business volume and stability of renovation and repair orders for old houses are relatively low, making few decoration companies willing to engage in such business.

Mr. Wang realized that there could be a tremendous business opportunity if he could connect consumer demands for repairs and renovations with decoration companies. The annual business volume of renovations in China amounts to billions, and although the exact scale of the renovation and repair market is unknown, it is conservatively estimated to be a market worth billions as well. Therefore, in 2015, Mr. Wang decided to establish a new company to engage in house renovation and repair services. With this idea in mind, Mr. Wang began contemplating the details of the project. He soon realized that relying solely on his decoration company and building materials store would not make a significant impact in the house renovation and repair industry. The local market for house renovation and repairs was limited, and even with efforts to expand the business area, based on the existing foundation, they would only cover a small area within a city. This was a far cry from their ultimate goal of dominating the market and influencing the entire industry. As a result, he started considering the possibility of leveraging the Internet to achieve his dream.

Case 11 "Response to Change"—Changes in the Organizational Structure of X Decoration Company

By 2015, the Internet industry in China had already flourished, and every aspect of people's lives had been profoundly influenced by the Internet. Mr. Wang wanted to adopt the model of Taobao, connecting thousands of home decoration companies with millions of consumers. Mr. Wang shared this preliminary idea with a young entrepreneur, Mr. Zhong, who also came from a family in the building materials industry. To their surprise, their ideas aligned perfectly. Moreover, Mr. Zhong had participated in several internet-related entrepreneurship competitions during his time at school, giving him a deeper understanding and proficiency in internet technology and the operations of internet startups. Therefore, Mr. Wang promptly invited Mr. Zhong to join, forming the core of the company's founding team. Together, Mr. Wang and Mr. Zhong further refined their business plan, aiming to establish an online platform that connects customers in need of renovation and repair for old houses with decoration companies and repair craftsmen. Customers would be able to place orders and specify their requirements on the platform, while decoration companies or repair craftsmen could accept orders and reach agreements within the platform's predefined price standards. The main source of revenue for the platform would be a commission from each order.

Ideas further refined, Mr. Wang and Mr. Zhong decided to continue expanding the team. On one hand, they lacked a background in information technology and needed to recruit a professional technical team to handle application development and platform maintenance. They also urgently required a partner with experience in internet operations to drive the smooth implementation of the platform project. On the other hand, the team's financial resources were insufficient. Internet projects require substantial initial investments, and the accumulated resources of the two founders alone would not meet the future financial needs. Therefore, they began recruiting a technical team and new partners. After great efforts, they successfully hired a technical team responsible for application development and platform maintenance. They also successfully invited the head of the technical team to become a partner within the core team. Additionally, they brought in two entrepreneurs with Internet operation experience as partners. With this, the company officially formed with five core partners and three programmers as initial employees.

Regarding strategic decision-making, the partners adhered to a system of mutual consultation. They required unanimous agreement among all core members for any important decision, rather than voting based on equity ownership. After making decisions, the core members of the company divided the work among themselves, focusing on fundraising, market expansion, employee recruitment, and technological development. During the startup phase, everyone was highly motivated, and they were able to progress quickly in their respective tasks without the need for constant supervision. With the collective efforts of the team, the initial version of the App, "X Bang Ge", took shape, and the company also secured a seed funding of 500000 RMB, greatly relieving the financial pressure.

3. Rapid Growth

With the support of funding, the company decided to accelerate business progress. At that time, several companies engaged in similar businesses were also emerging and receiving funding. Therefore, the company needed to expand its customer base quickly to gain market share. The core team of the company determined that the company with the largest market share, having the most customers and service providers, would dominate the industry competition in the future. Otherwise, companies with slower development would find it difficult to challenge the market position of the industry leaders under the premise of industry homogeneity. Therefore, the company decided to hire more employees to promote the "X Bang Ge" App offline. The aim was twofold: to increase consumer awareness and usage of the platform and to attract more decoration companies and repair craftsmen to join, enabling consumers to find service providers more quickly and conveniently. As a result, the company initially hired several new employees responsible for offline contact and cooperation with decoration companies and repair craftsmen in major cities. The goal was to ensure that consumers in major cities across the country could find renovation and repair service providers on the platform. If customer service could not be effectively met, consumers would quickly migrate to other platforms. Simultaneously, the company began collaborating with various websites and media outlets to increase the App's visibility, allowing more consumers to submit their requirements on the platform and thereby enabling service providers on the platform to receive more orders. As the company continued to grow, the original technical team also became busier. Platform maintenance consumed a significant amount of their time, preventing them from dedicating themselves to updating and improving the App. Consequently, the company recruited two more programmers to expand the technical team.

As the company's business grew, several entrepreneurs with resources such as funding and suppliers gradually joined the core team as partners. The core team expanded to 9 members. At this point, the company had grown to a size of 20 people, but problems also emerged. Firstly, with more partners, the division of labor became ambiguous. Each partner did not have a specific role, resulting in a lack of dedicated personnel for comprehensive tasks such as finance and human resources. Initially, these tasks were managed part-time by CEO Mr. Zhong, with Chairman Mr. Wang overseeing the coordination of the partners' work. However, as the business grew, Mr. Zhong and Mr. Wang dedicated more time to fundraising and expanding the business, and the increase in personnel made comprehensive tasks burdensome. This led to a strain on the two individuals. For example, initially, the company's financial tasks were primarily handled by an accounting firm, overseen by Mr. Zhong. At that time, with a small business volume, Mr. Zhong could manage it relatively easily. However, as the business volume increased, the lack of timely accounting became increasingly prominent. Additionally, Mr. Zhong did not possess the qualifications and experience to handle financial work, leading to confusion in the company's financial data to some extent. Moreover, the decision-making efficiency of the company also faced challenges. While the company had always adhered to a system of collective decision-making and consensus among partners, reaching consensus became more difficult with the increase in partners. Many times, the core team had to hold meetings for one or two days, totaling dozens of hours, without being able to reach a complete agreement on a decision. Some partners left because they could not accept this inefficient decision-making process, resulting in the reduction of the core team from 9 to 8 members.

To address these difficulties, the company recruited a new employee responsible for comprehensive tasks such as finance and human resources. Additionally, the core team decided to strengthen the power of the CEO and the head of the technical team. Most decisions and tasks unrelated to the company's strategy and direction were directly authorized to the CEO, while technical matters were mostly entrusted to the head of the technical team. These adjustments strengthened logistical support and reduced the need for collective decision-making by the core team, thereby improving efficiency. However, as the company's business rapidly developed, the organizational structure quickly became constrained. It is worth acknowledging that the market opportunity targeted by the company had great prospects. Renovation and repair of old houses indeed met the needs of many consumers, and the company's initiatives to expand offline service providers were showing remarkable results. The number of registered customers and service providers on the platform increased significantly, as did the volume of orders completed on the platform. Correspondingly, more people were needed to maintain the platform and handle customer complaints and disputes. The increase in personnel and business growth placed a greater burden on finance and human resources, among other logistical work. Consequently, the company had to further expand its scale.

Initially, the company established a customer service department to handle disputes and strengthen communication with service providers. Next, more technical personnel were recruited to augment the technical team, ensuring timely maintenance and updates to the platform. Finally, a comprehensive department was formally established to handle internal logistical work such as finance and human resources. With the establishment of new departments and the expansion of personnel, the company's employee count quickly exceeded 50 people. To ensure the smooth operation of these departments, the company assigned core team members to lead each department. However, it became apparent that the company had not accurately anticipated the complexity of management.

The company soon discovered that although departments such as Customer Service Department, Technical Department, and Comprehensive Department had been established, the boundaries between departments were not clear. For example, many complaints received by the Customer Service Department were related to technical malfunctions on the platform. Departments often passed on issues without clear responsibilities to the Comprehensive Department, resulting in complex and diversified work that went beyond the capabilities of the Comprehensive Department.

These issues created difficulties in the company's operations. Firstly, the management of departments by core team members led to conflicts among them. Some members consistently approached problems and expressed their opinions from the standpoint of their own departments, seeking to shift responsibility and reduce their department's workload, while disregarding the overall interests of the company. Secondly, there was a lack of consensus among departments on many fundamental issues of employee management. For example, some departments frequently required working late into the night, resulting in employees arriving at work close to noon the next day. Meanwhile, other departments insisted on the traditional working hours of 9 am to 6 pm, making it difficult to carry out many tasks due to insufficient staff. Thirdly, the company's compensation system and promotion mechanism had significant issues. When the company was smaller, employee rewards and promotions were relatively straightforward, and top-level management could directly observe employees' performance and provide appropriate rewards or promotions. However, as the company grew, top-level management had limited knowledge of the actual work performance of many employees, necessitating a more robust performance evaluation mechanism.

Therefore, the company decided to further refine the division of labor between departments and the overall regulatory system. Firstly, the company clarified the responsibilities and scope of work for each department and released an organizational chart formulated by the company's top management. Since it was difficult to completely differentiate the boundaries of responsibilities between departments through division of labor alone, the company also specified that if there were disagreements between two departments, the senior management responsible for overseeing the departments would be responsible for coordination. If a consensus was not reached, the CEO would intervene. Secondly, the company improved its evaluation system, compensation structure, and promotion mechanism. Regarding the evaluation system, the company generally required a 9-to-6 work schedule. However, departments with significant nighttime workload, such as the Technology Department and Customer Service Department, were allowed flexible working hours, but employees must be on duty during the working hours of other departments. Regarding the compensation structure and promotion mechanism, the company conducted monthly and semi-annual performance evaluations, and rewards and promotes employees who had performed exceptionally well for six months or more. Considering that the company's own cash flow was not abundant, the company stipulated that significant rewards would be given in the form of company stock options. Furthermore, outstanding employees would have the opportunity to be promoted as shareholders or partners of the company. The implementation of these systems has significantly reduced conflicts between departments and employee dissatisfaction while increasing employee motivation.

4. Further Development and Growth

Thanks to the standardization of systems and the expansion of the renovation and maintenance market, the company's business scale has further expanded. In less than two years, the number of employees has grown to 200. The company's office space has also expanded from four compartments in the startup incubator to a whole floor. The rapid growth of the company has attracted the attention of investment institutions, and it has received seed funding of RMB10 million and Series A funding of up to RMB100 million. The substantial investment has brought greater confidence to the core team members of the company, and they hope to further expand the company's market share in the Internet-based renovation and maintenance industry. The company ranked third in the industry in terms of Internet-based renovation and maintenance services and was closely approaching the second-ranked company in terms of market share, with a gap of nearly 10% from the industry leader.

Additionally, during its operations, the company has identified attractive market opportunities in the domestic Internet-based home decoration industry. On the one hand, the domestic real estate market remained hot, and consumers had a great demand for decoration. However, due to a lack of time and relevant expertise, most consumers can only rely on offline home decoration companies for their services. Some of these companies cut corners in their work or use sub-par materials in order to maximize profits. This has led to a general lack of trust among consumers towards home decoration companies. On the other hand, consumers' distrust also increased the customer acquisition cost. Due to the lack of trust, the low-cost methods such as customer referrals or direct sales are unable to meet the operational needs of home decoration companies. Consequently, these companies have to invest a significant amount of resources in offline promotion or advertising, as well as offer large discounts to attract customers. The rising costs for home decoration companies indirectly increase the possibility of engaging in unethical activities that harm consumers, further reinforcing consumer distrust. This vicious cycle continues within the domestic home decoration industry. For the company, becoming a platform that facilitates transactions between consumers and decoration companies would be a great development opportunity. On one hand, consumers can purchase quality-assured building materials, determine decoration plans, have the platform handle material delivery, and supervise the quality of the decoration through the platform. On the other hand, decoration companies can directly obtain orders online, greatly reducing customer acquisition costs. To seize this newly discovered opportunity, X Decoration Company decided to venture into the new business of Internet-based new home decoration. By becoming a platform that connects consumers and decoration companies, the company aimed to provide a solution to the challenges faced by both parties.

To expand market share and explore new business opportunities, the company further expanded its workforce. However, as the company grew, it encountered several problems. Previously, each department had only 3 to 10 employees, and work assignments were managed by the department heads, ensuring smooth operations. With the sudden increase in the number of employees in each department, some department heads began to feel overwhelmed. Additionally, a significant proportion of the new hires further increased the management challenges for the department heads. To address this issue, some department heads attempted to delegate their management responsibilities by appointing team leaders and issuing job descriptions. These measures partially alleviated the management pressure on the department heads. However, they also presented certain risks. Appointing team leaders below the department heads decentralized the management authority, reducing the department heads' control over their subordinates Some department heads of larger departments were unable to stay informed about the work status of frontline employees. In some cases, experienced team leaders, in an effort to enhance their own status within the department, made significant decisions without the knowledge of the department heads. Furthermore, while the attempt to provide job descriptions to employees yielded positive results, many new employees found that the actual job requirements often deviated from the provided descriptions. As a rapidly growing company, business operations and requirements were continuously evolving, causing job descriptions to become obsolete and lose their effectiveness in guiding actual work.

Moreover, the company faced challenges in launching new business initiatives. The resources and focus of the company were primarily dedicated to maintaining and expanding the existing renovation and maintenance business. Consequently, the company's investment in new business ventures was insufficient. Furthermore, there was a lack of enthusiasm and motivation among the team members for the new initiatives. Apart from the chairman and CEO, most core team members already held managerial positions within specific departments. Although they expressed support and agreement for the company's new business ventures, their limited resources resulted in minimal support in practice. Additionally, after achieving initial success, many team members expressed a desire for a relatively stable life and were reluctant to relive the challenges of the startup phase for a new business. However, the new business venture was time-sensitive. The company's launch of an Internet-based new home decoration platform was not the first in the industry.

Some entrepreneurial teams had already identified this market and secured investments. The relative stagnation of the company's new business in the previous months placed it at a disadvantageous competitive position. In the fastpaced and highly competitive Internet industry, speed and scale often determine the "first-mover advantage". If the company completely loses this advantage, it will face significant challenges in the subsequent competition, especially considering the ease of replicating and catching up with business models in the Internet sector.

To overcome the series of challenges faced by the company's growth, the senior management decided to seek further transformation.

5. Breaking Down the Whole

To address the aforementioned problems, the company engaged in multiple rounds of discussions. The ultimate conclusion was that the root of the current issues lies in insufficient management capabilities. In response to this problem, two proposed solutions were put forward.

Proposal A: "Formalize" the company by implementing various rules and regulations to standardize employee behavior, thereby reducing the pressure on managers and freeing their energy from daily management tasks. At the company level, this would involve clarifying the division of responsibilities among departments, improving coordination mechanisms between departments, and establishing a basic work charter to regulate employee behavior. At the department level, it would entail further refining job responsibilities and corresponding workflows based on the company's strategic needs, as well as establishing systems for information reporting and dissemination within each department. However, during the discussions, it became increasingly clear that this approach had drawbacks. Firstly, the Internet industry relies heavily on fast decision-making and responsiveness. While "formalization" made work more structured and predictable, it also restricted employees' flexibility and hindered the company's agility. The bureaucratic nature of command and control slowed down the company's actions and risked making it rigid, which is commonly referred to as "big company syndrome". Secondly, although the company had reached a certain scale, both the industry and the company itself were experiencing rapid changes, and there was a lack of experience in many aspects. This made it challenging to develop a set of regulations that truly aligned with the company's strategic needs. Even if such regulations were formulated, they would require constant updates due to the frequent changes in the company's business and strategy. It was difficult to expect employees to adhere to a constantly evolving system and work according to its guidelines. As the severity of the issues associated with this approach became apparent, more members of the team recognized the challenges, leading to the shelving of this proposed solution.

Proposal B: "Break down the whole into parts". This proposal received increasing support from the members. In the core team, a member proposed that since the leaders of each department lacked sufficient ability and energy to manage the expanded departments, it would be better to further divide the departments into small teams, with these teams serving as the basic working units. It was quickly realized that this idea was similar to the Amoeba Management Model by Kazuo Inamori. Therefore, the company combined the concept of the Amoeba Management Model with this plan. Firstly, teams were established as the basic operational units of the company, and the existing departments were divided into small teams. Some decision-making authority was delegated to the team level, allowing teams to make decisions regarding most specific operational matters. Secondly, team leaders were given greater power. The company no longer established specific workflows and job requirements, apart from the basic assessment system, compensation structure, and promotion mechanism. Lastly, the responsibilities of each team were clarified, and coordination mechanisms between teams were improved. The company divided its overall strategy and business processes among the teams, and larger-scale projects were completed through collaboration between several teams. The company dispatched executives to coordinate the cooperation between teams. Considering that many team operations were difficult to quantify, the company did not explicitly require each team to account for their input and output like the Amoeba Management Model, but annual evaluations of each team's performance were conducted, and corresponding rewards or punishments were given. To promote talent development and enhance management capabilities, the company established a weekly management teaching and sharing system, facilitating exchanges and interpretations among experienced managers, external experts, team leaders, and potential talents.

Regarding new businesses, the company continued the approach of "breaking down the whole into parts" and decided to separate a subsidiary from the parent company to take full responsibility for the new house decoration business. The company believed that instead of confining the new business within the parent company, it would be better to grant it greater autonomy and establish it as a separate entity. Eventually, the company assigned the two youngest and most vibrant members of the core entrepreneurial team to lead this subsidiary, forming a new entrepreneurial team with them at the core to drive the development of the new business. Initially, the new company shared some resources with the parent company but gradually became independent from the parent company's support and guidance after it started formal operations. It became responsible for its own profits and losses and continued to develop independently.

The implementation of the "breaking down the whole into parts" organizational transformation and the establishment of a separate entity for the new business propelled the company back into the "fast lane" of development.

6. Continuing the Rapid Development

The implementation of the "breaking down the whole into parts" organizational transformation propelled the company back into the "fast lane" of development. Thanks to improved operational efficiency and the ability to quickly respond to market changes, the parent company maintained its position in the top three in the market of renovation and repairs for old houses without conducting large-scale and high-cost marketing activities. Furthermore, compared to competitors, the company had healthy cash flow and profitability. The subsidiary also achieved rapid growth, becoming self-sufficient and generating a certain level of profit. It relocated from the parent company and quickly expanded to a size of nearly 200 employees, ranking among the top ten in the market of new house decoration. The next challenge for X Decoration Company is how to achieve better synergy between the parent company and the subsidiary in their business development.

Questions:

1. What are the reasons for the successive organizational changes in X Decoration Company?

2. Which elements of the organizational structure of X Decoration Company were adjusted in the past organizational changes?

3. How did the company achieve synergy between the organizational structures of the new business and the existing business after establishing the subsidiary?

Tips for Answering the Questions:

1. Analyze the first question by applying relevant knowledge of organizational structure design and influencing factors of organizational structure.

2. Analyze the second question by applying the knowledge of organizational structure dimensions.

3. Analyze the third question by applying the knowledge of organizational structure design.

Case 12

Why Is the Organizational Transformation of JNSP Property Center So Tricky?

Key Words:

Organizational transformation, organizational transformation model

Purpose:

Based on the analysis of the organizational transformation of JNSP Property Center, this case is intended to guide the students to understand organizational transformation and organizational transformation model.

Case:

1. Introduction

Mr. Zhou, head of JNSP Property Center, felt great pressure in the meeting held today. In the meeting, Mr. Hu, a senior property manager made a summary report on the issues encountered during the organizational transformation of JNSP in the past year, which was agreed upon by other participants of the meeting.

Faced with these problems, Mr. Zhou understood that he needed to calm down. First, he needed to maintain overall stability in management and carry out current tasks efficiently. Then, he should analyze the problems and find solutions.

Mr. Zhou gently opened the curtains and looked out of the window. He recalled every detail of this period. He pondered over the reasons behind the problems encountered during the reform of JNSP Property Center.

2. Cross-industry Cooperation

In 1999, Shanghai XYZJ Property Management Company (XYZJ Company) was established, taking the lead in initiating the "New Home Movement". This movement focused on environmental protection, embraced nature, and emphasized humanistic care. It became an influential innovation movement in the real estate industry. Seizing this opportunity, Shanghai XYZJ Company focused on managing and providing services for high-end residential properties in Shanghai. It boldly introduced mature and advanced service concepts, combined with local characteristics, and continuously innovated and improved residential management methods. It received high praise from homeowners and the industry, being ranked among the top 50 property management companies in Shanghai for five consecutive years.

Since assuming the position of General Manager of XYZJ Company, Mr. Zhang officially took on the responsibility of the "New Home Movement". Leveraging advanced international property management concepts, he established the "Capital Garden." The residential property management service model represented by the "Capital Garden" received numerous awards, and the scale of management increased 50-fold. Mr. Zhang was satisfied with this achievement, at least not disappointing the expectations of the previous General Manager. However, the "New Home Movement" with its emphasis on humanistic care became the focal point for homeowners to vent their dissatisfaction.

To enhance communication with homeowners and improve service capabilities, XYZJ Company, in collaboration with Jingjin Technology Company, launched a community App in 2013. It was widely promoted in communities managed by XYZJ Company and Jingjin Technology Company, actively incorporating user feedback for continuous improvement. In 2014, XYZJ Company and Jingjin Technology Company created the first SaaS community platform, "Warm Micro-community", which became a crucial step in developing cloud-based community property management and operational management.

In 2016, when XYZJ Company believed they could successfully apply Internet applications to community property management, they gradually realized that traditional community property management was incompatible with Internet thinking. The community application had rich and powerful functionalities, but traditional community property management struggled to keep up with the pace of the Internet era, necessitating transformation.

Mr. Zhou was the founder of Jingjin Technology Company. He had multiple discussions regarding the direction of collaboration with Mr. Zhang. Mr. Zhou believed that advanced technology was merely a basic service platform for the operation of "Warm Micro-community." He believed that genuine collaboration with established enterprises was the key to a truly promising future. Mr. Zhang believed that for a property management company, transforming its traditional DNA with Internet thinking was of utmost importance. If Jingjin Technology Company and XYZJ Company merged, it would present an opportunity for XYZJ Company to create a new property management mechanism. Therefore, XYZJ Company and Jingjin Technology Company decided to conduct cross-industry cooperation.

In 2016, XYZJ Company acquired Jingjin Technology Company. Mr. Zhou was appointed as Deputy General Manager of XYZJ Company and took on the important task of managing the JNSP community, shouldering the responsibility of transforming community property management. The JNSP community, managed by XYZJ Company, had been recognized as an excellent residential complex in Shanghai. The community covered an area of 200000 square meters with a building area of 400000 square meters, primarily consisting of multi-story buildings housing approximately 3000 households and 10000 residents. Zhou, having worked in the IT industry for many years, was a typical "outsider" in the property management industry. Faced with Zhou's concerns, Zhang patted Zhou's shoulder and said, "You should be an ambitious reformer from the outside."

3. Hidden Turbulence

Mr. Zhang and Mr. Zhou chose the JNSP community as a pilot project for several reasons. Firstly, JNSP was the first location under XYZJ Company to implement the community App, and Mr. Zhou was familiar with its situation. Secondly, JNSP was a flagship and high-end community of XYZJ Company, making it suitable for setting an example.

With his IT background, Mr. Zhou had a deep-rooted belief in flat management. Upon taking office, he abolished all functional departments and established four housekeeper teams, each led by a team leader who was previously a customer service manager in the Customer Service Department. The remaining employees were evenly distributed among the four housekeeper teams. Based on geographical location, the JNSP community was divided into four regions, with each housekeeper team responsible for the property operations in one region. Each housekeeper team had independent finances and was accountable for its own profits and losses.

However, Mr. Zhou underestimated the resistance from the traditional property management industry towards Internet thinking. The former management, represented by Mr. Hu, strongly opposed the abolition of functional departments, thus impeding the transformation.

In the first half of 2016, when Mr. Hu reported to XYZJ Company, he was already aware that the company was preparing to acquire an IT company.

However, what Mr. Hu did not expect was that Mr. Zhou would become the leader of JNSP Property Center and take full responsibility for the property management transformation, using the JNSP community as a demonstration project for XYZJ Company's property management transformation.

The contrasting backgrounds of Mr. Hu and Mr. Zhou often led to differing perspectives and created difficulties in the transformation of JNSP Property Center. Despite Mr. Hu's lower education level, his practical understanding of social dynamics exceeded what could be learned from textbooks. When Mr. Zhou decided to abolish the functional departments, Mr. Hu strongly opposed the decision and reported it to Mr. Zhang. However, Mr. Zhang strongly supported Mr. Zhou, leaving Mr. Hu feeling disappointed.

The establishment of housekeeper teams did facilitate communication between the

Case 12 Why Is the Organizational Transformation of JNSP Property Center So Tricky?

property management and homeowners, improving operational efficiency. However, in the past year, numerous problems also emerged. Based on the difficulties faced after the organizational change, Mr. Zhou decided to convene a meeting with two main agenda items: first, to summarize the problems encountered during the past year of transformation, and second, to gather ideas and direction for the next phase of transformation. Surprisingly, during this meeting, everyone started complaining and blaming Mr. Zhou for his reform measures.

4. Conflict Arises

As soon as Mr. Zhou requested everyone to freely express their thoughts during the meeting, someone stood up.

"Mr. Zhou, I am a military veteran, and I have something to say. Since the Security Department was abolished, all the security personnel were assigned to the four housekeeper teams. However, security work requires regular professional training. Now, the personnel are dispersed among different steward teams, making it difficult to manage effectively. In the past year, we haven't even had a decent training session. Additionally, we need to collaborate with the government on public safety, urban management, and fire inspections. Previously, government departments only needed to contact us, but now each steward team is not fully cooperative. I'm not against the transformation, but if this continues, there will be issues." said Mr. Yang, the former head of the Security Department, expressing sharp criticism.

"Mr. Zhou, before the Engineering Department was abolished, it was responsible for the maintenance work of the entire community. The maintenance supplies were purchased according to standardized procedures. Now, with each housekeeper team having financial independence and being responsible for their own profits and costs, there are four separate procurement orders, resulting in varying prices and quality. Homeowners feel it's unfair and cause disturbances. Once the Planning and Construction Committee notices this, we will be in a difficult situation. Can we come up with a solution quickly?" added Mr. Bian, the former head of the Engineering Department.

"Mr. Zhou, the cleaning staff has complained to me more than once. Now, each housekeeper team is assigned specific floors based on regions, resulting in varying workloads for the cleaning staff. If a cleaning staff member falls ill or needs to leave, there is no willingness among the other teams to help. Previously, I didn't encounter such problems because I could coordinate and assign tasks. The relationships among the cleaning staff are not as good as before. How do you propose to solve these issues?" continued the former head of the Cleaning Department.

"Mr. Zhou, the community landscaping work involves two aspects: regular pruning and periodic replacement. In the past, regular pruning was centrally arranged, but now it's divided among the four teams, resulting in inconsistent landscaping across the community. Additionally, the issue of periodic replacement is similar to the Engineering Department. In the past, nursery plants were purchased centrally, but now the procurement is delegated to the housekeeper teams. Some teams frequently replace plants while others don't replace them at all. The committee members have repeatedly raised concerns and asked me to take responsibility. Now that the Landscaping Department no longer exists, what do you think my role should be?" voiced the former head of the Landscaping Department.

Finally, Mr. Hu took a sip of water and said: "Let me also express my thoughts. When the functional departments were abolished, I disagreed. Functional departments shouldn't be easily eliminated, and property management should not solely focus on the community. There are public security, urban management, fire protection, industry committees, social work committees, planning and construction committees, and various social organizations that cannot be ignored. We need a unified management approach."

Mr. Zhou listened to these comments patiently. Despite the challenges of the transformation, he firmly believed that the traditional property management industry should adapt to the digital age and provide better services and experiences to homeowners.

5. The Right Way to Go

After the meeting, Mr. Hu and Mr. Zhou conducted a phase-wise summary of the transformation. They concluded that JNSP community should immediately halt the transformation. Subsequently, XYZJ Company decided to suspend the transformation and the dissemination of the experiences gained from JNSP Property Center.

During the Spring Festival of that year, Mr. Xing, the team leader of one housekeeper team, received a notification that water supply in the JNSP community would be suspended for eight hours starting from 9 pm. This was a significant event that would affect residents' daily lives, and the property center needed to report it promptly to the leadership and inform the community. Otherwise, it could lead to homeowner complaints. After hearing Mr. Xing's report, Mr. Zhou took immediate action. He instructed Mr. Xing to pay special attention to ensure that the water suspension notice was not only published on the community App but also posted on the community bulletin board and shared with the industry committee. Mr. Zhou also suggested that the security personnel engage in conversations with homeowners during their patrols to inform them in advance and advise them to prepare for water storage to minimize the impact on their lives.

After the report, Mr. Xing didn't immediately leave. Although hesitating for a moment, he couldn't help but ask: "Mr. Zhou, there have been rumors in the company that you will be leaving JNSP Property Center after New Year's Day. Is it true?" Mr. Zhou assured him not to worry and told him to focus on his work.

Mr. Xing graduated from university in 2014 and joined XYZJ Company through campus recruitment. He was assigned to JNSP community as a customer service manager. His daily tasks involved dealing with homeowner complaints and inquiries, categorizing and providing feedback to the functional departments. These tasks were not complex but rather tedious. In his work, Xing gradually observed the drawbacks of the traditional property management system, where functional departments operated independently, resulting in numerous issues. He believed that the transformation of the traditional property management model was an inevitable trend. However, he was only a customer service manager and could do little about it. Fortunately, in the second half of 2016, Mr. Zhou arrived at JNSP Property Center and started driving the transformation of the property management model.

With the abolition of the original functional departments, all staff members were assigned to the housekeeper teams, and Mr. Xing was promoted to a team leader, responsible for around 800 homeowners in the community. This was undoubtedly a significant affirmation for him, but it also brought considerable pressure.

Over the past year, Mr. Xing not only had to deal with daily tedious tasks but also manage the team. Since the housekeeper teams were financially independent and responsible for their own profits and losses, he needed to regularly monitor the team's financial status. At the same time, XYZJ Company had been closely monitoring the community transformation at JNSP, which added significant pressure on him. Despite all this, he tried his best to excel in his work. However, the results of the past year's transformation were not satisfactory. In fact, it seemed like the transformation had failed. Recent rumors within the company gave him a sense of foreboding that Mr. Zhang, the CEO of XYZJ Company, would visit the community during the National Day, and he worried that the community's transformation would not continue to progress, leading everything back to square one.

Upon receiving the water suspension notice, Mr. Yang, the former head of the Security Department, also fell into contemplation. He retired from the military in 2009 and joined XYZJ Company as a security guard. With his outstanding physical fitness and disciplined military style, he quickly stood out. In 2013, he was appointed as the head of the Security Department at JNSP community. Mr. Yang had mixed feelings about the transformation led by Mr. Zhou. On one hand, he recognized the drawbacks of the traditional property management model, and he admired Zhou's bold and decisive transformation, which required courage. On the other hand, he wasn't optimistic about the transformation pushed by Zhou. Based on his intuition, he believed that Mr. Zhou's hasty implementation of the transformation without sufficient understanding of the property management industry was very dangerous.

After the water supply interruption issue was resolved, Ms. Tang came to Mr. Zhou's office and submitted the financial statements of the previous month.

Observing the anxiety on Zhou's face, she asked if there was anything she could help with. Mr. Zhou looked up, sighed, and Ms. Tang, a highly experienced community finance staff member, commanded his respect. He also wanted to hear her thoughts on the community transformation over the past year.

Ms. Tang replied: "I see that you've been extremely busy this past year, truly wanting to do a good job with this matter. However, I think there were some issues with the transformation method, especially the abolition of all functional departments. The various groups in the original structure of community property management, whether it was the Security Department, Engineering Department, Landscaping Department, or Cleaning Department, each department gradually formed its own invisible relationships and patterns. A radical transformation would disrupt the existing relationships and patterns, which is hard for people to accept. Although the transformation can improve service efficiency, it will also face significant resistance."

6. Things Will Mend in the End

After communicating with Ms. Tang, Mr. Zhou conducted a detailed investigation into the details of the JNSP community's transformation work over the past year. The research results confirmed Ms. Tang's statement and even overturned Mr. Zhou's perception. Mr. Zhou had to admit that the issues the employees complained about did exist. At the same time, Mr. Zhou received a phone call from Mr. Zhang, expressing his desire to discuss and hear Mr. Zhou's thoughts on the organizational transformation of JNSP Property Center. Mr. Zhou also felt it was time to develop a new plan with Mr. Zhang.

After listening to Mr. Zhou's report, Mr. Zhang felt shocked but also somewhat surprised. Although the transformation might not have appeared successful, it truly made them understand the internal interests of traditional community property centers. Being in a high position, Mr. Zhang didn't have enough opportunity or energy to understand the internal interests of grassroots community property management. It was precisely these factors that rendered their efforts for transformation ineffective, directly hindering the progress of management transformation.

Mr. Zhou said: "Additionally, I noticed that the employees in community property management lack sufficient incentive mechanisms. The community is seen as a market of resources, and employees want to secure more benefits for themselves. In this situation, discussions about management concepts and service awareness are futile."

"What are your plans moving forward?" Mr. Zhang asked. "I have two ideas at the moment. The first one is to consider appropriately retaining functional departments and combining them with the steward team model. Looking back, I initially believed that directly abolishing functional departments would be more efficient, but that was a bias in my understanding. After abolishing functional departments, the housekeeper teams would need to simultaneously handle management and operations, which would place excessively high demands on their capabilities. So, I believe the transformation should progress gradually and functional departments should be retained as needed." Mr. Zhou explained.

"This idea is interesting. Please continue." Mr. Zhang encouraged.

"My second idea is to strengthen internal employee training within the company. Previous training primarily focused on job skills, although management concepts and service awareness were also emphasized, the results were poor. Based on the actual situation, the overall educational level of employees in the property management industry is low, so we should reform the training system for talent development. However, before that, I think we should temporarily suspend the transformation and address these internal issues!" Mr.

Zhou further explained, and Mr. Zhang's eyes also lit up.

One afternoon in October 2017, Mr. Cao, head of the Human Resources Department of XYZJ Company arrived at the conference room of JNSP Property Center.

Mr. Cao said: "I have come here with a mission. The main purpose is to announce two decisions from XYZJ Company. Firstly, from now on, Mr. Zhou will take full responsibility for the property management of JNSP Property Center. Secondly, Mr. Hu will no longer serve as the property manager of JNSP Property Center and will be relocated. Mr. Zhang emphasized repeatedly that JNSP community is a demonstration community of XYZJ Company, representing the image of XYZJ Company. He hopes that everyone will cooperate with Mr. Zhou and strive to create an exemplary community."

Mr. Zhou then delivered a speech: "I would like to express my gratitude to XYZJ Company for their support, as well as to all colleagues for their support over the past year. JNSP community is a demonstration community of XYZJ Company, which means that our every action represents the future direction of XYZJ Company. In the digital age, the transformation of traditional property management is a general trend and also a strategic choice for XYZJ Company. I sincerely hope that everyone can continue to support my work." Mr. Zhou's tone was calm, his eyes bright, and he looked sincerely at everyone.

7. Epilogue

After the meeting, Mr. Zhou sat in his chair, recalling the frustrations of the past period. Although he had experienced ups and downs, he always firmly believed in the inevitability of the transformation of community property management in the digital age. The combination of the Internet and community property management would bear fruit, and this was also his dream.

Mr. Zhou slowly stood up, knowing full well that Mr. Zhang's support did not mean that everything he did was correct. Currently, everything seemed to be improving, but it was not so much Mr. Zhang's trust in him as it was recognition of his transformation concept. However, this did not guarantee success. All future management transformations of JNSP Property Center must withstand the test of practice. He had to work hard, not to disappoint Mr. Zhang's trust, and build the "ideal community" in his heart.

Questions:

1. How do you perceive and evaluate the organizational transformation measures taken by Mr. Zhang and Mr. Zhou? What are the main driving factors for the transformation of JNSP Property Center?

2. What problems did JNSP Property Center encounter during the transformation? What were the causes of these problems?

3. There are many characters in the case, each playing different roles during the transformation. What attitudes and positions did the different characters of JNSP Property Center have when facing the transformation? Analyze the underlying reasons.

4. Did the transformation of JNSP Property Center succeed or fail? If you were Mr. Zhou, how would you proceed with the next steps of the transformation of JNSP Property Center?

Tips for Answering the Questions:

1. Analyze the first question by applying the organizational transformation theory.

2. Analyze the second question by applying the organizational transformation theory.

3. Analyze the third question by applying the organizational transformation model theory.

4. Analyze the fourth question by applying the organizational transformation theory.

Case 13

Organizational Transformation of ZL Corporation

Key Words:

Organizational transformation theory

Purpose:

Based on the analysis of the organizational transformation of ZL Corporation, this case is intended to guide the students to understand the organizational transformation theory.

Case:

1. Introduction

Since its establishment, ZL Corporation has been in operation for over sixty years. Despite the 2008 financial crisis, the company experienced significant sales growth from 2009 to 2013. It successfully resolved internal and external crises and gradually developed its operations.

2. Background

2.1 Overview of ZL Corporation's Current Status

Established in 1950s and headquartered in Beijing, ZL Corporation is a large transnational metal mining corporation engaged in exploration, development, smelting, and trading of metal minerals and other emerging businesses including financial service, real estate construction, and R&D of metallurgical technology. Adhering to the development concept of "To found a corporation of vital and lasting importance and build a green future", it is committed to providing high-quality services across the globe. At present, it is engaged in the business covering 26 countries and regions worldwide, has almost 200000 employees, and holds 13 domestic and foreign listed companies. Before China's reform and opening-up, ZL Corporation was the main supplier of imported metal minerals in China. After the reform and opening-up policy, ZL Corporation extended the businesses into over 40 countries and regions worldwide and became one of the earliest companies that started international business under the "going out" strategy in China. In 2000, ZL Corporation engaged a well-known international consulting firm to formulate its first development plan. In the development plan, a business structure based on 7 business segments (raw materials, steel, non-ferrous metals, comprehensive services, financial, real estate, education) and 2 business units (freight transport and bidding).

2.2 Historical Development of ZL Corporation

2.2.1 Development during the Period of Policy Monopoly

ZL Corporation was one of the first large-scale state-owned foreign trade companies specialized in the import and export of metal minerals in China. In the 1950s, under the centralized planned economy system, it enjoyed absolute monopoly over the export of mineral products and procurement of steel throughout China until after the reform and opening-up. From the company's establishment until the mid-1980s, its revenue maintained a good growth momentum. In 1985, ZL Corporation's revenue reached 7.5 billion USD, setting a record high in its development history.

2.2.2 Development during the Market Transformation Period

With the deepening of China's reform and opening-up, reforms in foreign trade systems also progressed. The monopoly position of ZL Company in the field of hardware and mineral imports and exports was gradually abolished. In 1985, the import and export rights were delegated to local governments. The provincial and municipal branches of central enterprises were completely decoupled from the headquarters. Central ministries and commissions, as well as provinces and cities, established their own foreign trade companies and obtained the foreign trade operation rights for hardware and mineral products. This brought a significant impact to ZL Company, and simultaneously, the multichannel operations of many foreign trade companies greatly affected the variety of sustainable operations for ZL Company. After the implementation of the steel import agency system, the number of foreign trade companies engaged in steel import increased in various provinces and cities, causing the proportion of ZL Company's steel imports in the country to decline from 100% before 1979 to 60.2% in 1990.

In response to these changes, ZL Corporation entered a period of market transformation from 1988 to 1999. In 1988, based on its main business, ZL Corporation merged 13 departments and established secondary companies, including non-ferrous metal trading company, rare mineral product import and export company, industrial development company, and ZL Trade Limited. These newly established secondary companies operated independently, had independent accounting, and were responsible for their own profits and losses. At the same time, ZL Corporation established branch offices in coastal areas and economic zones, and began to diversify its operations, investing in projects in various fields. During this period, although ZL Corporation conducted a series of explorations and reforms, most of the projects failed due to investment dispersion, long frontlines, and weak management. In 1999, ZL Corporation's export volume dropped to the lowest level since the reform and opening-up, reaching only 1.48 billion USD.

2.2.3 Development during the Strategic Formation Period

In 2000, ZL Corporation entered a new period: strategic formation. With a strategic orientation, ZL Corporation implemented internal resource integration and established a clear "7+2" business model, determining the development direction of extending the metal mineral industry chain, controlling upstream mineral resources, and developing downstream distribution networks. The focus of this stage was the comprehensive implementation of a new development strategy, deepening strategic transformation and internal reforms. From 2000 to 2004, ZL Corporation's business scale began to grow rapidly, with a compound annual growth rate of 45% in revenue, 62% in total profit, and 26% in total assets. Its comprehensive strength significantly improved.

As the reform and opening-up further deepened and the trend of economic globalization became increasingly evident, competition for mineral resources intensified, the international metal market continued to heat up, and there were significant changes in the world trade circulation pattern. ZL Corporation's internal operations also faced unprecedented challenges. For ZL Corporation, the systemic and structural contradictions that constrained the transformation of its development mode were not fundamentally resolved. It had weak independent innovation capabilities, and compared to other state-owned enterprises, there was a considerable gap in development speed and profitability.

On December 27, 2004, Mr. Li was appointed as the General Manager of ZL Corporation. At the beginning of his tenure, Mr. Li proposed to continue adhering to strategic transformation and strengthen the control of metal mining projects and the construction of a global marketing network.

In 2005, ZL Corporation signed strategic cooperation agreements or special agreements with several provinces, municipalities, and autonomous regions, completing the preliminary deployment of the strategic layout of regional economic cooperation in western, central, northeastern areas and Bohai Rim Economic Circle. With the promotion of regional economic cooperation, ZL Corporation acquired a metallurgical corporation in the central region and entered the field of metallurgical engineering construction, achieving a new extension of its industrial chain.

In 2007, ZL Corporation first proposed the development of six major main businesses, forming a distinct and clear development pattern that includes ferrous metals, non-ferrous metals, finance, logistics, real estate construction, and education.

In 2009, taking advantage of the industrial adjustment opportunities brought by the financial crisis, ZL Corporation successively acquired and restructured a batch of industrial and mining enterprises and research institutes, improving the integrated industrial chain layout of science, industry, and trade. It gained control of eight listed companies at home and abroad. The company adjusted its strategic vision, changing it from "an internationally leading metal mineral corporation" to "an internationally competitive metal mineral corporation", emphasizing the construction of competitiveness. It proposed a business system structure featuring "macro-mining" "macro-circulation" "synergistic diversification", guiding the reform and development for the next three years and laying a strategic foundation for subsequent organizational transformations.

3. Motivation for ZL Corporation's Organizational Transformation

The motivation for ZL Corporation to implement organizational transformation stems from the change in company strategy, namely the strategic transformation.

3.1 Background of Strategic Transformation

In 2005, ZL Corporation formulated a five-year development plan for 2006—2010, setting the mid-term strategic development goal of "building a rejuvenated ZL Corporation in five years". After three years of development, ZL's Corporation's strategic transformation showed initial results, and in 2008, the company's business scale and profitability doubled ahead of schedule. The black metal business established a complete layout of the steel industry chain, while the non-ferrous metal business developed a multi-metal and full-industry chain pattern. ZL Corporation owned over 60 industrial and mining enterprises and 24 mines, with mining capabilities in iron ore, tungsten ore, leadzinc ore, and smelting and processing capabilities in steel, alumina, tungsten products, ferroalloys, antimony, tin, and aluminum. The contribution of production-type businesses to ZL Corporation's revenue increased from 4% in 2005 to 26% in 2008, and the profit contribution rate continued to rise.

However, in 2008, the international financial crisis erupted and spread to the real economy. As the crisis spread, ZL Corporation's main businesses were severely affected in 2009, especially the black metal and non-ferrous metal core businesses. In February 2009, ZL Corporation's revenue dropped by over 50% compared to the previous year. The international financial crisis led to a dual impact of rapid decline in demand and tightened liquidity in the industry, with most metal mineral prices experiencing a significant downturn. In the context of relatively sluggish international economy, metal demand did not increase significantly, and the metal cycle was in a relative low. Meanwhile, the long-term contradiction of excess energy in China's steel and nonferrous metal industries gradually surfaced, and the market shifted from "resources-oriented" to "order-oriented".

How to fully leverage ZL Corporation's overall advantages, adjust its operational strategy, and adapt to the characteristics of the new situation became important issues for ZL Corporation to maintain its industry competitiveness.

3.2 Strategic Transformation Process

In this context, ZL Corporation carried out learning and practice activities using the scientific development concept, clearly recognizing that the company still had many deeprooted contradictions and problems in the reform and development process. In the second quarter of 2009, ZL Corporation held several strategic seminars to discuss the company's future development. The group was facing the sharp contraction of business scale and profitability, as well as a sharp increase in risks. This was not only the result of the financial crisis but also the outcome of the company's extensive operations in the metal boom cycle without significant improvement.

Through discussions and analysis, ZL Corporation identified nine issues from development models, resource security capabilities, business structure layout, corporate governance, talent security, technological innovation, and basic management. In particular, by benchmarking against leading international metal mining companies, ZL Corporation found that there were still significant gaps.

Therefore, ZL Corporation embarked on a self-transformation once again: reevaluating and adjusting its strategic vision and initiating a three-year rolling plan. The three-year rolling plan departed from the previous practice of simply revising the original five-year plan at the group headquarters and adopted a combination of top-down and bottom-up approaches, incorporating development ideas proposed by the secondary companies from their respective industries' perspectives. ZL Corporation hired an external consulting firm to assess the feasibility of the company's initial strategic vision. After several rounds of communication, ZL Corporation defined its strategic vision as: becoming an internationally competitive metal mining enterprise group based on trade and relying on resources.

4. Organizational Transformation of ZL Corporation

On April 14, 2009, during a symposium on learning and practical activities in some central enterprises, Mr. Li, CEO of ZL Corporation, reported to the central leadership on the learning and practical activities of implementing the Scientific Outlook on Development. He proposed that ZL Corporation would consider dealing with the international financial crisis as an important component of their learning and practical activities. The guiding principle of their activities would be to "improve the level of scientific development and achieve a new leap in three years" aiming for stable development and promoting transformative adjustments.

Mr. Li believed that learning the Scientific Outlook on Development should be combined with practice, advancing practice through learning and deepening learning through practice. The metal mineral resource field where ZL Corporation operates was heavily affected by the international financial crisis, being a "disaster area". In 2009, the prices of steel and non-ferrous metals dropped by more than 40% compared to 2008. Market trading was sluggish, and business growth was hindered. Mr. Li considered the international financial crisis as a practical lesson and emphasized the importance of closely observing the trends and dynamics of the crisis, understanding the regularities and destructive nature of the crisis, analyzing the changes in power balance within the crisis, reevaluating corporate governance and management under the conditions of global economic integration, actively exploring the patterns and effective approaches of "turning crises into opportunities", and preparing for higher levels of international competition.

Mr. Li's report received a positive response from the State-owned Assets Supervision and Administration Commission (SASAC). With the support of SASAC and relevant ministries and commissions, ZL Corporation initialized a step-by-step organizational transformation. At the end of April 2009, ZL Corporation launched comprehensive restructuring, taking an important step in institutional reform. In mid-October, ZL Corporation submitted the proposal for comprehensive restructuring and listing to SASAC. At the end of October, ZL

Company reviewed and approved the three-year plan for 2009—2011, proposing a "macro mining" "macro-circulation" "synergistic diversification" commercial system structure. In January 2010, ZL Corporation adjusted its main business by adding metal and mineral product engineering design, technical research and development, and related services. In February 2010, ZL Corporation set up a special team to study business structures and management models, and they visited Baosteel, COFCO, CSCEC, Sinochem, and other enterprises to learn from their experiences. By the end of March, a preliminary overall plan was formed. Through reporting to the corporation's leadership, communication, and incorporating suggestions for adjustments and improvements, the overall plan for business structure and management model adjustments was formulated and approved in April.

5. Analysis and Diagnosis of the Organizational Transformation

The strategic transformation has driven ZL Corporation onto the development path of transitioning from traditional foreign trade to a resource-based enterprise. Over the course of ten years of transformation, ZL has experienced continuous significant growth in business scale and efficiency. Operating revenue increased from 24.7 billion yuan to 185.3 billion yuan, and profits increased from 380 million yuan to 7 billion yuan. The industrial structure improved significantly, with 25% of revenue and 50% of profits coming from production enterprises. Technological strength has greatly enhanced, laying the foundation for the integration of industry, technology, and trade. The rapid development of ZL Company is evident and inspiring.

With the continuous advancement of strategic transformation, ZL Corporation's business scope and scale have expanded. ZL Corporation has undergone revolutionary changes in its business structure, personnel structure, corporate composition, operational model, and industrial layout. However, the existing organizational structure has become increasingly inadequate to meet the new development requirements of the company, resulting in a series of operational management issues. During the rapid business expansion, the company faced challenges in coordinating management across business lines, functions, and regions, leading to increased managerial span and complexity. The strategic transformation based on various business sectors had a phased nature. There was overlapping of operational activities among some business sectors, causing internal competition within the company. The overseas network was marginalized, and the traditional advantages were not fully utilized. These problems may be summarized as follows.

5.1 Problems with the Original Organizational Structure

According to classical strategic management theory, strategy determines organizational structure. If a company wants to achieve its strategic objectives, it must have a matching organizational structure for implementation. However, as of the end of 2009, except for logistics, ZL Corporation did not have a unified management body for its other main business sectors, and the main business models were not in line with the organizational structure. In addition, exploration, scientific research, and other activities were outside the framework of the main business and required clarification of their corresponding relationship with the organizational structure. Due to the mismatch between the organizational structure and strategic goals, serious issues of cross-operations emerged within ZL Corporation, resulting in resource waste.

The waste of resources was primarily manifested in the unreasonable structure and regional distribution of customers and suppliers. ZL Corporation had a large number of customers and suppliers, with scattered regional layouts. Internal financial and human resource allocations were not rational, hindering efficient resource utilization. Both suppliers and customers had structural problems, with a high proportion of random customers and the stability of channels needing improvement.

5.2 Problems with the Original Management Model

Firstly, ZL Corporation established six business centers through adjusting its business structure, which initially resolved the issues of excessively wide management scope and long management chains. However, different types of business centers required matching management methods.

Secondly, there was room for improvement in functional management at ZL Corporation. In terms of functional management division, ZL Corporation had not yet established a standardized, unified, and clear management and control system, leading to overlapping and misalignment of responsibilities, resulting in unclear responsibility subjects. For example, in the establishment, alteration, or disposal of subsidiary companies, multiple departments issued relevant management regulations and participated in the work. This multiple management, lack of unified systems, led to confusion in responsibility allocation and control systems.

Lastly, the hierarchical management and authorization system within the company was imperfect. Headquarters had highly centralized functional management authority, and core management decisions within subsidiary companies, such as operating plans, investments, and changes in human resources, required approval from the headquarters. This hindered the development of business activities, and there was a need to optimize the division of rights and responsibilities and operational mechanisms. According to the feedback from a survey conducted by consulting firms, which included questionnaires on control management to over 100 general managers and deputy general managers of ZL Corporation's functional departments and subordinate units, 36% of respondents believed that the overall control situation of ZL Corporation was good, 61% believed it was average, and 3% believed it was poor.

The diverse types of business, overlapping operations, and chaotic business lines became factors limiting the company's overall listing.

6. Further Implementation of Organizational Transformation at ZL Corporation
6.1 Optimization and Re-structurin
To establish a clear organizational structure and address the issues of cross-operations and internal competition, ZL Corporation needs to tackle a series of significant problems.

Regarding the problem of organizational structure design, based on the main businesses approved by the SASAC and referring to the management model of international metal mining companies, ZL Corporation separated exploration and mining from distribution and circulation, establishes an independent marketing platform, closely integrated logistics and trade, established a shared technology research and development platform within the group, restructured subsidiary companies, integrated cross-business activities, and divided the company into seven major business centers: non-ferrous metals, ferrous metals, logistics of ferrous metals, finance, real estate construction, technology, and education.

After clarifying the organizational structure, it was necessary to determine the positioning and control models of each business center, design the detailed business and functional structures, formulate specific operational plans, develop business processes for human resources, operations, finance, and other core management systems, propose information system connectivity and subsequent development plans to support the new architecture and management model.

To achieve this, ZL Corporation established a dedicated corporate transformation working group and separate working groups for each business center to drive the transformation and develop detailed implementation plans. From the establishment of working mechanisms, relevant organizational planning and advancement systems were put in place, management methods for adjusting the company's business structure and control model were formulated, overall objectives were clarified, tasks were allocated, and communication mechanisms were established. Work meetings were held weekly to report on the progress of the transformation, discuss and coordinate various issues in a timely manner.

Cross-business issues involve the division of interests among the different business centers, requiring coordination at the group level. Therefore, the corporate transformation working group stepped in to address disputed assets and business boundaries, coordinate relevant business centers, and clarify the assets and business boundaries of each business center to avoid cross-operations.

In terms of operational mechanisms, general principles for supply chain coordination and operational mechanisms for each link were formulated as follows.

(1) Production enterprises purchase raw materials in bulk through relevant business departments based on sales plans. The products are then sold by the respective business departments and regional centers, settled at market prices.

(2) Given equal conditions, production enterprises should choose logistics services provided by the logistics department.

(3) Freight forwarding and warehousing services are primarily implemented by the warehousing department and logistics department, settling at market prices. The concentration of import and export freight forwarding and warehousing services falls under the scope of centralized business collaboration assessment. Transport and insurance services are entrusted to the respective business departments such as the chartering department and insurance department under equal conditions.

(4) Regarding bidding business, relevant units should promptly provide bidding information and notify the involvement of the bidding business department in advance. The bidding business department should actively follow up, provide high-quality services, and meet the needs of internal and external customers.

(5) Overseas enterprises serve as ZL Corporation's sales organizations overseas and are responsible for local market, customer, and business development. In principle, the sales operations of domestic entities overseas should be carried out through local overseas enterprises, settling at market or agreed prices. If procurement business cannot be conducted through overseas enterprises, timely notification should be given. The procurement business and domestic sales operations of overseas enterprises should generally be carried out through domestic business divisions.

To address the issue of funds not being centrally utilized, the commercial unit has developed a centralized and unified fund management system. Regarding fund allocation, it is stipulated that funds should be centrally arranged by the commercial unit, and the business departments should use them with compensation. In terms of capital budgeting, it is stated that capital budgets have binding constraints, and any budget adjustments must follow the approval process. Regarding external financing and guarantees, it is specified that external financing and guarantees cannot be provided without written consent from the commercial unit.

6.2 Further Strengthening of Management and Control Model

To establish a management and control model that aligns with the business, it is necessary to determine the scope, depth, and methods of management. As the business scopes of the various business centers differ, the focus and challenges of control may vary. The company should establish the relationship between the headquarters and the business centers based on the characteristics of each business. Since management and control models are highly specialized and involve the allocation of responsibilities between the headquarters and the centers, it is advisable to involve external consulting firms, as their designs carry strong persuasiveness. Therefore, the design of ZL Corporation's management and control model scheme is mainly completed by a consulting firm.

Considering that ZL Corporation had determined the development direction of multiple main businesses, and the operating models and core competitiveness differed significantly among the main businesses, with a moderate level of business synergy between them, the consulting firm believed that the strategic control model is suitable for ZL Corporation's management and control model. Considering the different operating models and business characteristics of the 7 major business centers, the 4 centers—non-ferrous metals, ferrous metals, logistics of ferrous metals, and technology—adopt an operation-oriented strategic control model, while the other 3 centers—finance, real estate construction, and education—adopt a finance-oriented strategic control model. Under the operation-oriented strategic control model, the headquarters of ZL Corporation focused on controlling the strategic direction of the business centers, monitoring the execution of the centers, and ensuring the comprehensive implementation of ZL Corporation's strategic intentions. Under the finance-oriented strategic control model, the headquarters of ZL Corporation focused on controlling the strategic direction of the business centers while granting them higher autonomy in business, budgeting, and investment.

In terms of management and control methods, ZL Corporation formed 6 core management and control methods including strategic planning, planning and budgeting, performance assessment, investment and capital operation, key position management, and risk management and auditing. Through strategic planning, the headquarters could ensure the strategic direction and implementation of the business centers. Through planning and budgeting, the headquarters could manage and monitor the operation of the business centers. Through performance assessment, the headquarters could monitor the operation effects of the business centers. Through investment and capital operation, the headquarters could have the main investment approval authority for the subordinate business centers and delegate general investment approval authority based on the principle of hierarchical authorization. Through key position management, the headquarters could manage the key positions of the business centers. Through risk management and auditing, the headquarters could conduct audit on the business centers and formulate a unified risk management system.

In terms of department function optimization, the concept of core functions was introduced, and the necessary core functions for the headquarters control were established and improved, addressing the issue of function overlap. Through the horizontal integration of core functions between departments, the misalignment and gaps in function management were resolved, achieving organic connections between departments. For example, the investment management department should primarily be responsible for investment project review, tracking, and evaluation, but its original functions also included investment enterprise management, resulting in the investment management department "playing the role of both referee and player". After function optimization, ZL Corporation eliminated the function of investment enterprise management.

6.3 Restructuring

In April 2009, ZL Corporation initialized a comprehensive restructuring and established a joint-stock company by the end of 2010. After the overall restructuring, the functional departments were mostly transferred to the joint-stock company, operating under the model of "one team, two brands."

7. Operation of ZL Corporation after Organizational Transformation

7.1 Achievements after Organizational Transformation

Through the establishment of the business centers, ZL Corporation's business structure became more scientific and rational. The company's operational specialization and integration advantages were significantly strengthened, consolidating the favorable situation of strategic transformation and taking the comprehensive competitiveness of future development to a new level.

The operating performance of ZL Corporation in 2010 was significantly improved. Revenue soared to $43 billion, operating income reached RMB 255 billion, a year-on-year increase of 49.62%. The total profit amounted to RMB 7 billion, a year-on-year increase of 123.2%. Total assets exceeded RMB 200 billion, net assets exceeded RMB 50 billion, both with a year-on-year increase of over 50%. The asset-liability ratio further decreased, indicating good asset quality. In 2011, the effect of transformation further manifested, with the company's scale and economic benefits reaching the best level in history. Operating income reached RMB 355.18 billion, a year-on-year increase of 39.7%, and the total profit amounted to RMB 12.77 billion, a year-on-year increase of 98.5%. ZL Corporation achieved leapfrog development.

7.2 New Situation after Organizational Transformation

After the organizational transformation, the operational and managerial powers of the headquarters were delegated. Under the new management and control model, the headquarters only managed the strategy, planning, budgeting, and evaluation of each business center, while each business center managed its subordinate business units. After two years of operating under this management relationship, the headquarters' management personnel gradually felt disconnected from the business. Mr. Wu of the Business Analysis Department at ZL Corporation's headquarters lamented, "In the past, conducting business analysis allowed us to obtain first-hand information about the business, but now I feel that much of the information is being shielded."

Additionally, due to the recent establishment of the business centers, many management personnel in functional departments are fresh graduates lacking managerial experience, which hinders business operations.

Although ZL Corporation's overall operational situation improved, and financial performance was enhanced, there were still many new issues that need further improvement. As the main leader of the organizational transformation, Mr. Li has also heard about these new problems. Some issues can be resolved through coordination, while others are significant structural issues that require comprehensive thinking. How to address these new issues has left Mr. Li deep in thought.

Questions:

1. ZL Corporation implemented organizational transformation at the key time when the internal and external contexts changed and has achieved remarkable results. Based on the case, please analyze what transformation strategy ZL Corporation adopted in the process of organizational transformation.

2. In the case, Mr. Li thought that although the external context posed pressure, it was a good opportunity for ZL Corporation to promote organizational transformation. Please analyze the reasons and the roles of internal culture and values in the process of organizational transformation?

3. In the organizational transformation, most proposals for ZL Corporation were given by

external professional consulting firms. How do you think about the role of consulting firms in the organizational transformation of ZL Corporation?

4. In the process of organizational transformation of ZL Corporation, the senior leaders played an important role. Based on the case, analyze the role of leadership and communication mechanisms during the organizational transformation process.

Tips for answering the questions:

1. Analyze the first question by applying the organizational transformation theory.

2. Analyze the second question by applying the organizational transformation theory.

3. Analyze the third question by applying the organizational transformation theory.

4. Analyze the fourth question by applying the organizational transformation theory.